IMAGES
of America

Newaygo County 1920–2000

On the Cover: Like so many camps and resorts throughout Newaygo County, Browns Landing on Hess Lake offered rental cabins and boats. Visitors can enjoy the relaxing water sports that the area offers. The county is known for its great fishing and boating, as well as its nice beaches, where a vacationer can relax and take in some sun. (Terry Wantz Historical Research Center.)

IMAGES
of America

NEWAYGO COUNTY
1920–2000

Sandra Vincent Peavey and the
Terry Wantz Historical Research Center

ARCADIA
PUBLISHING

ISBN 978-1-4671-1205-5

Published by Arcadia Publishing
Charleston, South Carolina

Printed in the United States of America

Library of Congress Control Number: 2013955314

For all general information, please contact Arcadia Publishing:
Telephone 843-853-2070
Fax 843-853-0044
E-mail sales@arcadiapublishing.com
For customer service and orders:
Toll-Free 1-888-313-2665

Visit us on the Internet at www.arcadiapublishing.com

The book is dedicated to the men and women who worked to settle Newaygo County, making it into the county we know and love today.

Contents

ACKNOWLEDGMENTS

We would like to thank the settlers who developed Newaygo County, making it what it is today. These include Native Americans, early lumbermen, and early merchants and businesspeople who helped the county grow and prosper. Also deserving thanks are the farmers and immigrants who farmed the land and kept the county fed and enabled Newaygo County to become a leading agricultural center.

We also would like to thank the volunteers who helped make this book possible: Belva Bouwsma, for her countless hours of putting together this book and for her day-to-day help at the center; and Robin Peavey, who cleaned up the photographs, taking them from originals to usable prints, and helped with the photography in general.

Preserving local history has always been important for residents throughout the county. We work daily at the nonprofit Terry Wantz Research Center at preserving and saving the county's rich history for future generations, as well as the stories of the families who pass through. We like to say we are "genealogists without borders." We assist residents with their family trees, and we accept copies of genealogies for the center to help us preserve family histories, regardless of where the person is from. We work actively at preserving family histories, cemetery information, and obituaries, along with the history of Newaygo County in general. We are currently working on an oral history project, recording interviews with as many Newaygo County residents as we can. We need to remember that everyone has a story worth telling.

We work with the local chapter of the National Society of the Daughters of the American Revolution. The Whispering Pines and Prairies Chapter has a desk at the center, opening up more resources for people to utilize in the search for family histories. The society plays an important part at the Wantz Center, and without its regent, Belva Bouwsma, this book would have taken a lot longer to finish. Thank you, Belva.

Unless otherwise noted, all images are courtesy of the Terry Wantz Historical Research Center.

INTRODUCTION

An area of western Michigan was, until 1836, the home of Native Americans. That was the year the first white settlers started coming to what would become, in 1851, Newaygo County.

Most of the early towns were built along the many rivers, streams, and railroads, thus allowing them to develop in proximity to transportation. Workers could send logs to the sawmills, which in turn provided water and energy to the community. The railroads opened the world to rural areas, allowing new residents to come in, while conversely allowing more access to those who had already settled in the area.

In 1837, the first permanent home was built in Newaygo. With its location next to the beautiful Muskegon River, it was an ideal place to establish a new town. Newaygo was the first county seat until one was established at the center of the county in White Cloud. Newaygo grew over the years and has gone through many changes.

Hesperia is on the Newaygo and Oceana County line, which runs through the middle of town. It is located along the White River, home to some of the best salmon and trout fishing in the state.

It would be easy for people driving through the city of Grant on M-37 to miss all that it offers. In the heart of the city is the new Water Tower Park. It features the last wooden water tank in Michigan and one of the last in the United States. The water tower was used in the 1973 film *Scarecrow*, starring Gene Hackman and Al Pacino. There is also an original 1927 Chessie System caboose in the city.

Fremont is known as the "Baby Food Capital of the World." In 1927, Dorothy and Dan Gerber came up with the idea of processing food for babies. In 1928, the Gerber Baby made its debut—and the rest is history. Many people, however, still miss the blueberry buckle baby food that they grew up with. Fremont became the main center of commerce for the county. Every July, the city celebrates the National Baby Food Festival. Fremont is also home to the nonprofit Terry Wantz Historical Research Center. Readers of this book who find themselves in the area are encouraged to stop by and say hello.

White Cloud is home to the county seat and all of the county offices related to it. The city prides itself with the sign "Welcome to White Cloud, where the north begins and the pure water flows." Located along the White River, the town offers fishing and swimming at the millpond.

There are many small communities throughout the county that have stood over the years, producing many crops or serving as a lumber town. Many have fallen along the wayside, such as Fox, Park City, and Ryan's Corners. Many, however, are still holding on as small farming communities, including Reeman and Brunswick, Bitely, Brohman, Woodland Park, and Lilly. They provide an important thread that holds the county together.

Croton is a scenic little town that is home to the Hardy Dam. Construction began in 1929, and the dam opened in 1931, making it at the time the largest earthen dam east of the Mississippi River. The Muskegon River backs up behind the dam, creating a large pond that offers swimming, boating, and fishing. Natural beauty surrounds Hardy Pond and the Muskegon River. Croton is often referred to as a "hidden diamond."

Some of the small communities have held on by taking advantage of their natural resources, such as Loda Lake, which offers a trailhead to the North Country Scenic Trail and is a wildflower sanctuary. Many of the nature trails have native Michigan plants marked off for preservation, allowing their beauty to be enjoyed by future generations.

Bitely and Woodland Park offer a rich history and provide many lakes for visitors' enjoyment. Big Prairie once was the largest desert east of the Mississippi River. Hungerford Lake is a cross-country skier's mecca, with miles of trails. These, and many other natural wonders, play an important part in making Newaygo County what it is today.

The county has been blessed with beautiful land and bountiful forests. It has 234 lakes, 356 miles of rivers and streams, and over 100,000 acres of national forest. Newaygo County has long been known as a vacation spot for families. For visitors looking for morels, fishing, or hunting, the county offers it all. Often, people who come to the history center while visiting the county explain how they came here as a young person while camping or visiting a cottage or one of the many private or church camps, such as Camp Newaygo, Camp Henry, and Camp Echo, among others. They tell us of their fond memories, making us proud of our county. They are now continuing the tradition by bringing their children and grandchildren.

Newaygo County is a four-season recreation destination. In the spring, wildflowers and mushrooms draw people into the woods. In summer, water sports and camping are the big attractions. Newaygo County in the fall offers majestic colors on the trees and pumpkins in the fields. It also brings hunting season, with everyone hoping to get that trophy buck. Winter means snow and cold, but thankfully Lake Michigan keeps temperatures a few degrees warmer than areas farther inland. Winter also brings with it ice-skating and ice fishing. Newaygo County also offers many miles of cross-country skiing and sledding.

Newaygo County has quite the heritage when it comes to its natural resources, and it is also true when it comes to its residents and businesses, which create the backbone to life in the area. It is our hope that this book will offer a glimpse into that rich heritage.

One

Events and Festivals of Newaygo County

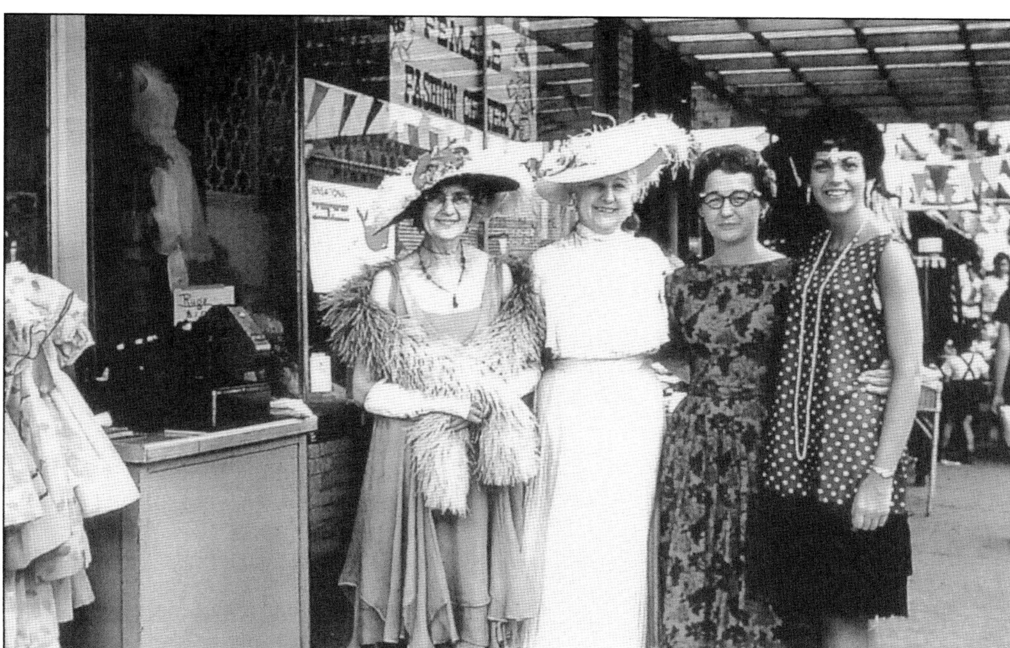

For many years, the city of Fremont celebrated Old Fashioned Days during the month of July. The two ladies on the left in this photograph are dressed for the occasion.

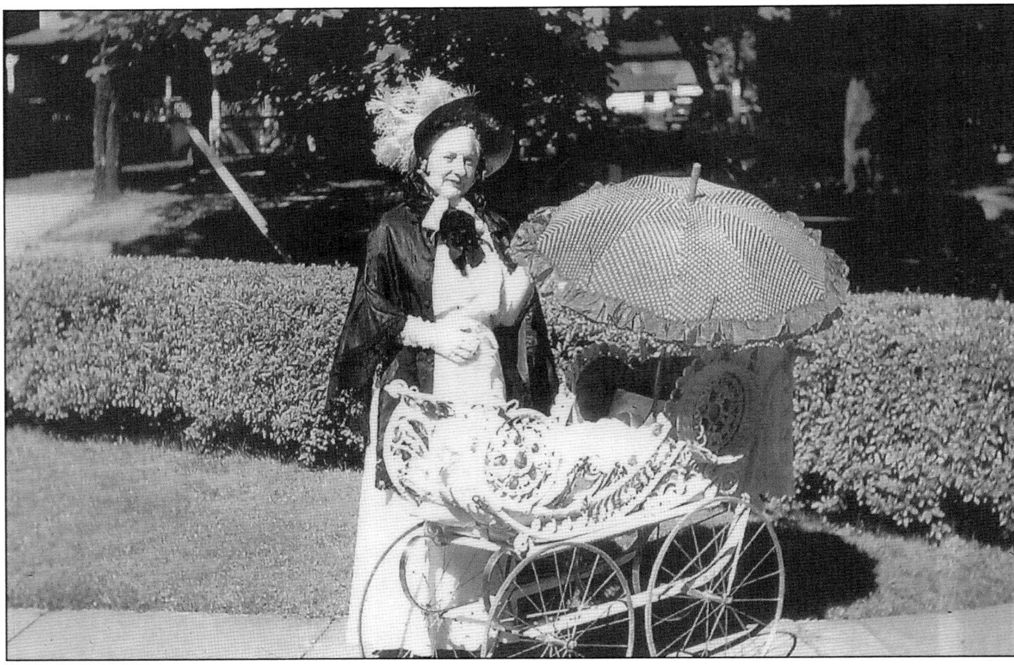

Starting in 1990, the Old Fashioned Days event was changed to the National Baby Food Festival, celebrating Fremont and Newaygo County's status as the home of Gerber Baby Foods.

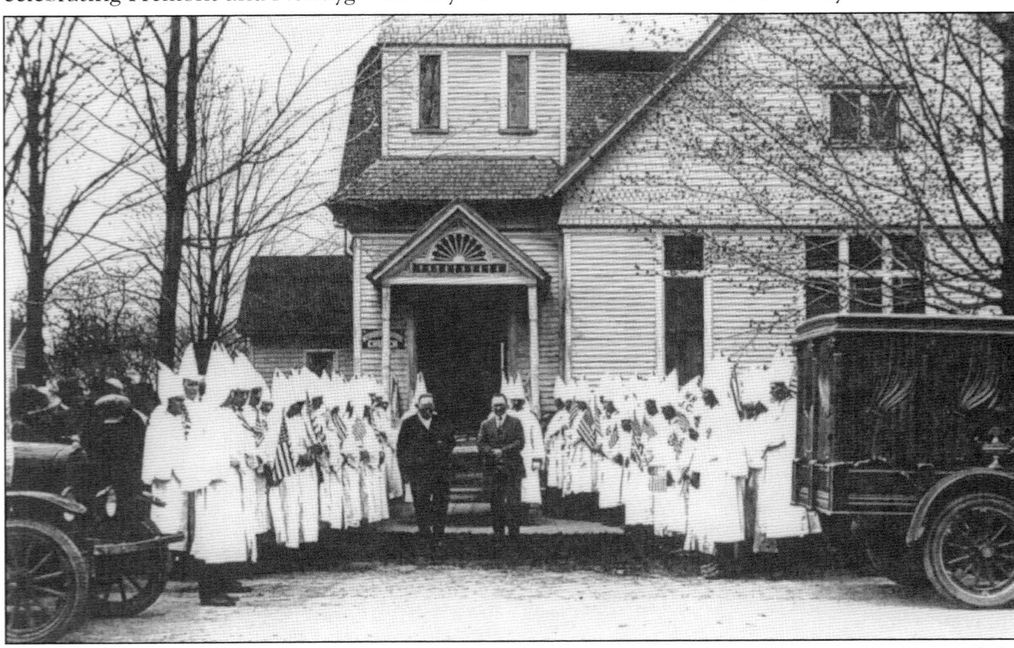

Shown here is a funeral for a Ku Klux Klan member in Hesperia. Note that the faces of the attendees are not covered. Michigan law allowed members of the Klan to wear their robes as long as their faces remained exposed. With the discovery of a hidden room in the Anderson home in 1992, many relics of the KKK came to light that had been long forgotten. The items date to 1925 and 1926 and brought national attention to Newaygo County. They were sold at a public auction that was attended by over 1,000 people.

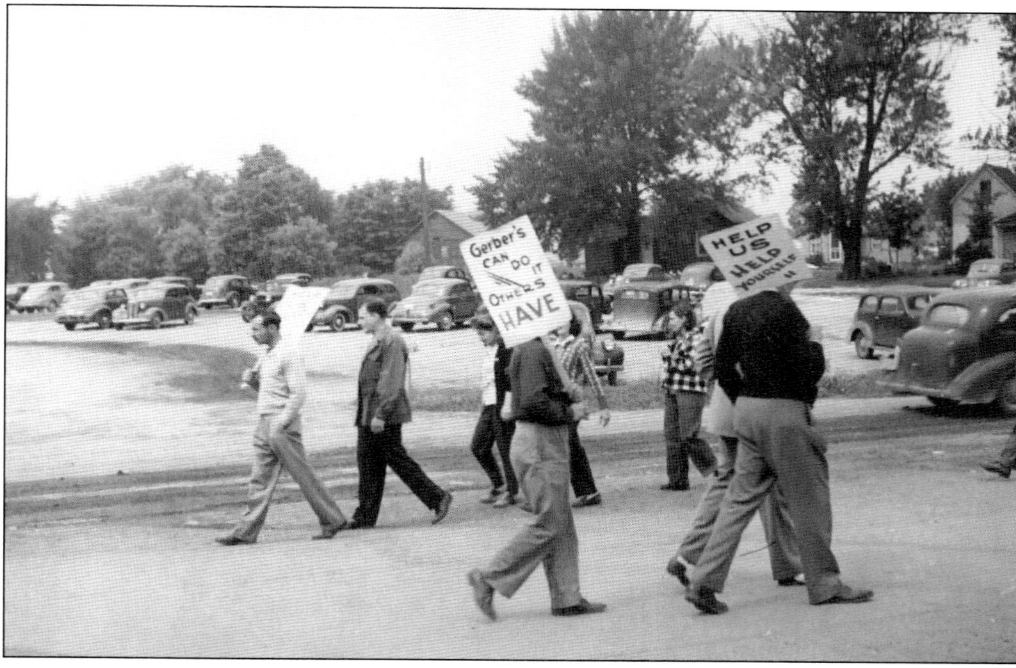

One of the largest employers in Newaygo County, Gerber Products Company in Fremont, has not been without its share of discontent. A few times in its history, the firm's workers have gone on strike and walked the picket line. These photographs show one of the strikes, with employees pounding the pavement.

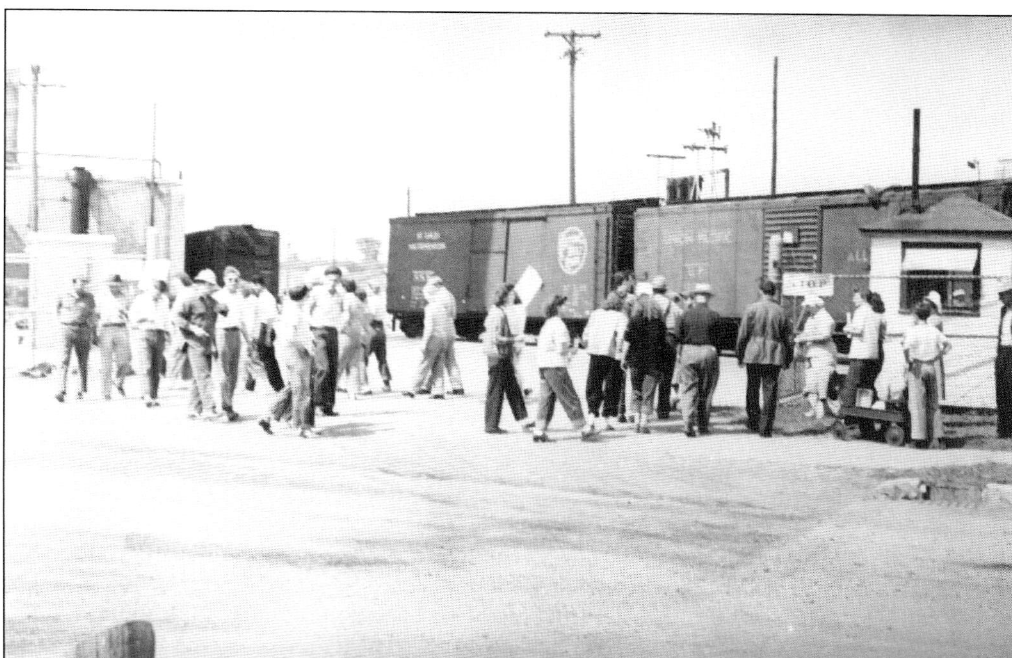

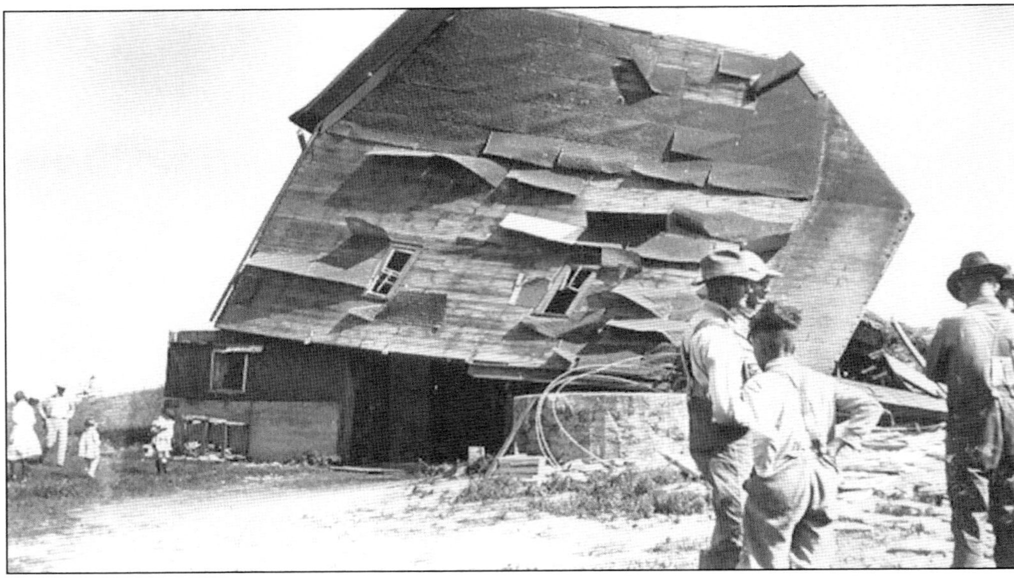

In 1923, the east side of Fremont was hit by a devastating tornado. It leveled many barns, including the one owned by Harry Stroven (shown here). It also destroyed and damaged some homes, including the residence of Gilbert Doris. As soon as the storm was over, people came to help those in need, showing how the community and county comes together in times of hardship.

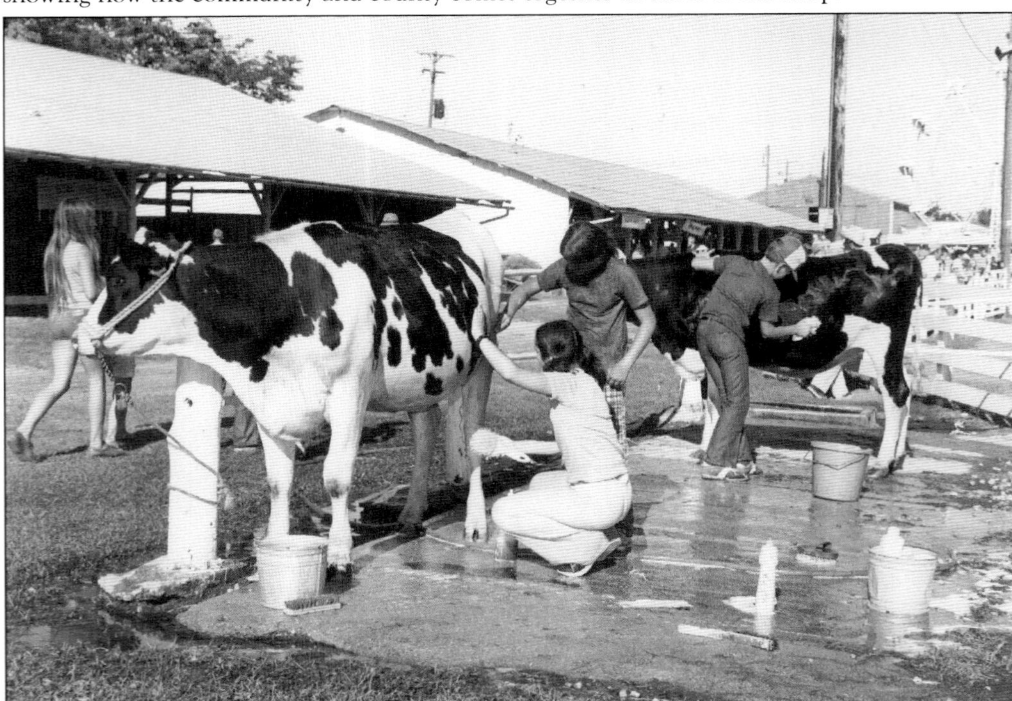

The Newaygo County Agricultural Fair, which began in 1955, has given many Newaygo County 4H youths a start in farming. The event also showcases youth achievement and hard work. It started in the parking lot of the old high school before moving onto the present fairgrounds, which offered more space to erect barns and show arenas.

Two

The People of Newaygo County

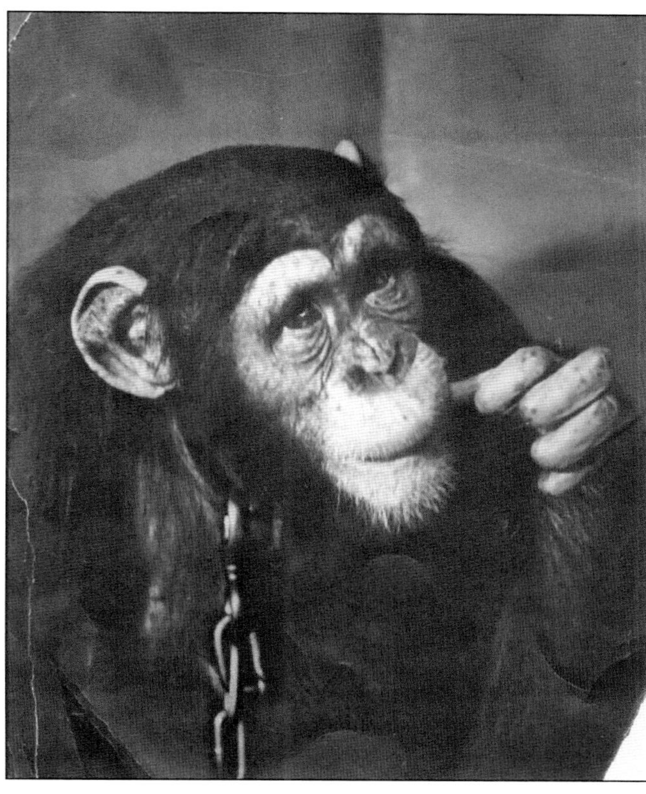

The Mankin family kept a variety of exotic animals on their farm south of Fremont. The menagerie included a camel, which Harlan Mankin rode around the neighborhood. The chimp shown here often accompanied Harlan to the 7 Mile Inn and sat at the bar. It is not known if the chimp drank, and if he did, what beverage he preferred.

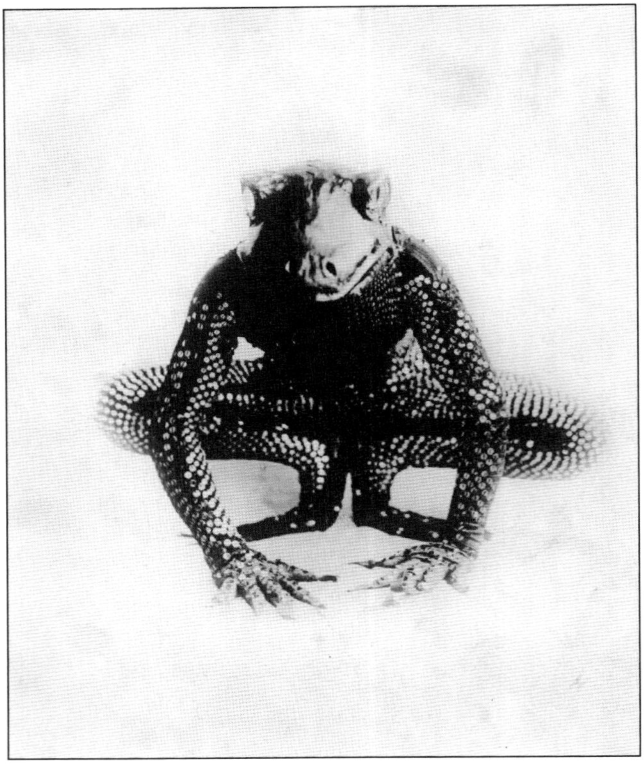

Harlan Sanford Mankin, seen here in his frog costume, was born in Grand Rapids and later became a Fremont resident. He was a popular vaudeville performer.

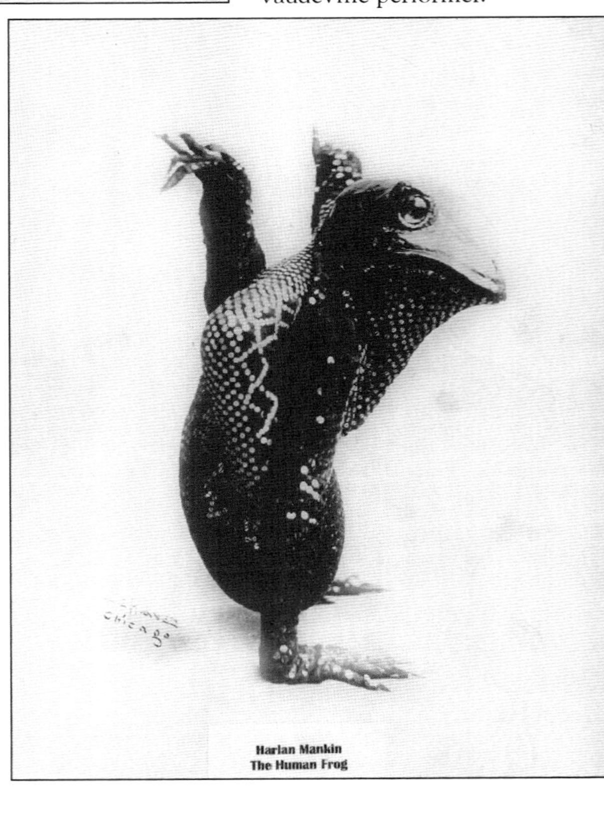

Harlan Mankin
The Human Frog

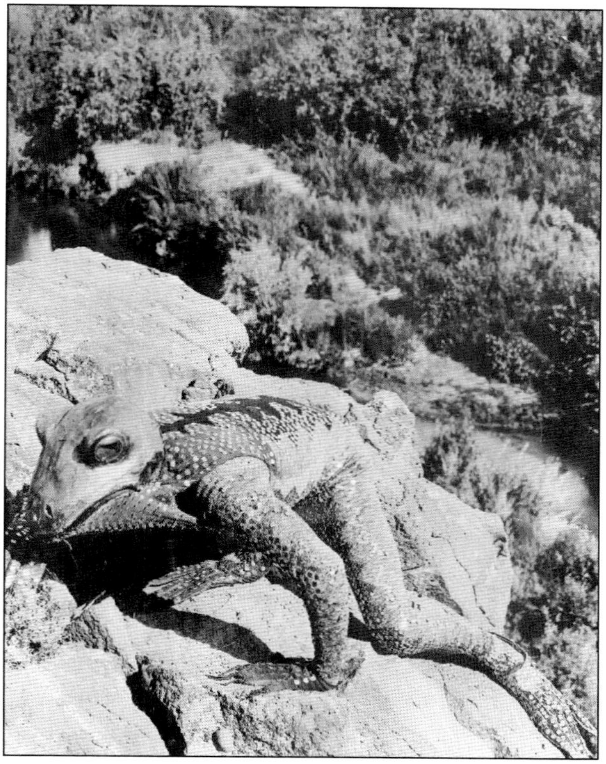

Mankin, known as the Human Frog, performed feats of acrobatics and contortion. He traveled the world with his act, finally retiring to his farm near Fremont in 1930.

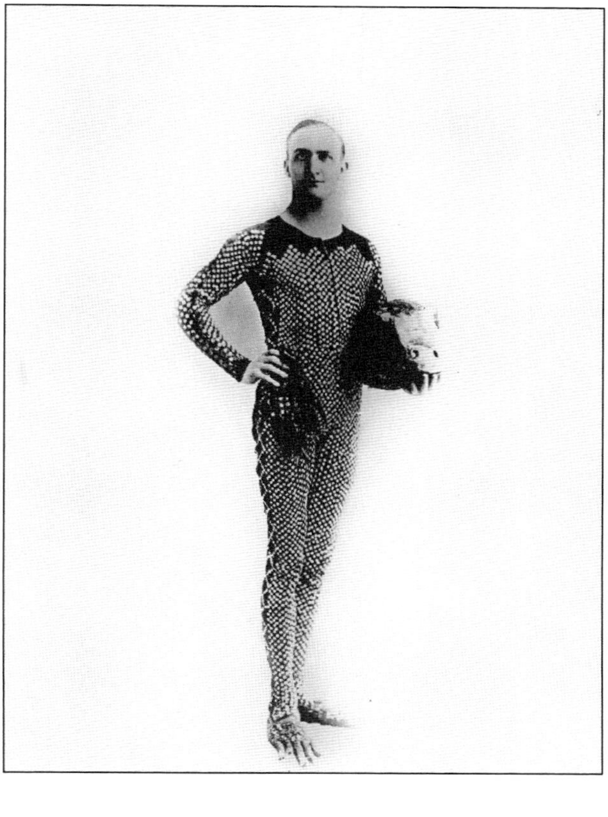

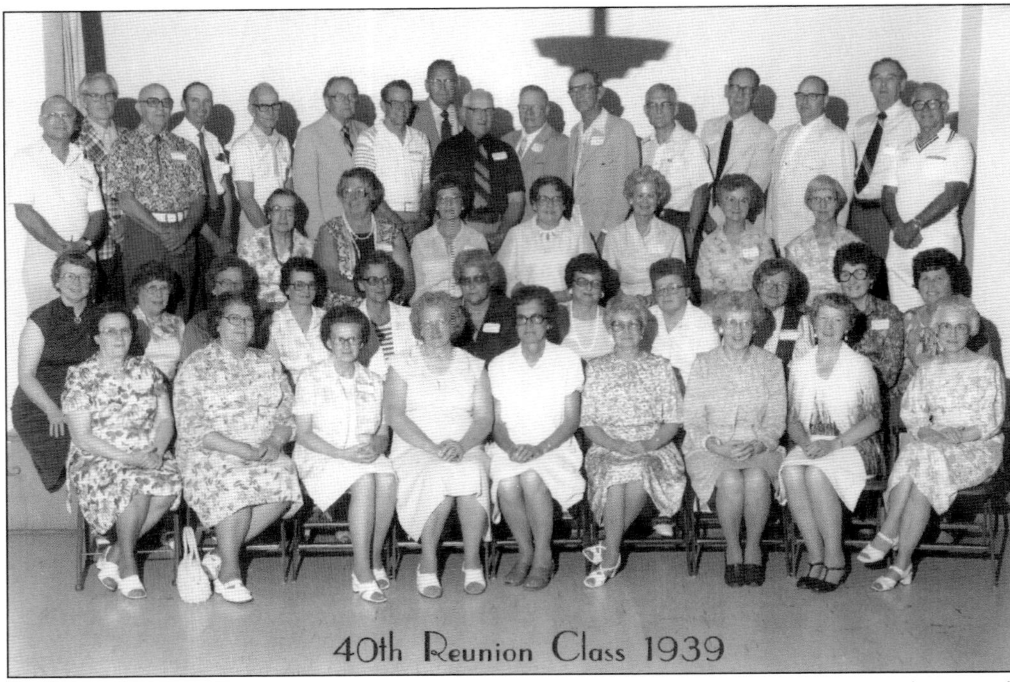

Participants in the 40th reunion of the Fremont High School class of 1939 pose for a photograph. Each year, reunions take place for alumni, and they meet to enjoy memories of the "good old days" of high school. Many families remain in the area. Perhaps some of people pictured here are familiar to readers of this book.

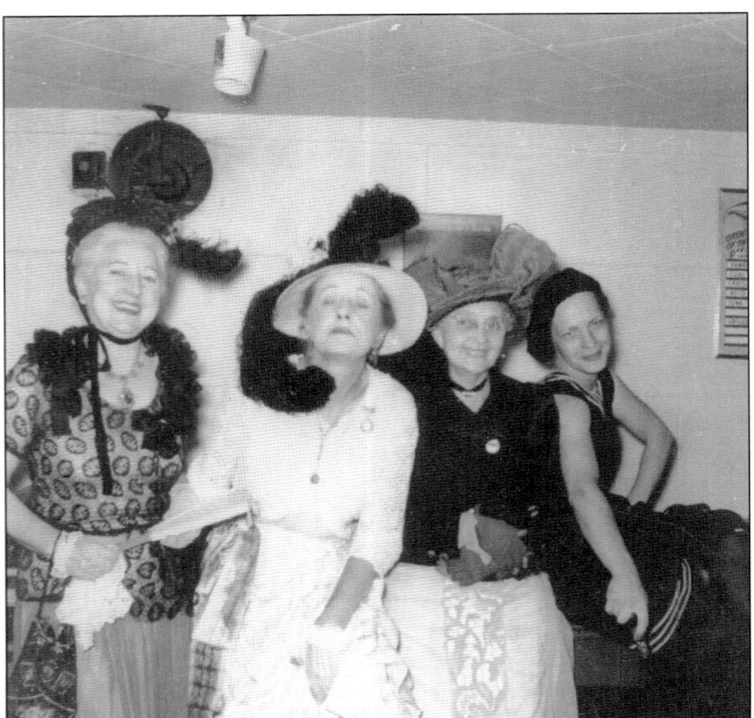

These ladies of the original Old Fashioned Days pose in their period dresses, one of the most popular parts of the event. People came from all over to see the costumes and decorated windows. The festivities were followed up by a parade, which included antique cars and floats from many local organizations.

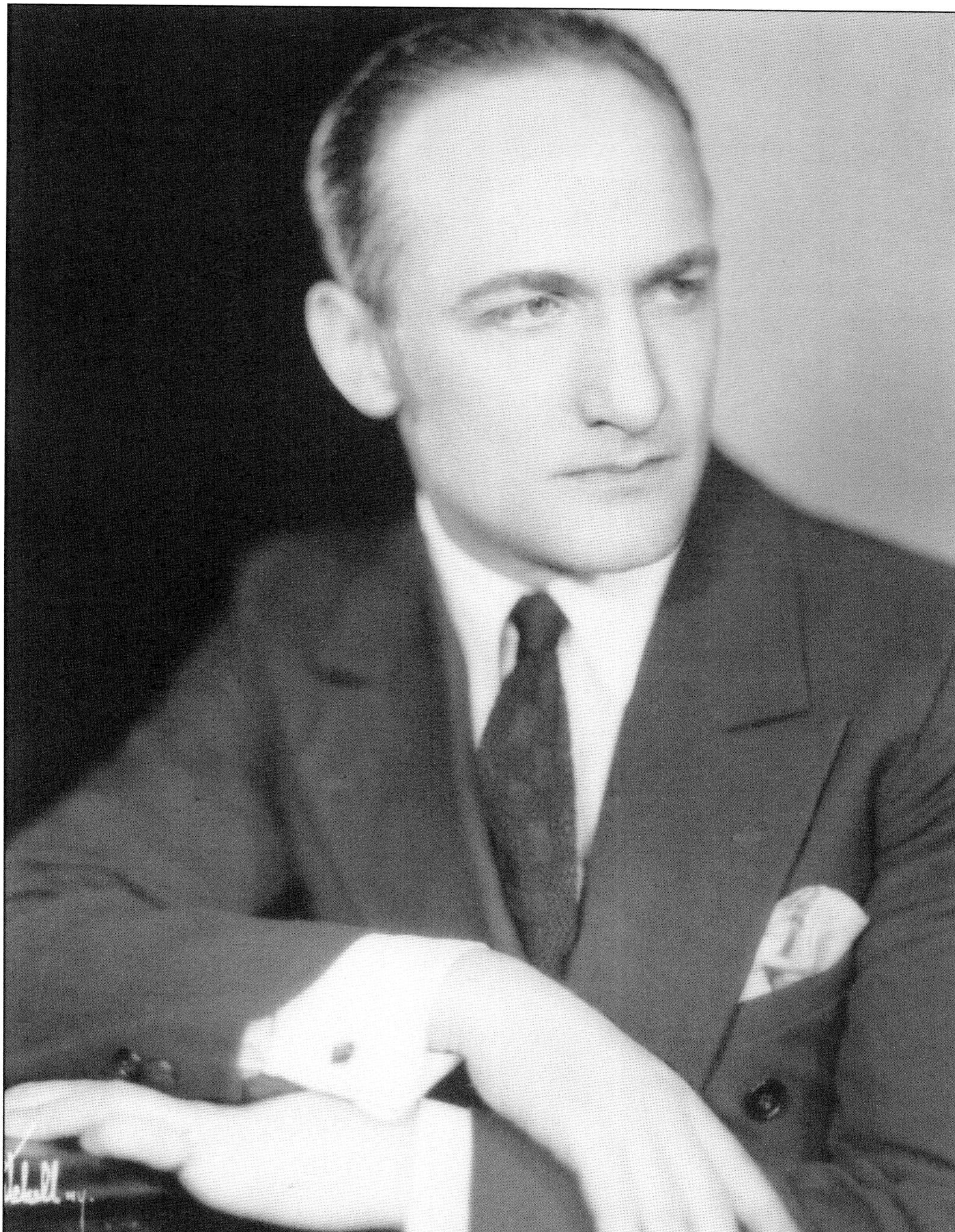

Harlan Mankin, the "Human Frog," billed his performances as the "World's Greatest Contortion Act. Positively the most daring contortion act ever performed before the public. New, novel, and sensational, this is an original being done on a seven-inch plate, 15 feet from the ground, and is the only act of its kind in existence."

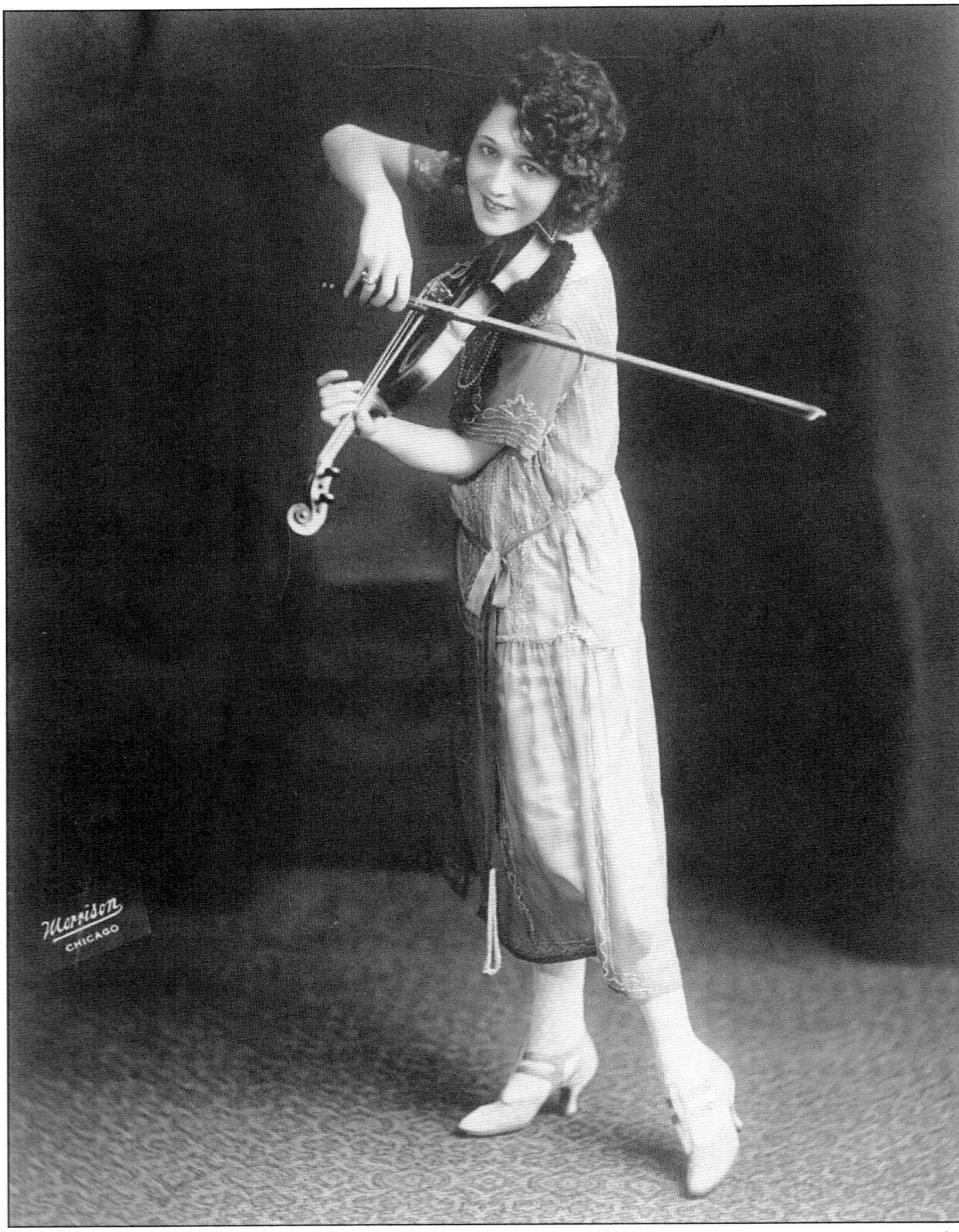

Menette Mankin, wife of Harlan Mankin, toured with the "Human Frog" for many years on the vaudeville circuit. She played her violin on stages around the world, bringing fame to herself in her own right. She and Harlan lived in the house they built south of Fremont with their many animals. Several of their vaudevillian friends would stop by over the years.

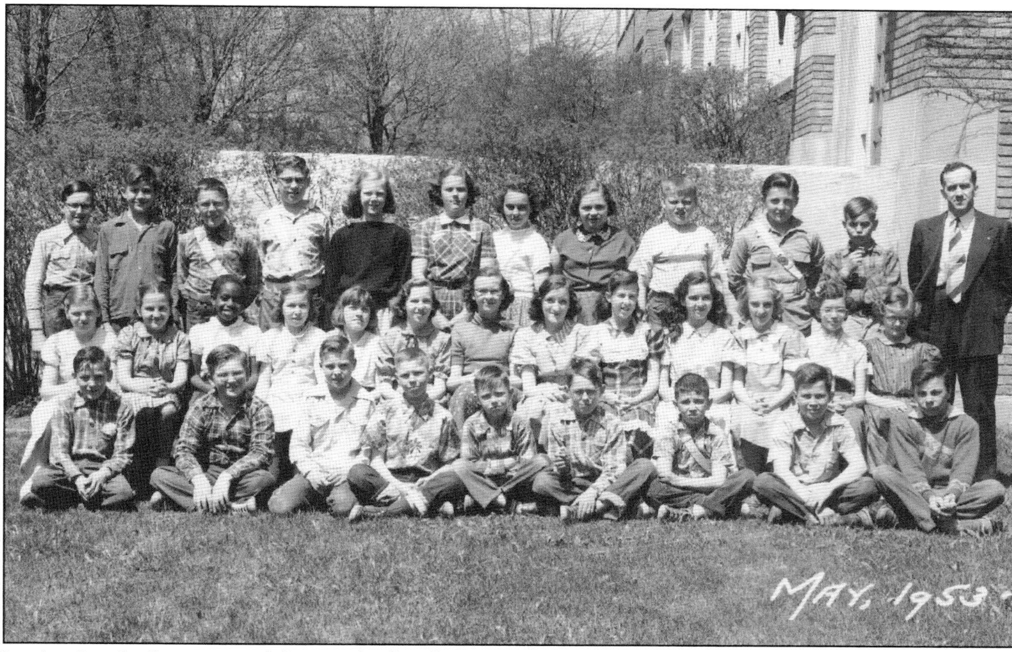

In the days before most of the rural schools were consolidated in Newaygo County, the elementary students of Fremont attended the same school as the high school students. Here, students of Mr. Leckrone's class pose along the side of the high school building in 1953.

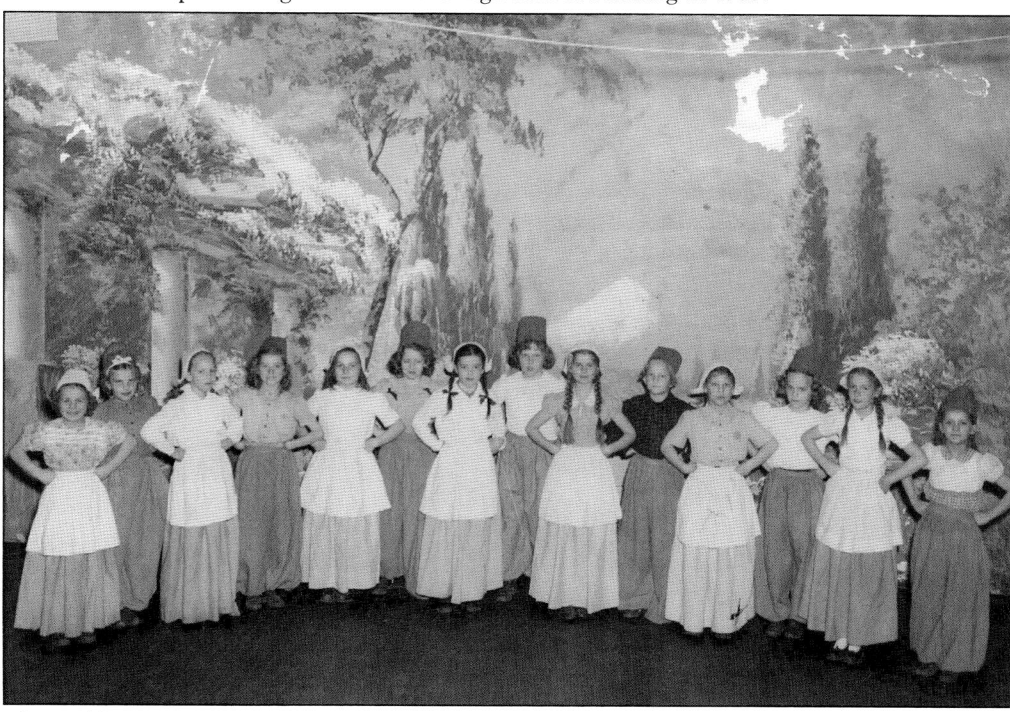

The Soldiers Memorial Community Building in Fremont hosted many performances by local schools and civic groups. The building had bowling lanes in the basement and a large stage upstairs. In this photograph, the child fourth from right is Karlene O'Dell.

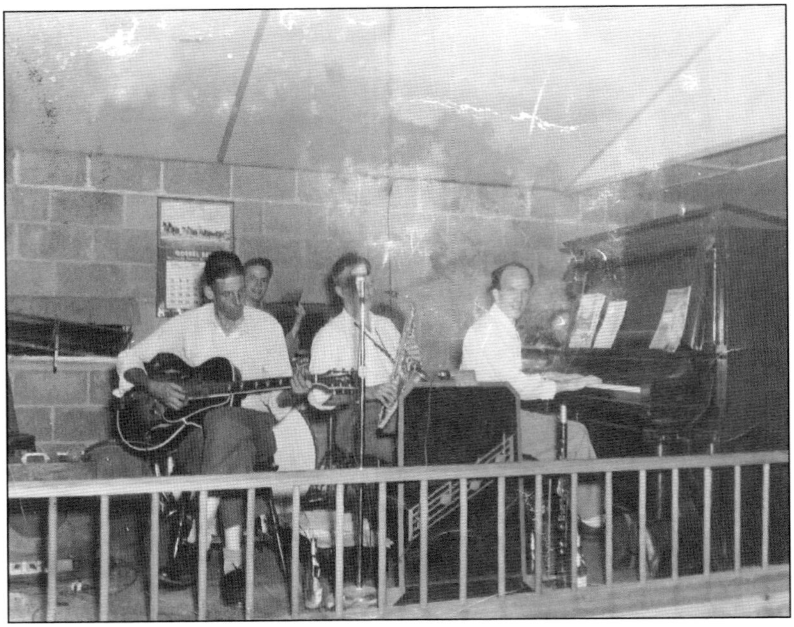

Many bands and musical groups formed in the area, playing wherever and whenever they could. This band is composed of a few county residents, including Morris Robins (right) and Karl O'Dell (left).

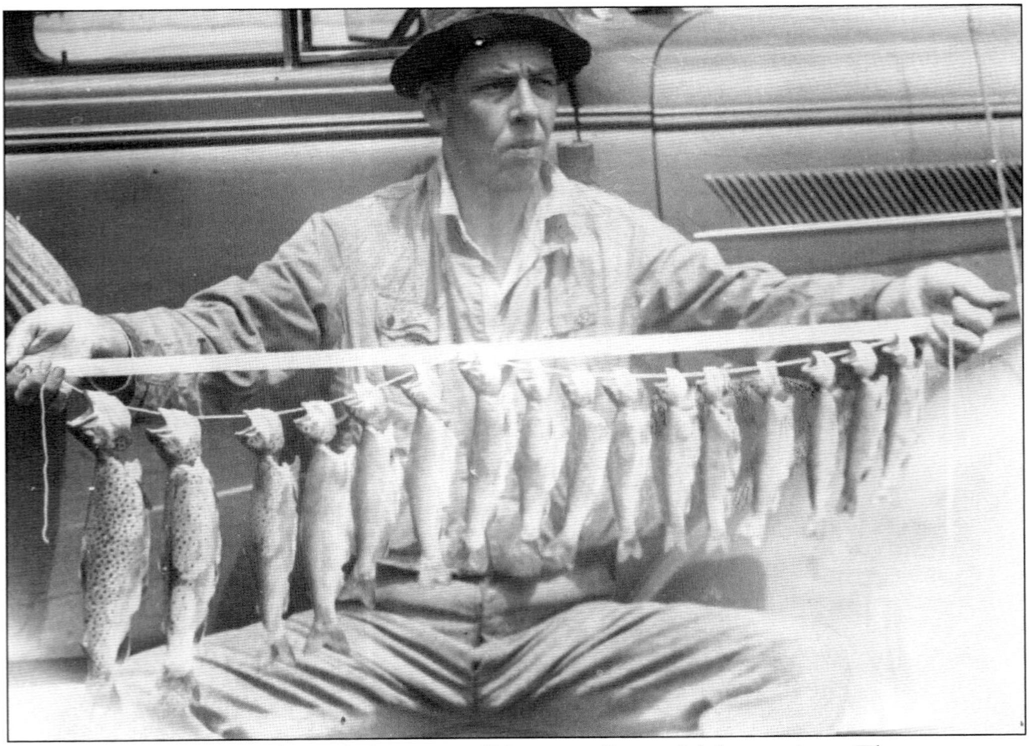

Karl O'Dell shows his daily catch from one of Newaygo County's lakes or rivers. The county was and continues to be a sportsman's paradise. Karl had a love of fishing, music, and the goings-on in the area. Many of the photographs of Fremont saved through the years are due to him.

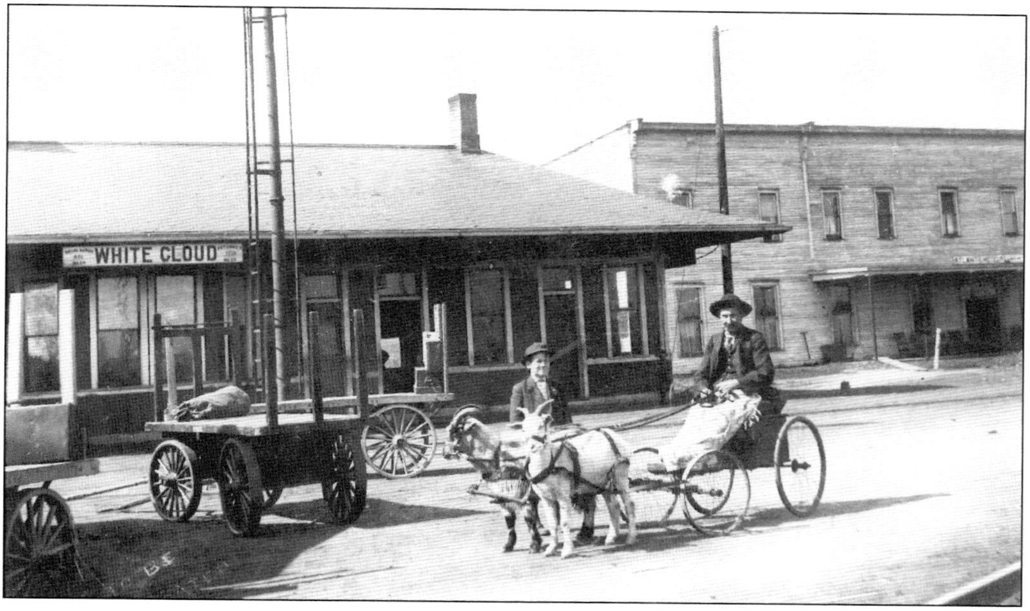

William "Billy" McGowen passed away in 1935. He was paralyzed from a shooting accident when he was stealing a chicken. He was self-employed, meeting trains with a goat-pulled cart from which he sold snacks to hungry travelers. He rapidly became a local character, and people looked for him when they arrived in White Cloud during train stops on the way north or other destinations. "Billy the Goat Man" is a much-loved part of Newaygo County's history.

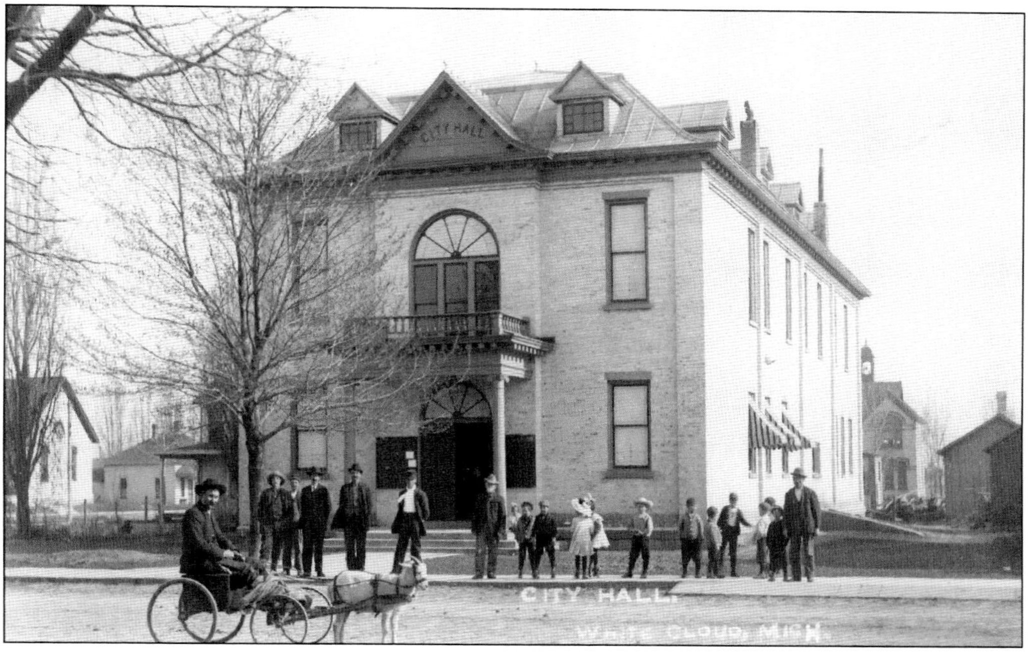

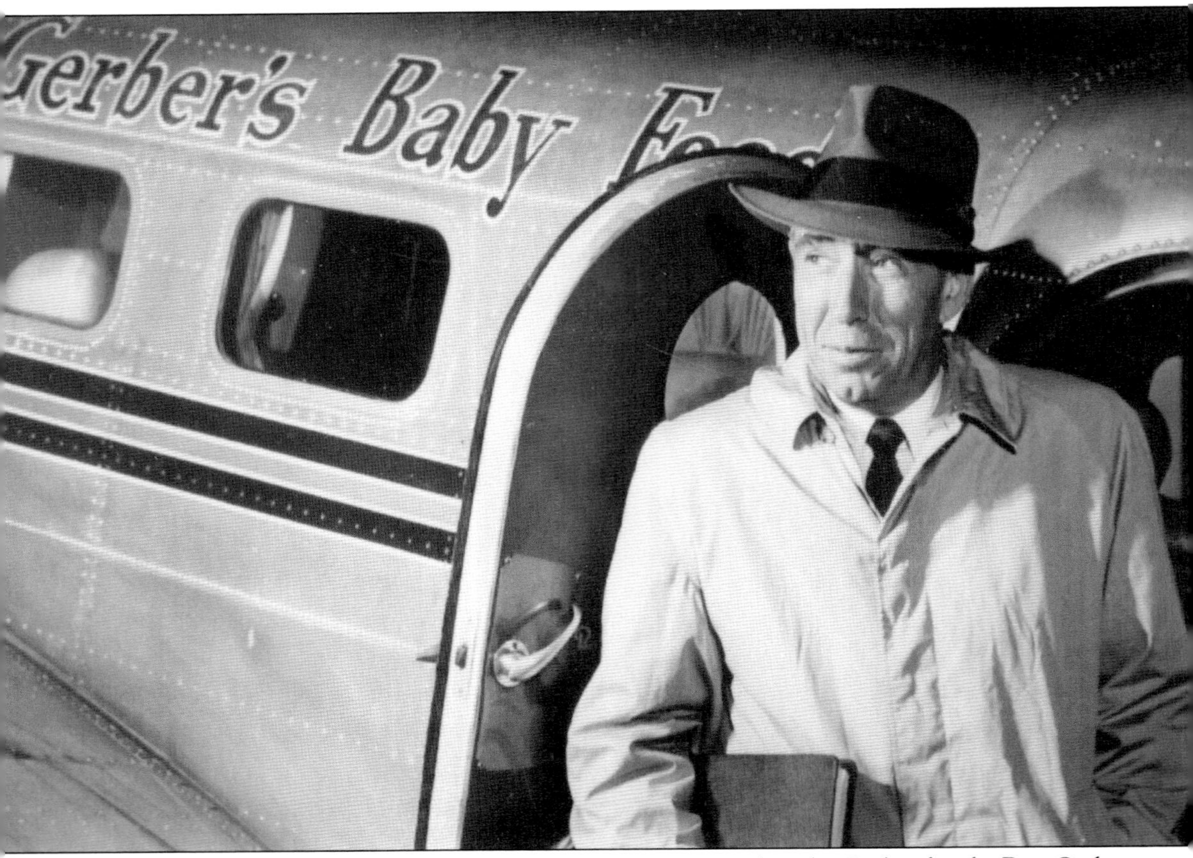

Few clans have left as immense an impression on a county as has the Gerber family; Dan Gerber stands out among them. The president of Gerber Products Company, he was also the inventor of Gerber baby food, when his wife, Dorothy Scott Gerber, requested a simpler way to strain solid foods, which she had been doing for their daughter. Dan Gerber realized the business opportunity, thus making history and parents happier.

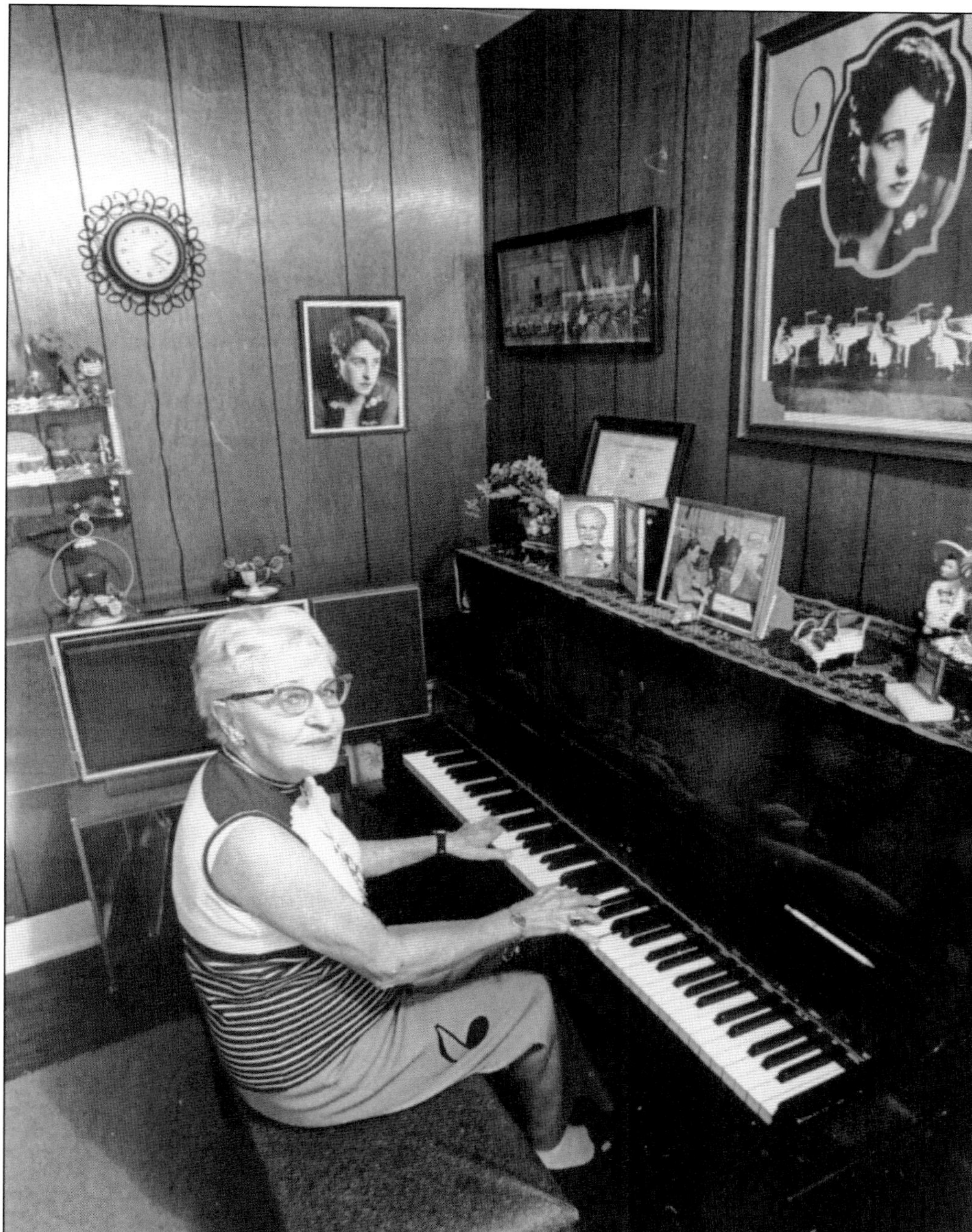

Gerry Valliere and her Baby Grand's played at the opening of the Chicago Theater in 1920, and from there she traveled the world with her vaudeville act. Born in Fremont, Valliere enjoyed a career that crested during the vaudeville era. She returned to Fremont in later years and taught piano to many people in the community.

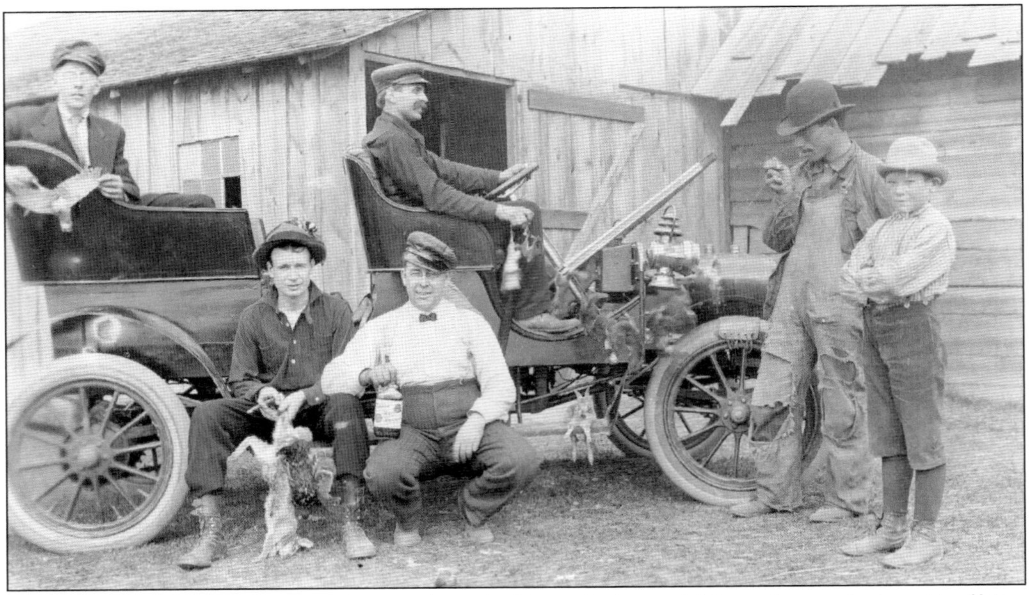

Among the group seen here on the north end of Long Lake are Milton Hoppook, Len Graff, Dr. Webber, and M.W. Odell (in white shirt, holding a whisky bottle). Judging from what one of the men is holding, this group had been rabbit hunting.

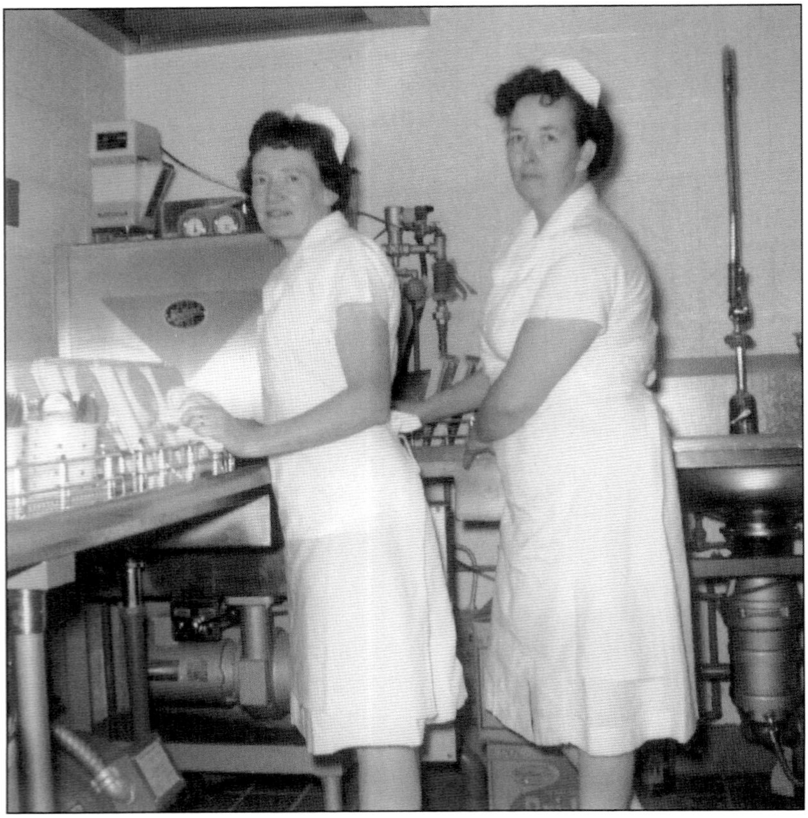

Every student can remember the hot-lunch ladies. Each school in the county had many employees who worked behind the scenes to keep the schools clean and the students fed and healthy. The two ladies pictured here are Laura Tjalma (left) and Betty Vincent. They worked for many years in the Newaygo school system.

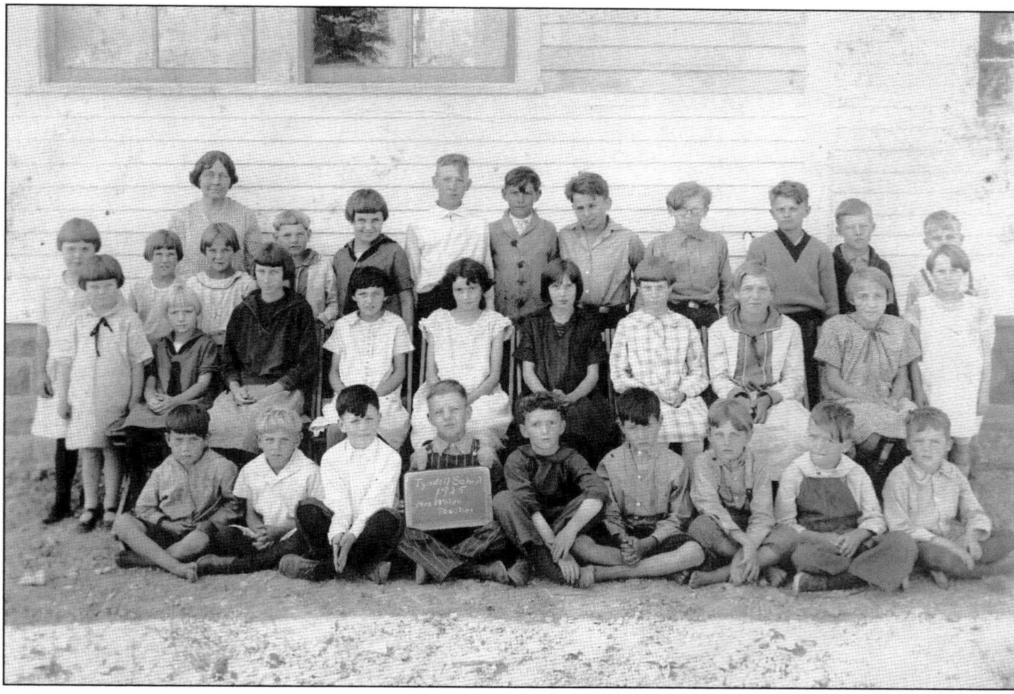

In 1925, rural schools were the main source of elementary education in most of the county. Secondary education was only available in high schools in the towns. This photograph shows students of Tyndall School. The teacher is identified as Mrs. Waldo, in the back row on the far left.

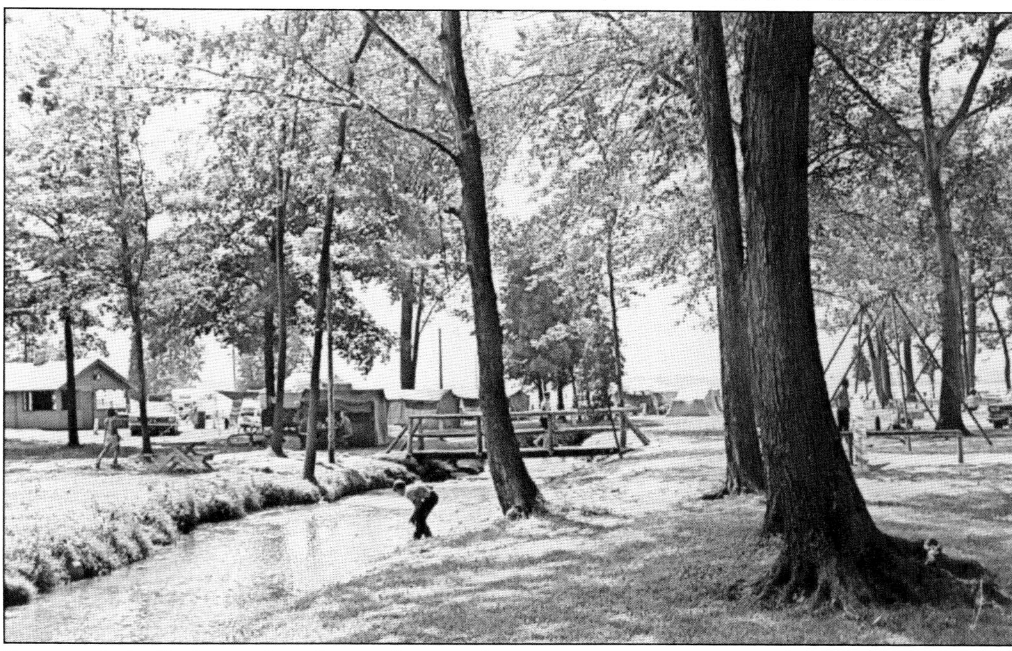

Fremont Lake Park is a place for residents and visitors to picnic, swim, and camp. It continues to be a popular site. It originated as a location where Civil War veterans held their annual Grand Army of the Republic (GAR) reunions. Even as the old soldiers passed away and the GAR posts were disbanded, the park remained.

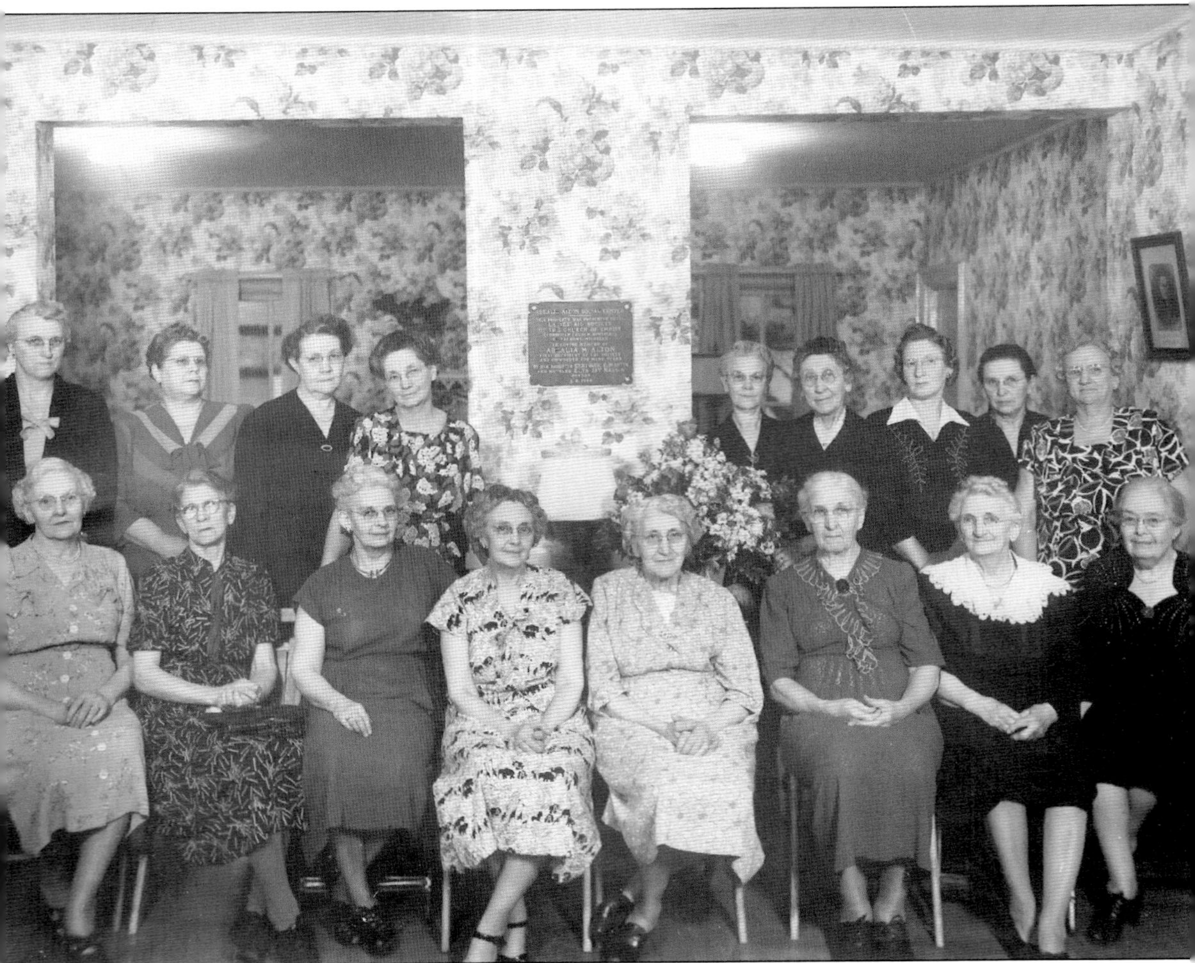

This group photograph was taken on April 18, 1949. The church represented here is not mentioned, but all of these ladies were members of the Ladies Aid Society for 25 years or more. The sign behind the women states in part: "Adealia Alton Social Center. This property was presented to the Ladies' Aid Society of the Church of Christ (Christian Church, Disciples) of Fremont Michigan."

In 1950, the city of Fremont began celebrating its past with Old Fashioned Days. Every summer for 40 years, it was marked by parades, rides, and sidewalk sales by downtown merchants. Many of the workers dressed in costumes of an earlier period. The Reber and Reber Law office was no exception, as seen here. In 1991, the event became the National Baby Food Festival, creating a new chapter of Fremont's heritage.

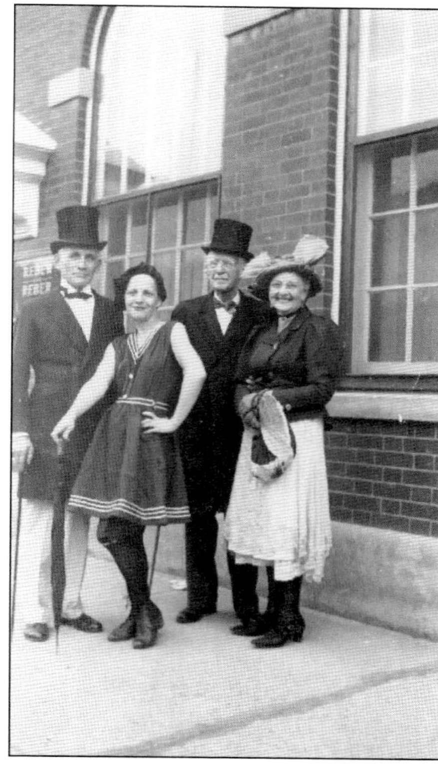

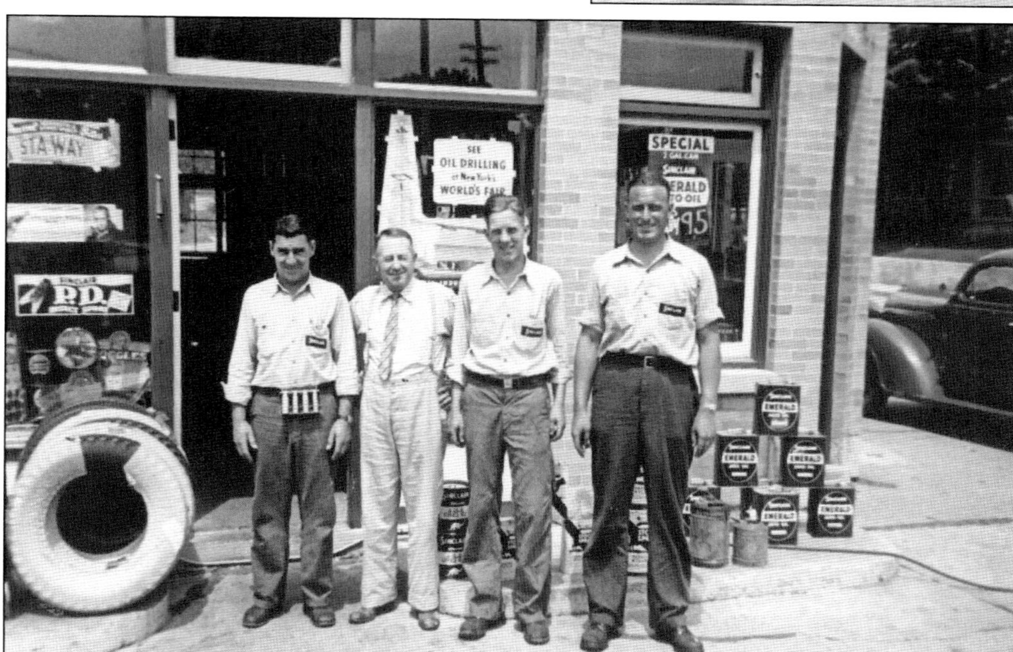

Fast and friendly service was the way to keep customers happy in the early decades of the automobile. Newaygo County had many gasoline service stations to serve increasingly mobile residents. Shown here are, from left to right, Harry Westra, Henry Blont, Tom Hady, and Bill Maynard. They were among the friendly gas station attendants who served customers.

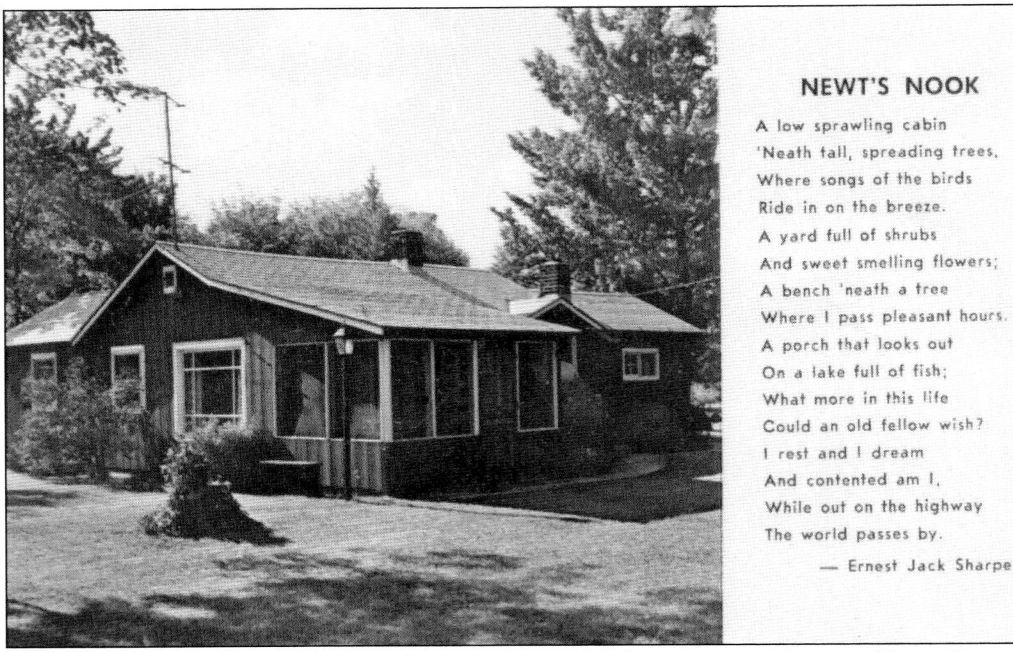

Earnest Jack Sharpe gained fame by writing verses under the pen name Newaygo Newt. He was born Earnest Sharpsteen on July 8, 1888, in Kent County; he later changed his name to Sharpe. Earnest spent his early years as a circus clown and in vaudeville as an actor. He purchased some land on Robinson Lake, retiring there in 1931. A friend sent him a little green jug shortly after he moved in, and soon more and more jugs came; he decided to line his driveway with them. Soon, his resort acquired the name Jugville.

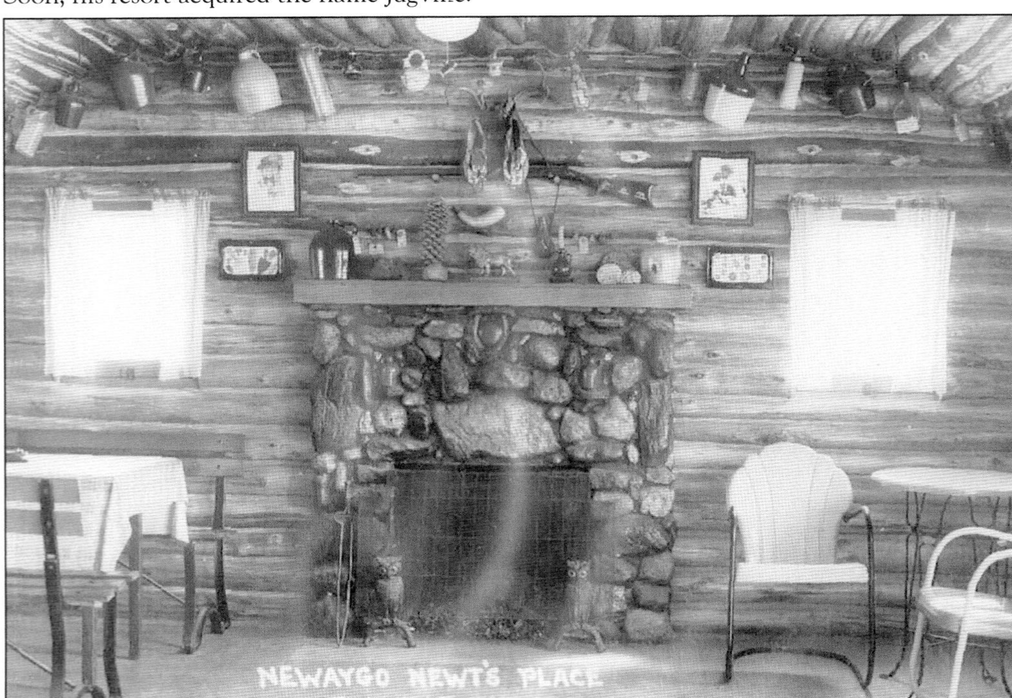

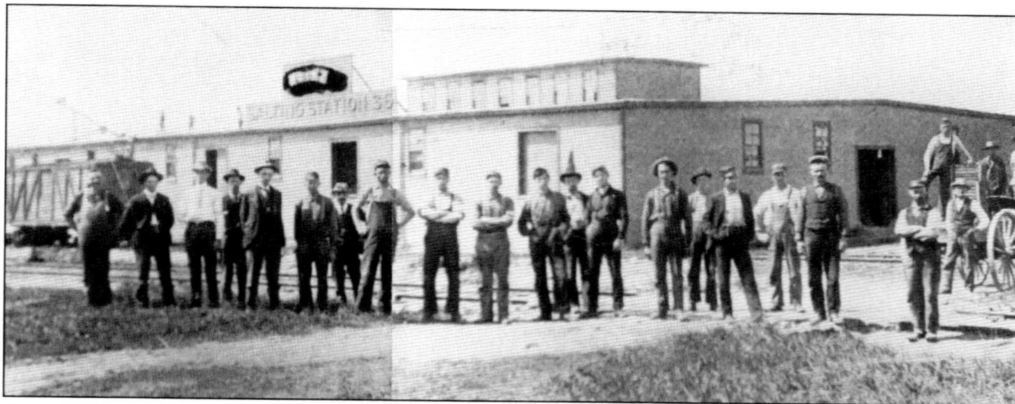

Another business in the county was the Heinz Salting Plant. Here, pickles were packed in salt and prepared for transport to be further processed and canned. The large Heinz pickle sign is a prized piece of memorabilia. One of the few remaining signs in the country is owned by a nearby private collector.

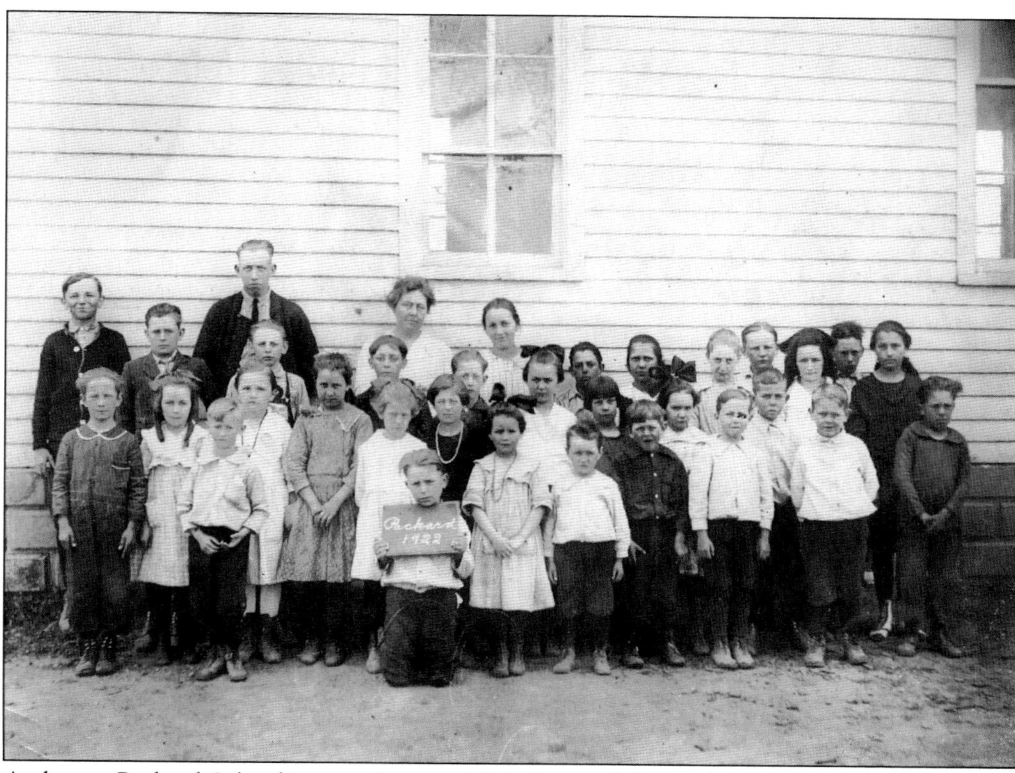

A class at Packard School in seen here in 1922. Some of the students do not look very happy, who range in age and grade. The one-room schoolhouse is a thing of the past, but it is a memory that many people still cherish.

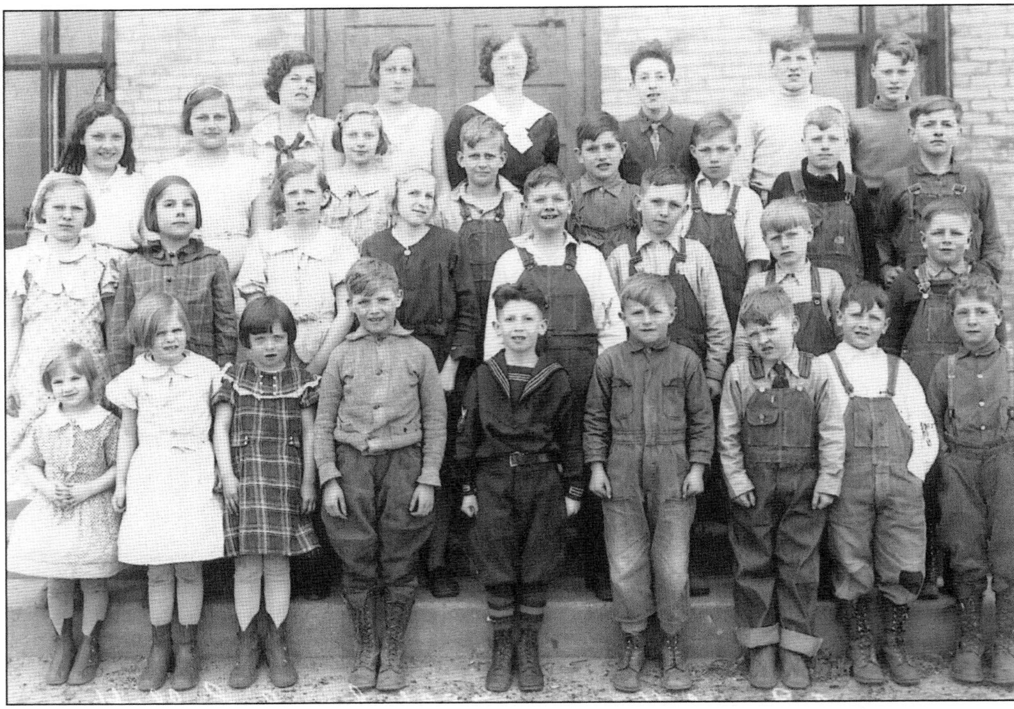

Many one-room schoolhouses appeared across rural America in the late 19th century, and Newaygo County was no exception. As the populace was so spread out in the area, there were many of these schoolhouses. This is a 1935 photograph of Hill School and the class of Helen Hill (back row, center).

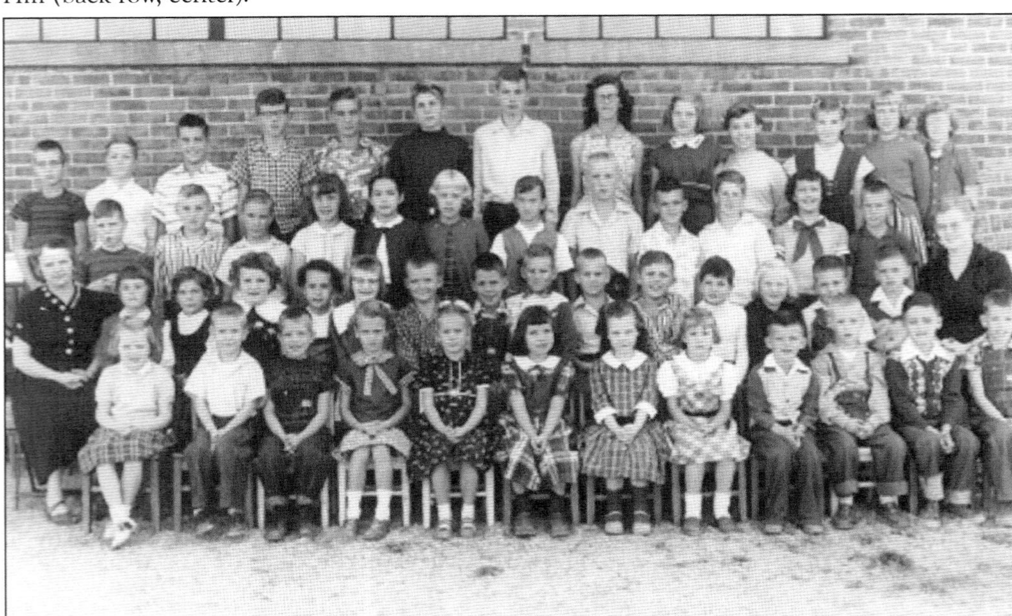

Before the consolidation of country schools, a few of them were multi-room buildings, including Roottown School. The large, impressive brick structure, though shabby, remains standing today. This photograph shows the student body and their teachers posing outside the school.

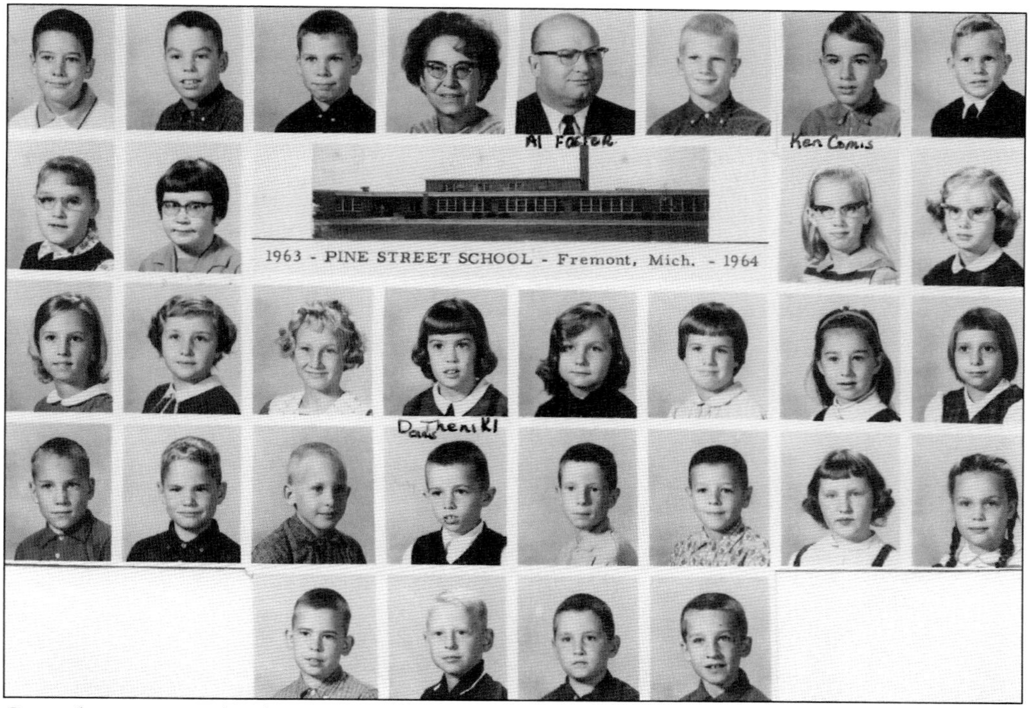

Once the country schools were consolidated into Fremont, newer primary schools were created. Prior to that time, all grades in Fremont were taught in the same building, now known as the Old High School. These students were from one of the classes attending the Pine Street School in 1963–1964.

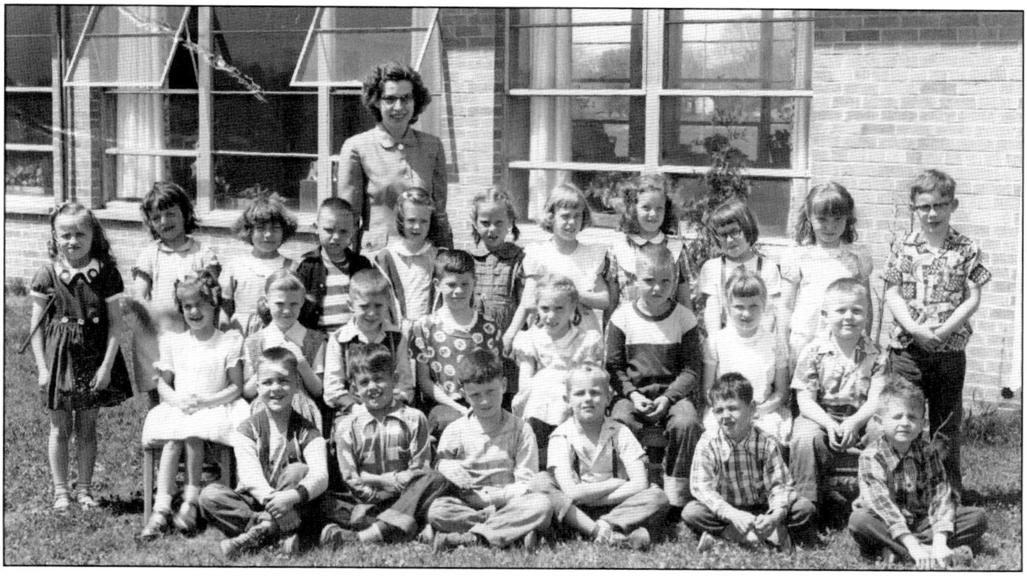

This is the Fremont Elementary School class of 1953. Fremont has gone through many changes over the years, but residents have always stood behind their teachers and support and transportation staff. Everyone feels personally responsible for each and every student. Picture-taking day was always an exciting event. The best part was that the children were allowed to keep the little black comb given out for last-minute touch-ups.

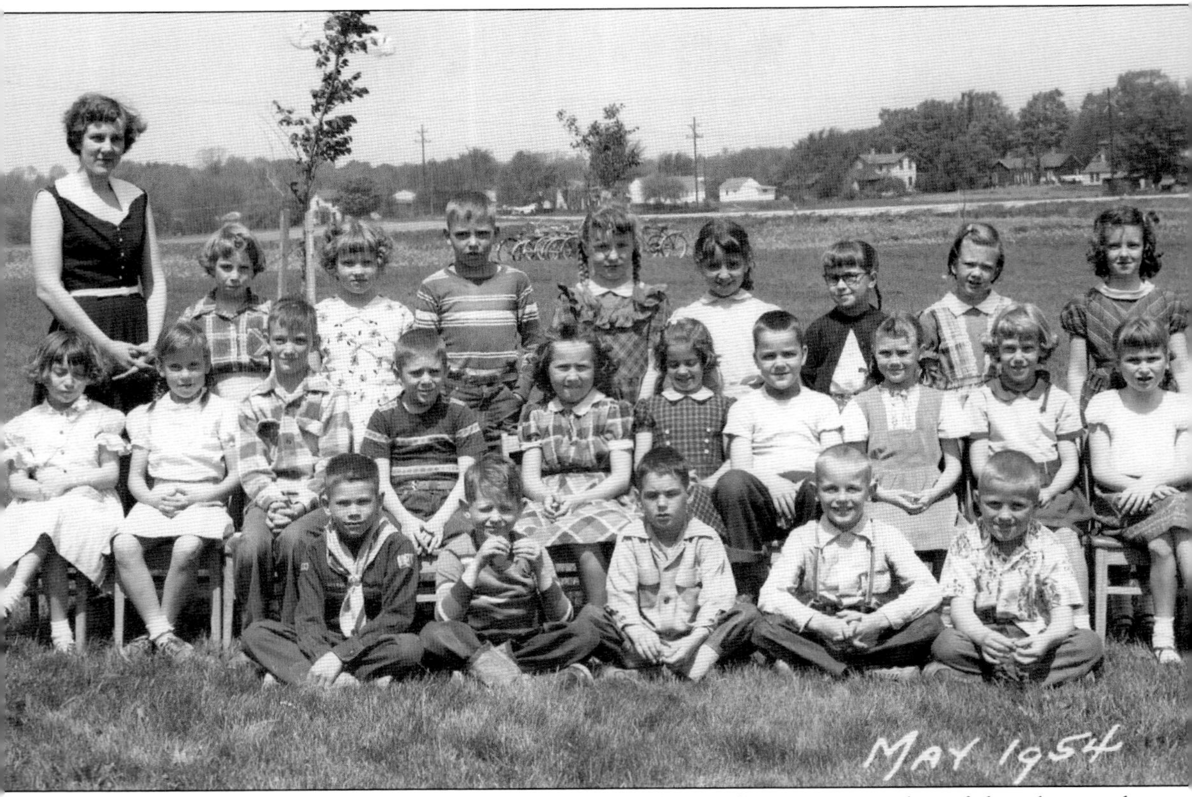

The same class is seen here a year later in 1954. John Darling was a member of this class, and he will long be remembered in the community for giving his life defending the country in the Vietnam War.

Three

Businesses and Organizations of Newaygo County

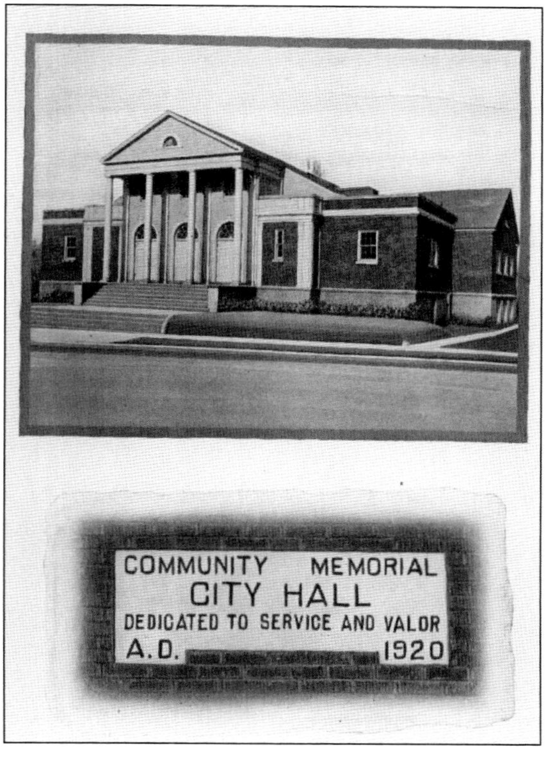

The community building in Fremont was erected after World War I. Its official name was the Soldiers Memorial Community Building, and it was dedicated to the nine men from Fremont who gave their lives in service during the war. The building contained the city clerk office, a small bowling alley, a gymnasium, and a billiards room in the basement. The upstairs held a kitchen, stage, and large auditorium that hosted many community performances.

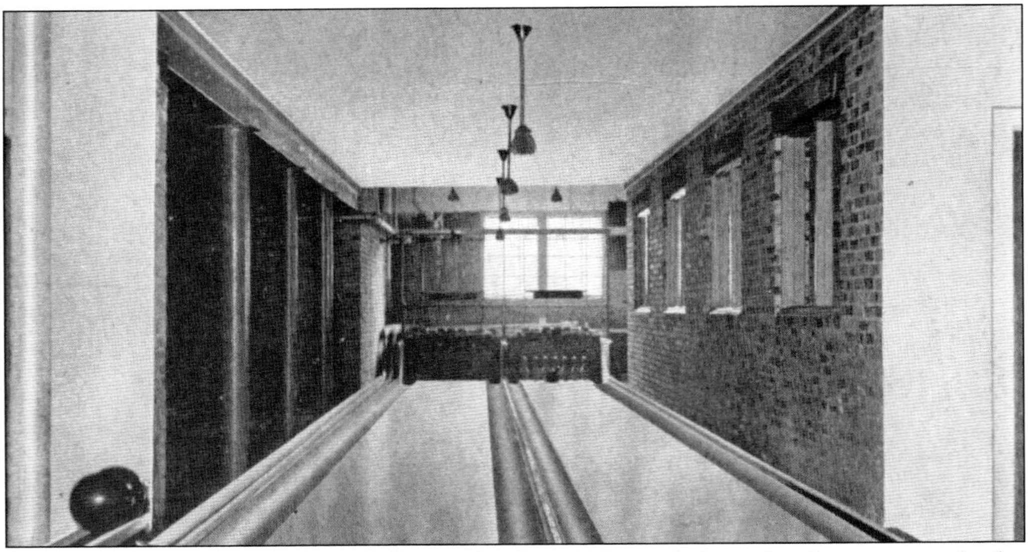

The Community Memorial City Hall, completed in 1920, was dedicated to the service and valor of Fremont's World War I soldiers, in particular those who died while in service. Not only were the city offices housed there, but also within its walls were an auditorium with a balcony, a library and reading room, and even a two-lane bowling alley (pictured).

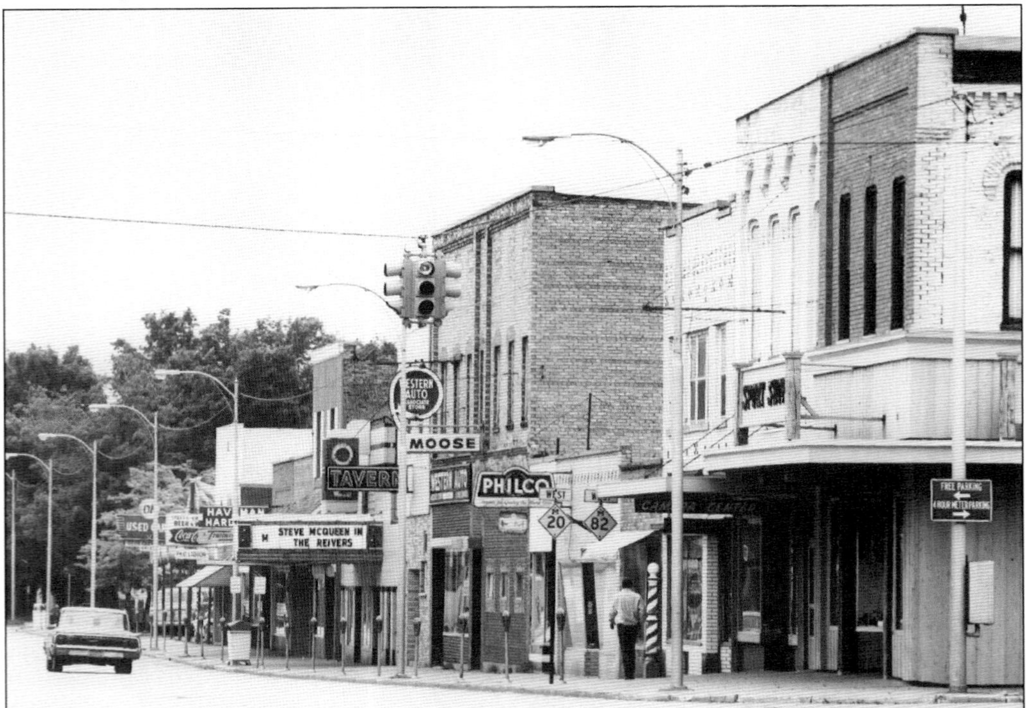

This photograph of downtown Fremont was taken when there were parking meters along Main Street. This is the northwest section of town, looking toward Veterans Park. The image was taken in 1969 or shortly later, as the Steve McQueen movie *The Reivers* is being advertised on the marquee of the old Oz Theatre.

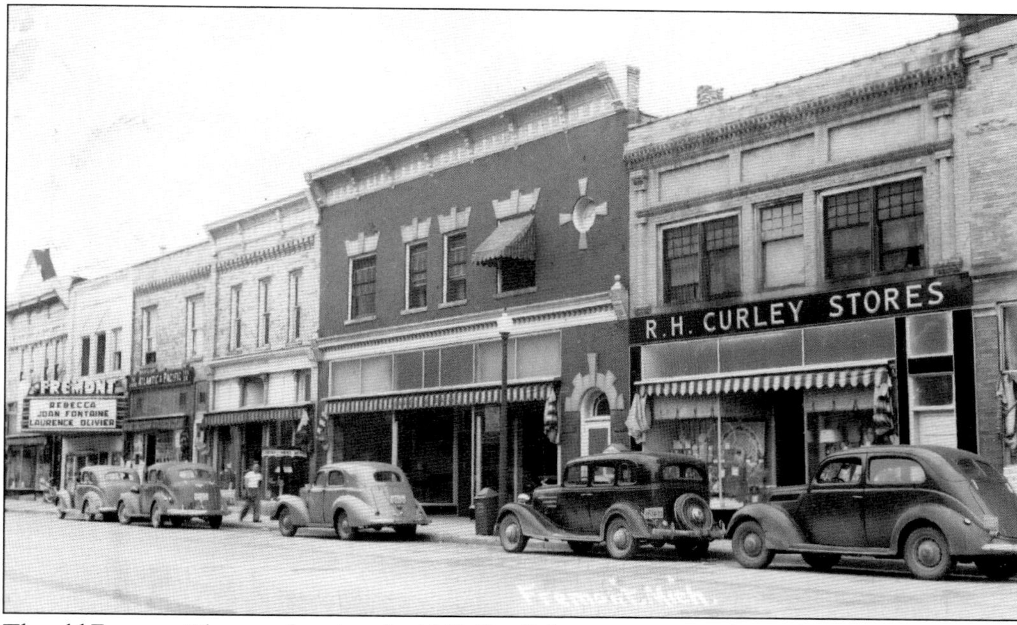

The old Fremont Theater, showing the 1940 film *Rebecca*, entertained people visiting downtown. After the movie, stopping at Caruso's ice cream and candy parlor was a welcome treat. R.H. Curley, with stores in Newaygo and in Fremont, offered shoppers many special and necessary items.

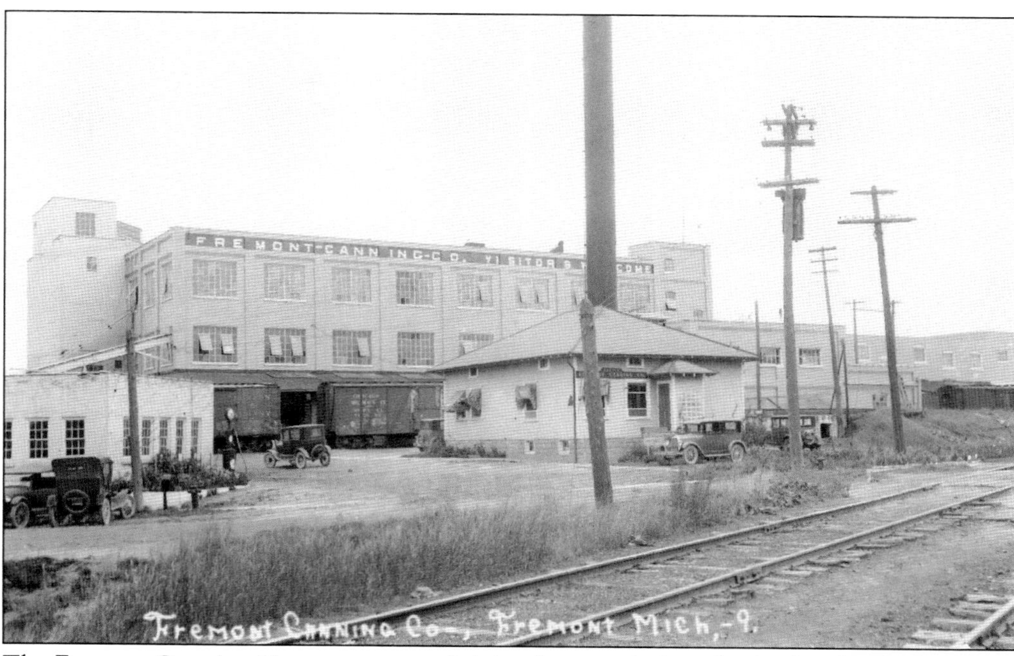

The Fremont Canning Company was a thriving business before the Gerber family discovered the market for prepared canned baby food. It had been operating for many years before it was rebranded as Gerber Products Company in 1941. Before long, frazzled mothers everywhere were welcoming the product into their homes. Gerber babies can now be found around the world.

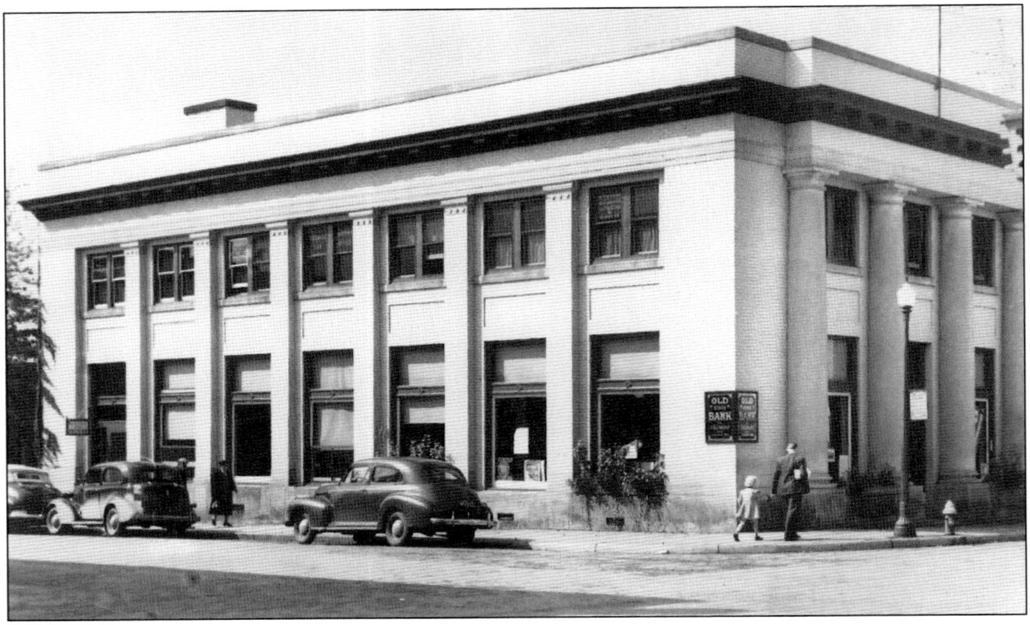

Old State Bank, shown here, was a longtime institution in Fremont. Many prominent citizens served as directors. The bank was established in 1883, and the building at 2 West Main Street was constructed in 1915. It is still in use at the present time, although Old State Bank merged and is now Huntington National Bank.

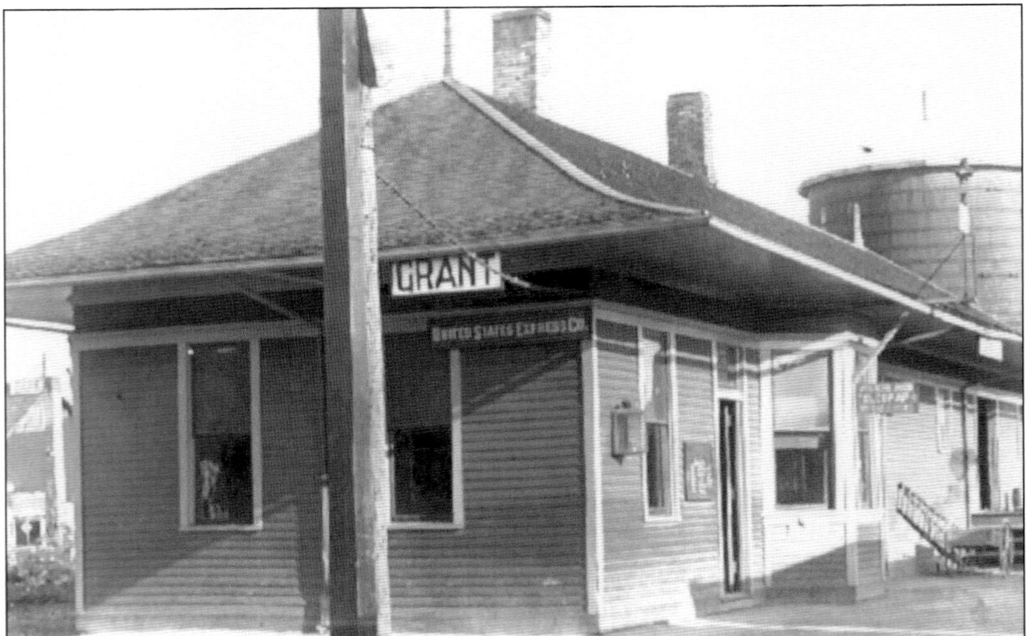

The railroad was an important resource in the community. In the early part of the 20th century, Grant shipped a lot of produce by rail. In 1915, ten to twelve cars of peaches a day were shipped. In the 1930s, carloads of onions became part of the produce exported out of town via rail. As late as 1940, there were still two passenger trains going through town, between Grand Rapids and Traverse City. The last passenger train ran in 1963.

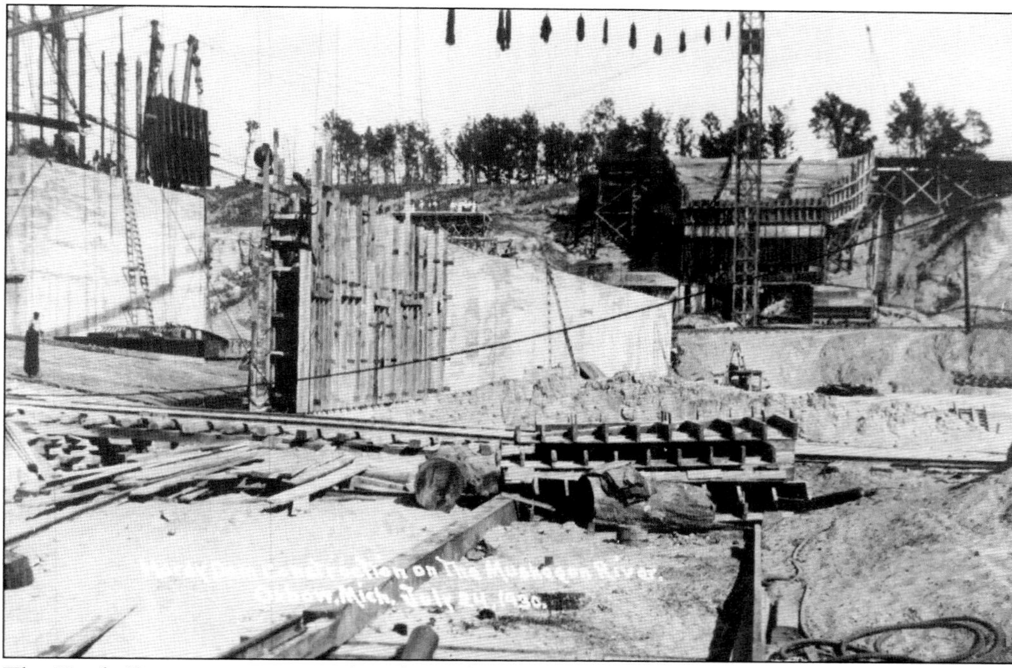

The Hardy Dam was constructed in the early 1930s to help provide electricity by harnessing the power of the Muskegon River. By July 1930, part of the structure was already in the process of being poured. Located in what was considered the Oxbow region of the river, the power plant went into service in 1932.

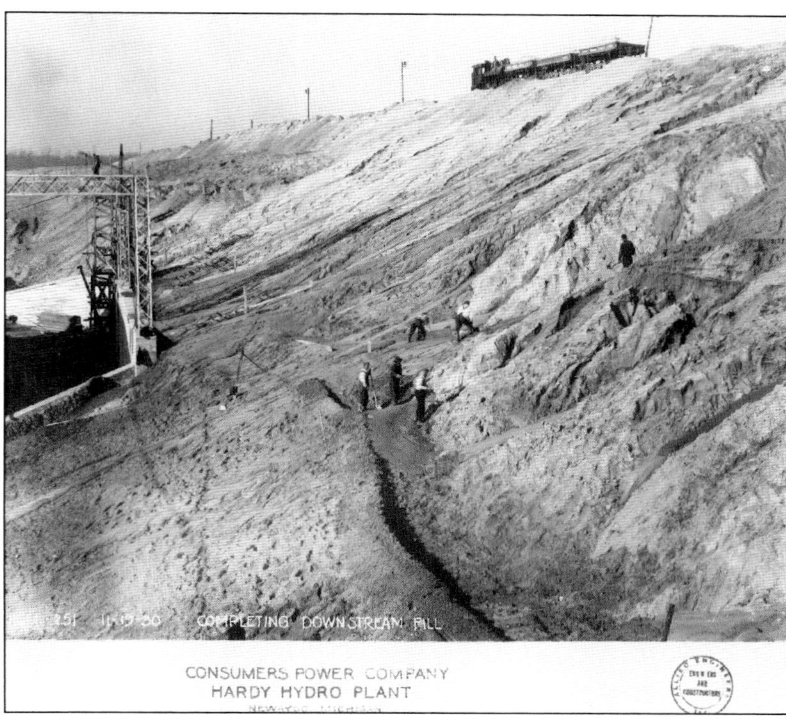

The construction of the Hardy Hydro Plant was a very unique project, and many people made it a Sunday outing to see what was taking place. This November 19, 1930, photograph shows the process of completing the downstream fill for the dam. Note the men digging with hand shovels.

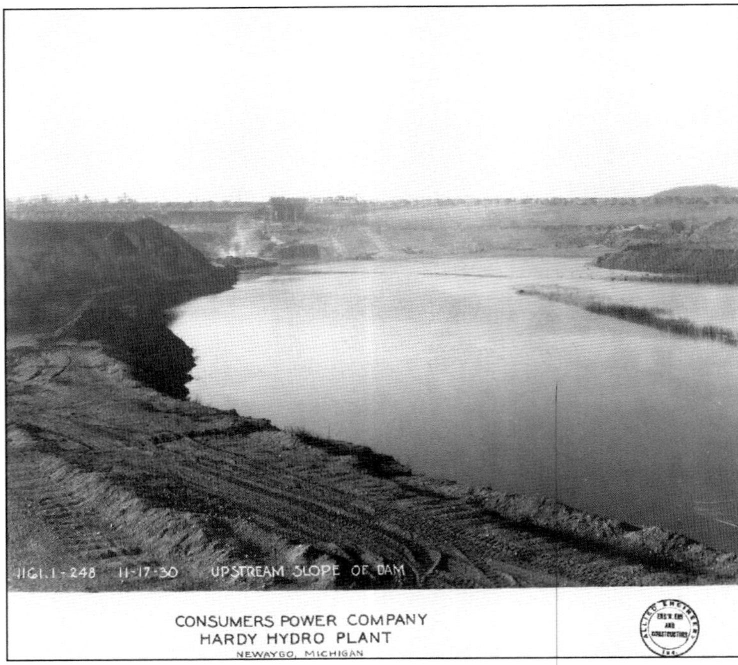

Here is the upstream slope of the Consumers Power Company Hardy Hydro Plant during construction on November 17, 1930. This series of images provides a sense of how large the dam project was.

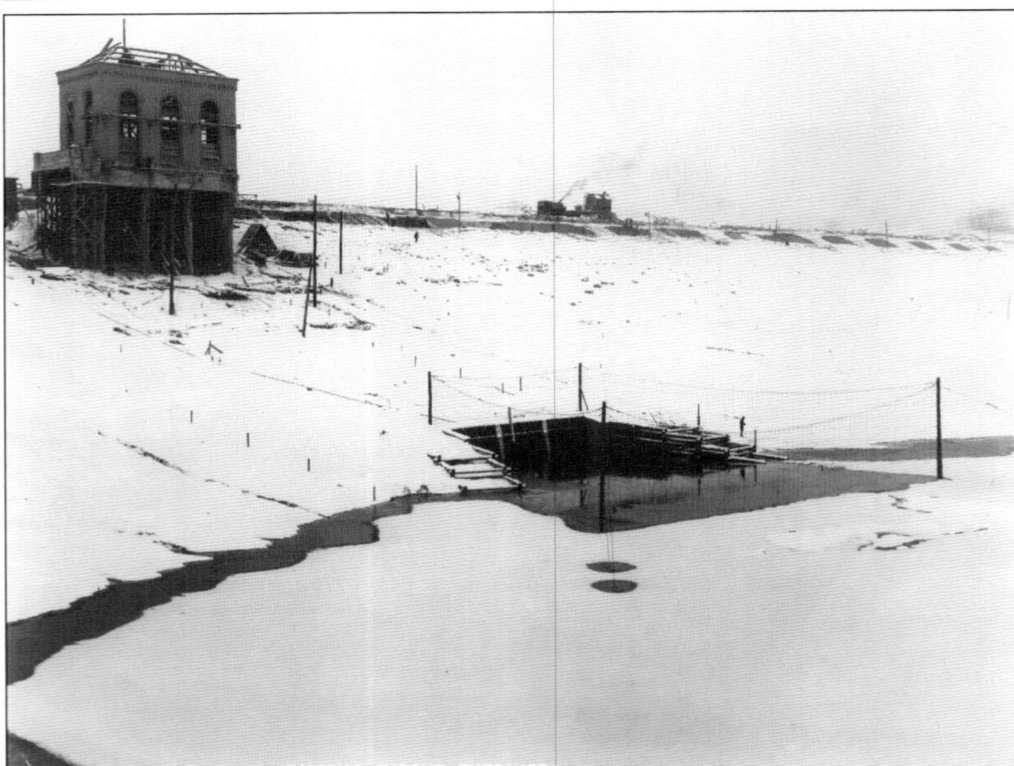

This photograph of the upstream intake entrance offers a view of the dam not commonly seen. It also shows that the men worked year-round, not stopping for the snow and cold. It would be a cold job in January, when this photograph was taken in 1931.

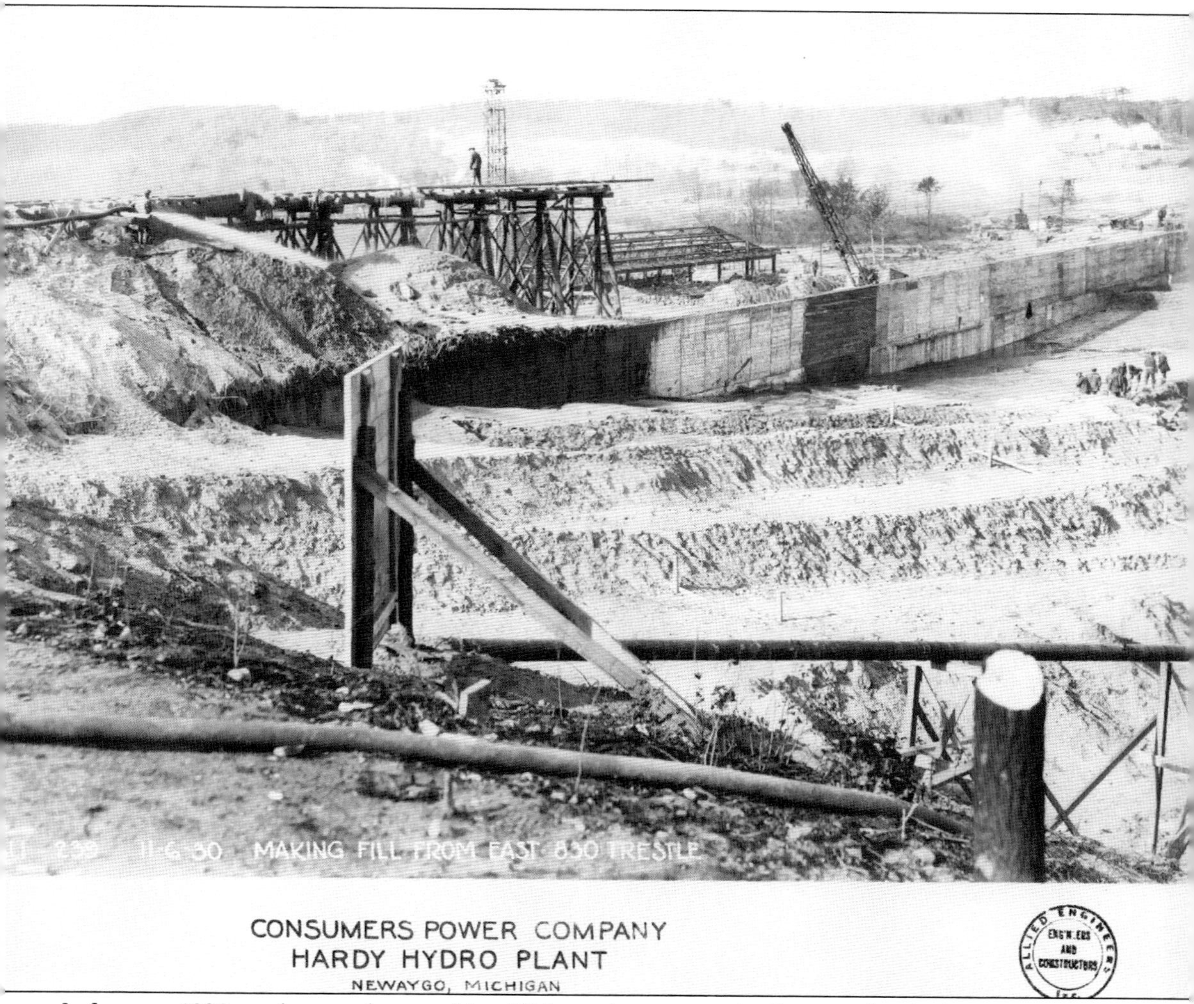

In January 1930, workers are busy making fill from the east trestle. During what looks to be hard labor, one wonders if the men ever thought of the future impact the dam would have on the area. The dam created over 50 miles of shoreline that would become dotted over the years with campgrounds, beaches, and cabins, becoming a favorite vacation spot.

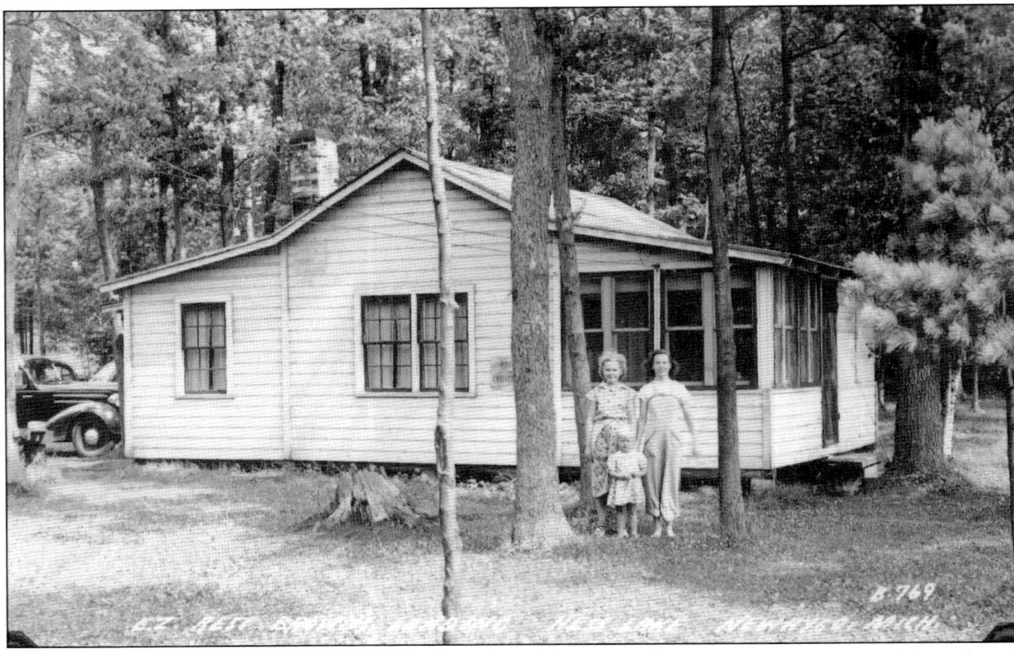

With the many rivers and lakes to be found in Newaygo County, it is not surprising that it became a popular vacation spot. Resorts and cottages sprang up near area lakes and rivers. Many families could rent a cottage by the week or month for a relaxing summer vacation. Hess Lake, near Newaygo, was one popular destination, as these vacationers can attest.

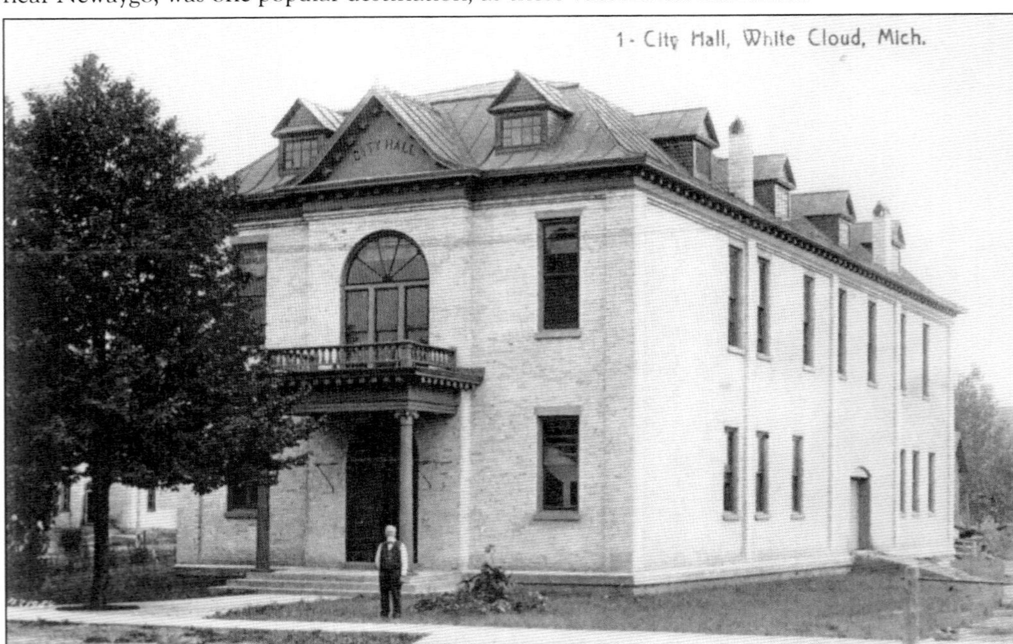

The original White Cloud Courthouse was built in 1910 and served the county until 1993, when it was torn down. A new courthouse was built for the county in 1992–1993. Today, the county complex is made up of several buildings. By 2000, Newaygo County's population had grown to 47,874 people.

Tourism is the most important economic activity in Newaygo County, followed by a blend of agriculture and small manufacturing. International baby food manufacturer Gerber Products Nestlé is currently the county's largest employer, with approximately 1,300 employees. Newaygo County also has a large number of summer residents. Fishermen can find steelhead in the spring and salmon in the fall in the county's rivers and streams. Camping, hunting, cross-country skiing, bicycling, bird watching, and off-road racing are common in the Manistee National Forest. (Courtesy of Camp Newaygo.)

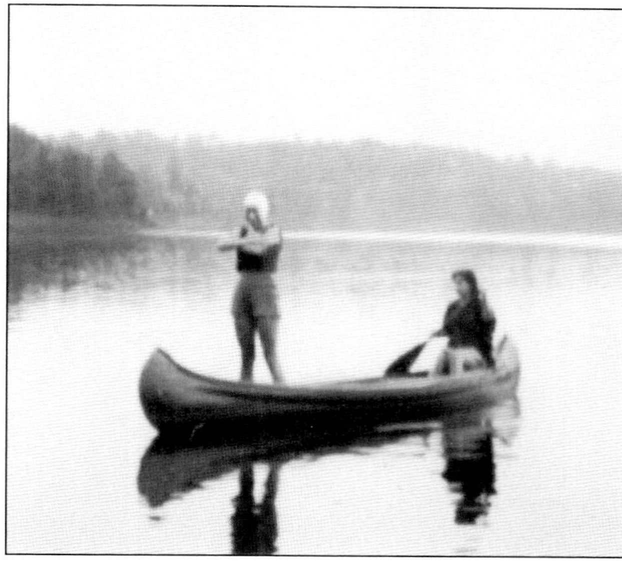

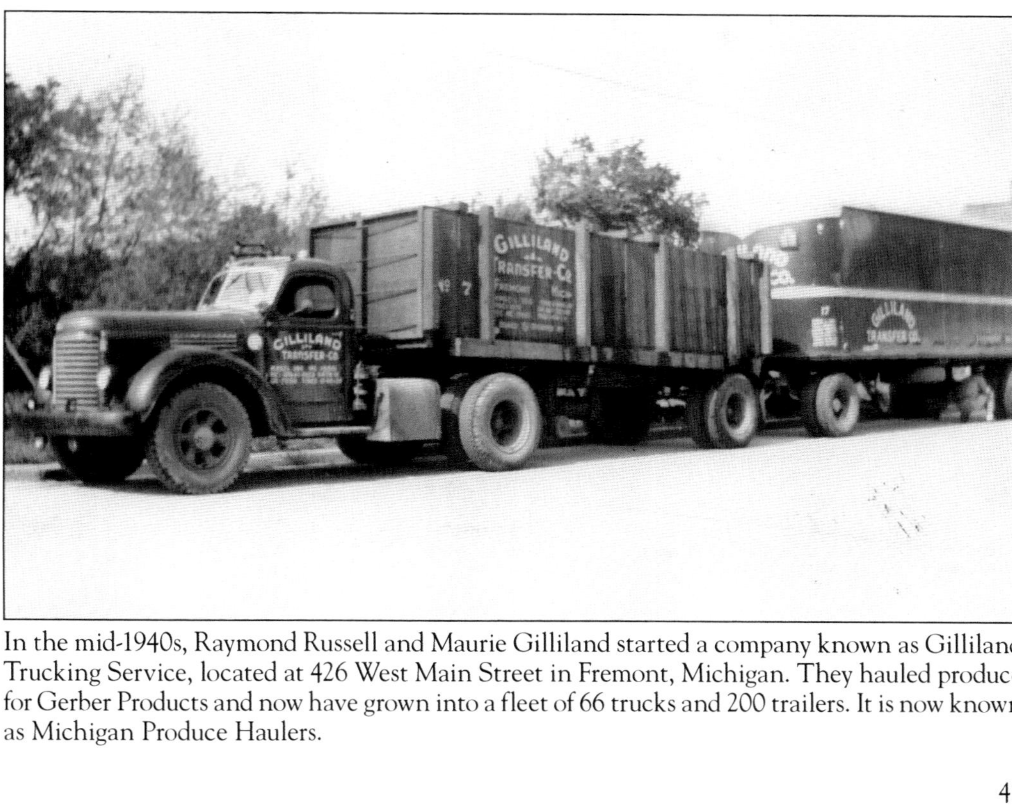

In the mid-1940s, Raymond Russell and Maurie Gilliland started a company known as Gilliland Trucking Service, located at 426 West Main Street in Fremont, Michigan. They hauled produce for Gerber Products and now have grown into a fleet of 66 trucks and 200 trailers. It is now known as Michigan Produce Haulers.

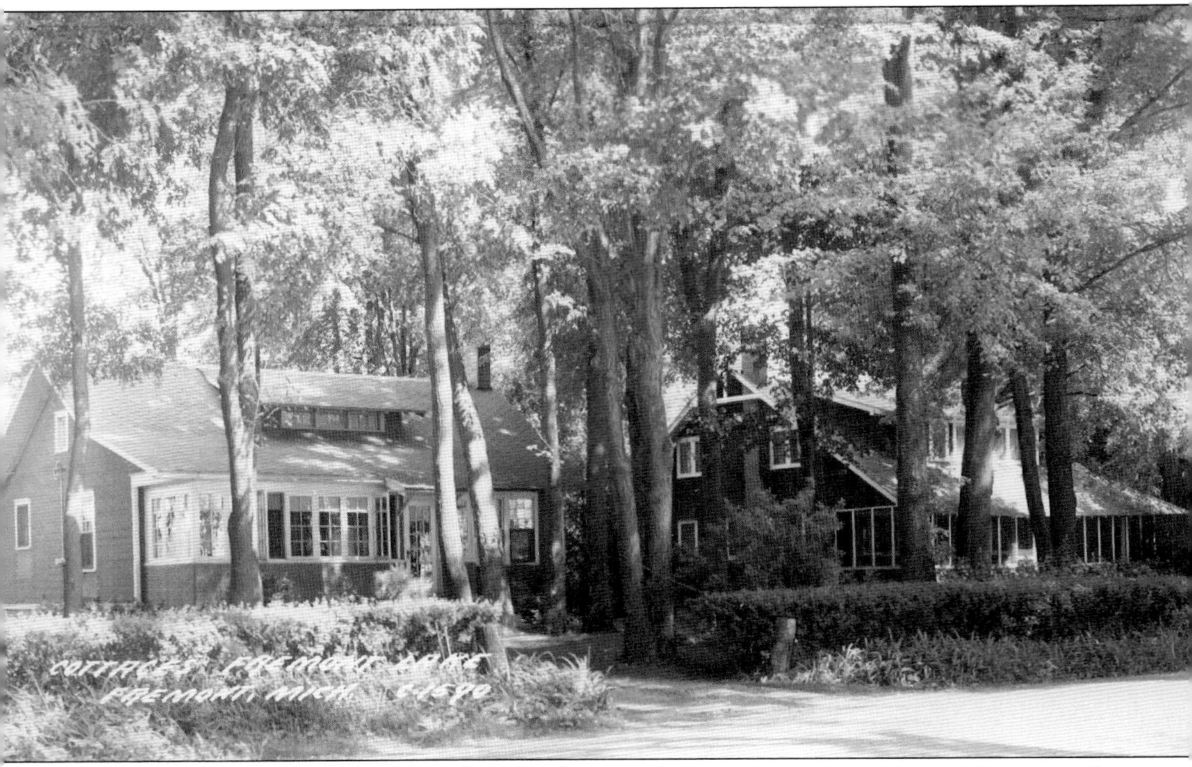

With its proximity to Fremont, Fremont Lake is very popular with residents. The area offers camping, as well as swimming and boat launches. Many cottages surround the lake. Families have built homes for year-round use on its shores, as it provides the best of town and rural life.

The Muskegon River has played a large part in the development of Newaygo County, from transporting logs, to fishing, to electric power in the present day. Hardy Hydroelectric Plant is the largest of its kind in Michigan. Its completion in 1932, with state-of-the-art equipment, has helped provide electrical power to much of west Michigan.

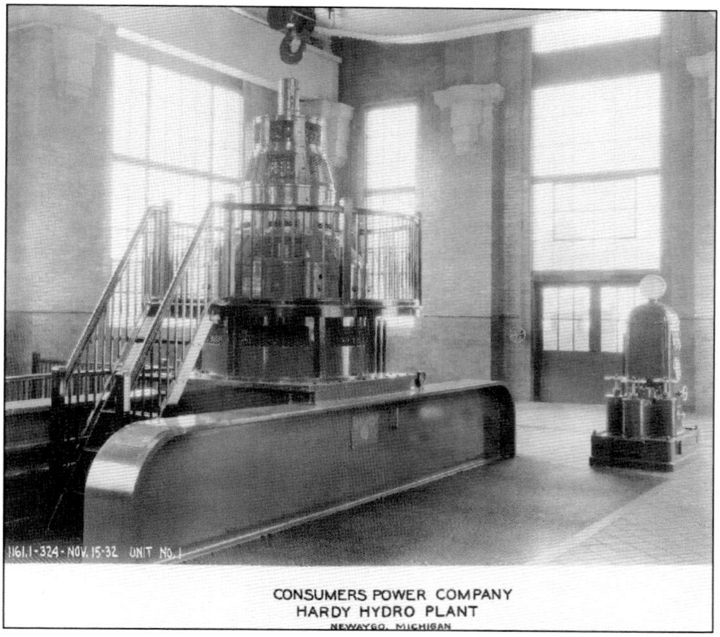

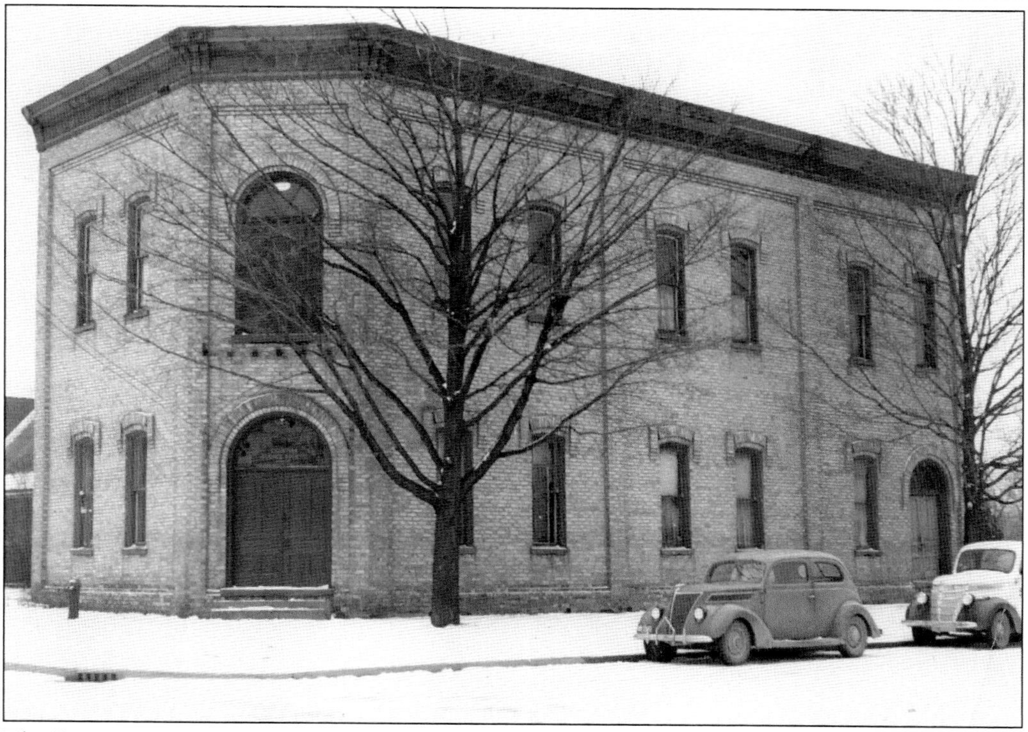

The Fremont Grange was granted a charter in November 1874. In 1876, it purchased the Carlisle property at the corner of Merchant and Sheridan Streets. The new hall was built in 1897. This was a much-loved landmark in the county as a symbol of the farming community. In 1949, the grange celebrated its 75th anniversary. After several years of increasing costs and with fewer grange members, the bottom floor was leased to the county historical society, which was unable to keep up the cost of repairs and maintenance. The grange was burned down in 1979 by arsonists.

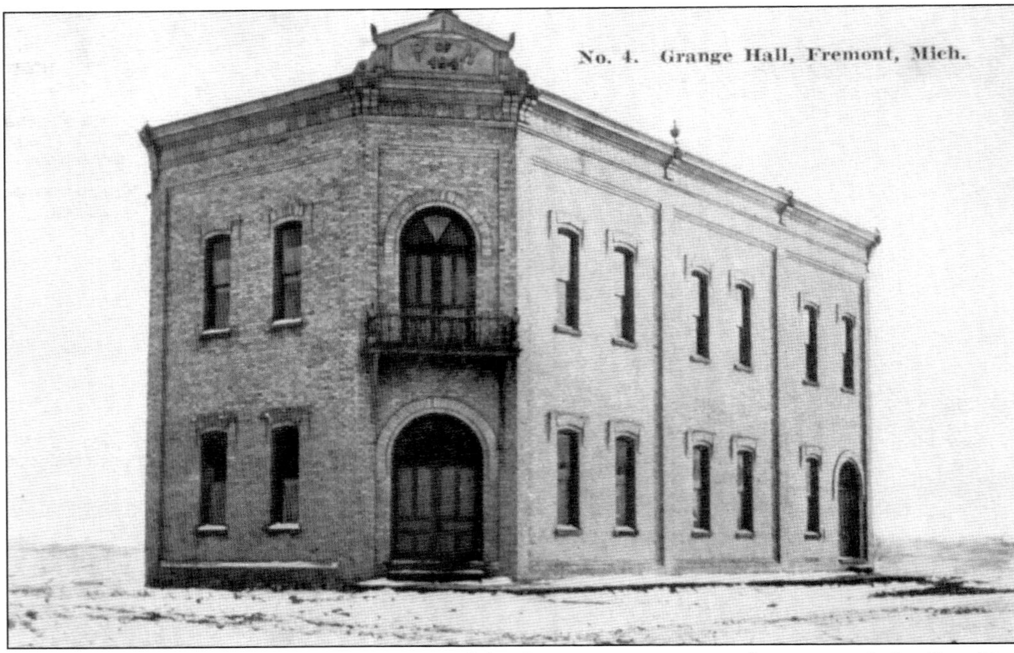

The Fremont Grange was an active part of the farming community. It instituted the first Cow Testing Association in the United States. There were roller-skating facilities in the building, and the Grangers helped clean and repair the old Pioneer Cemetery west of Fremont. The building was home to the Historical Society of Newaygo County, and the 105-year-old building eventually burned down in an act of arson.

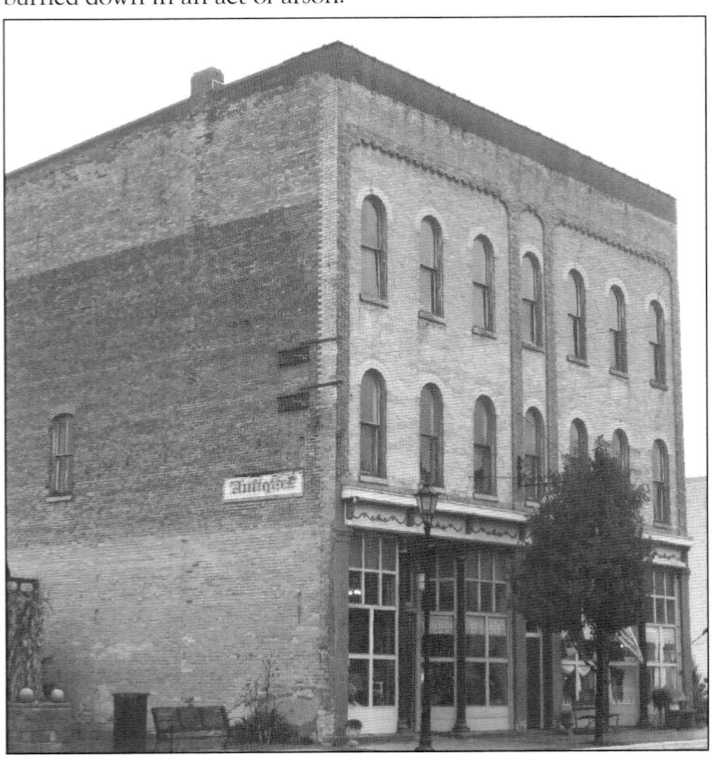

Romeo Noel Lemire started the Lemire Drug Store in 1920 when he purchased the Raider Block, later known as the Lemire Block, on State Street in downtown Newaygo. Lemire hired a high school student, Elizabeth Peacock, to help in the store. The two were later married. The Lemire Drug Store was also the location, in the 1930s and 1940s, of the North Star Bus Line, which stopped at the drugstore to pick up and drop off passengers.

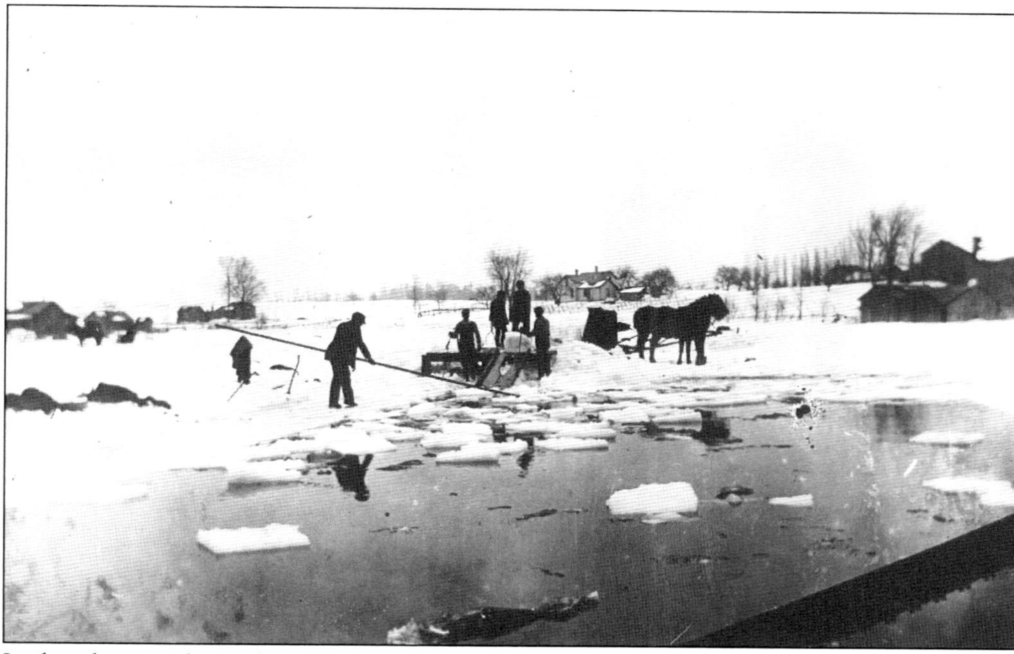

In this photograph, residents are putting up ice on Second Lake near Fremont. In the days before household refrigeration, ice was cut and stored in icehouses. Industrial and commercial refrigeration started in the 1800s, but not until the 1940s did residential refrigerators begin to become commonplace. The need to cut ice was thus eliminated, making life easier for everyone involved.

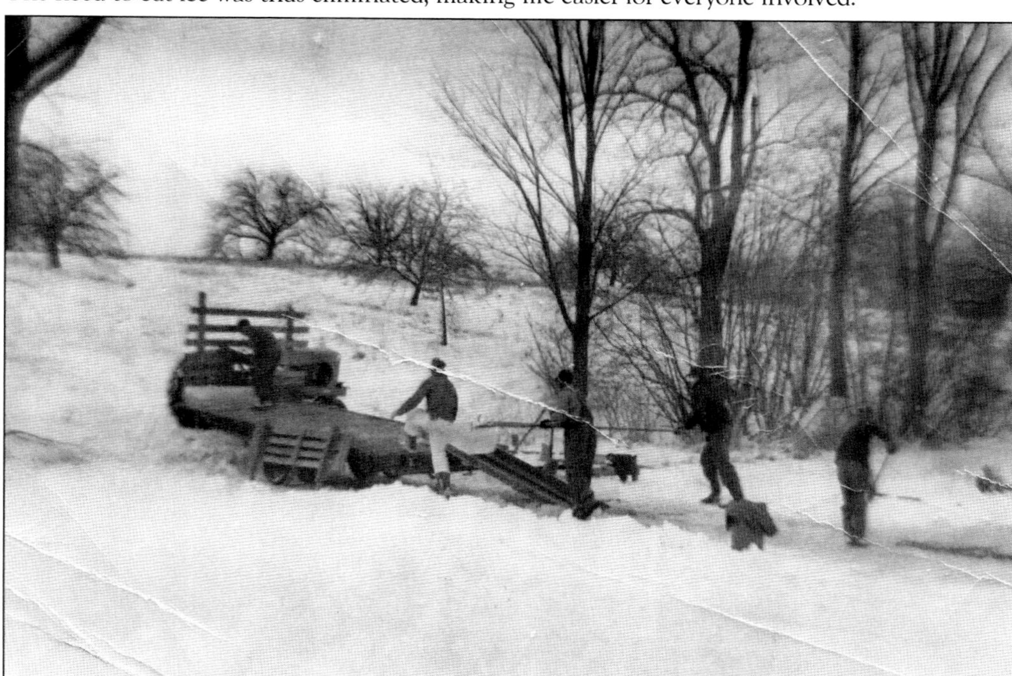

After ice was cut from the lakes, the big slabs were fished out of the water. They were then pulled to a ramp and slid onto a wagon to be hauled to the icehouse. The cold and wet work was necessary in order to furnish iceboxes in the summer.

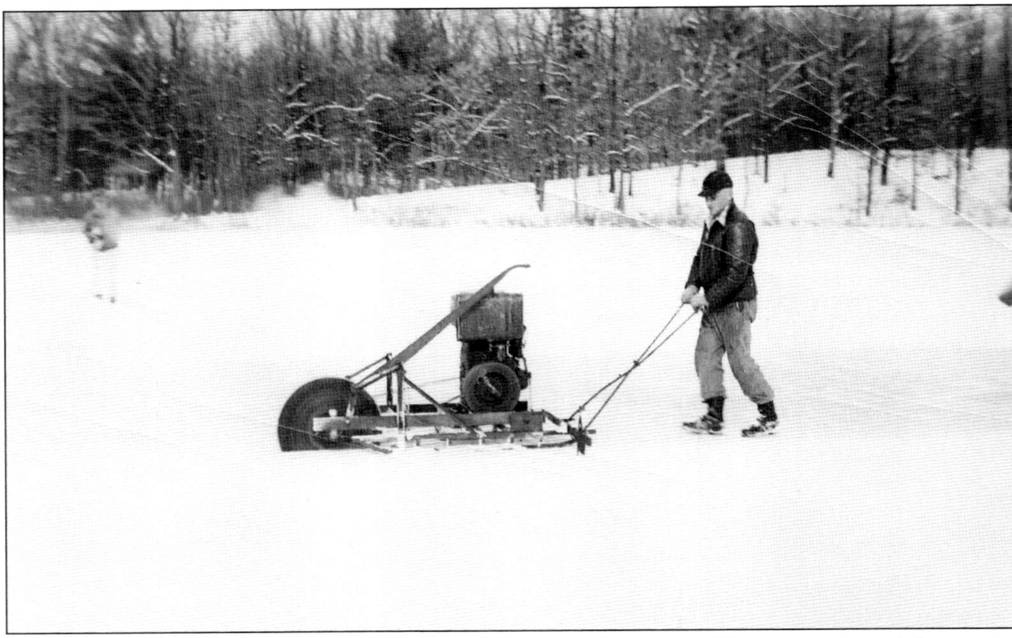

Before refrigerators gained wide usage, the icebox reigned supreme. They necessitated the cutting of ice to be packed away in winter and stored for use in the summer months. The powered ice cutter shown here would slice large blocks, which were then hauled to icehouses. Diamond Lake had a large icehouse for such storage.

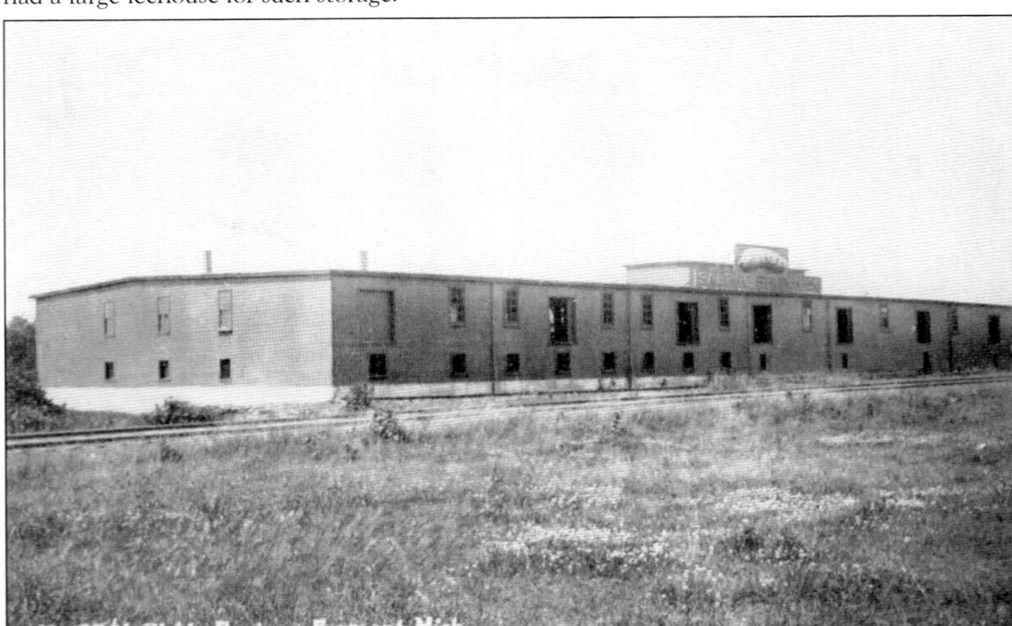

Heinz pickle factory No. 2541, located in Fremont, was an employer for many years in Newaygo County. Many area residents worked in the counting, dill, and salting rooms. When the pickle barrels were rolled out and stacked to await shipment, local youngsters would be happy to look for leaky barrels, sampling the juice and pickles as they escaped. This photograph was taken around 1921.

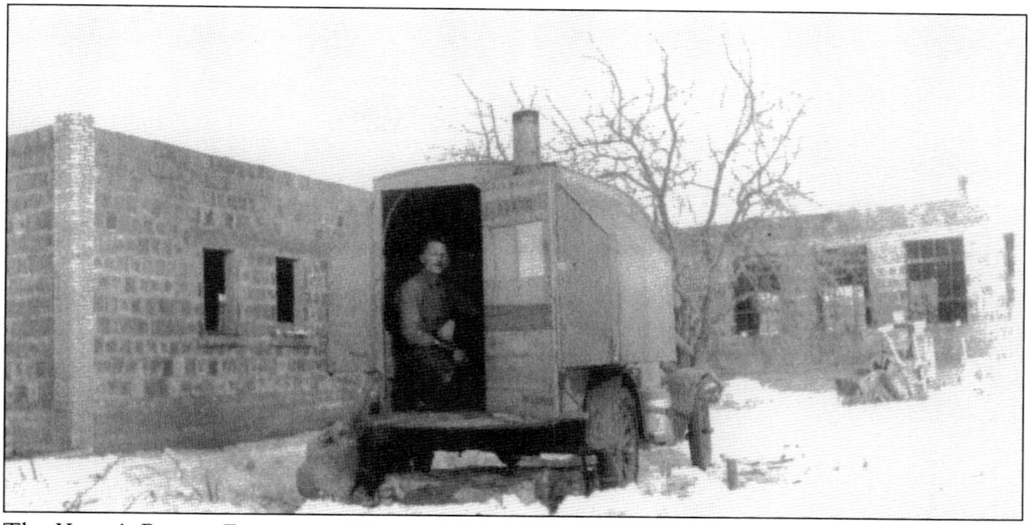

The Knott's Button Factory on West Maple Street in Fremont provided employment for many residents during the Depression years. Originally, the clamshells used to make buttons came from rivers in Michigan. The Muskegon River was considered to have the best shells for the buttons. When Michigan shells became scarce, railroad cars full of shells from the Wabash River in Ohio and the Mississippi River were brought in. Many local driveways still have remains from the shells today.

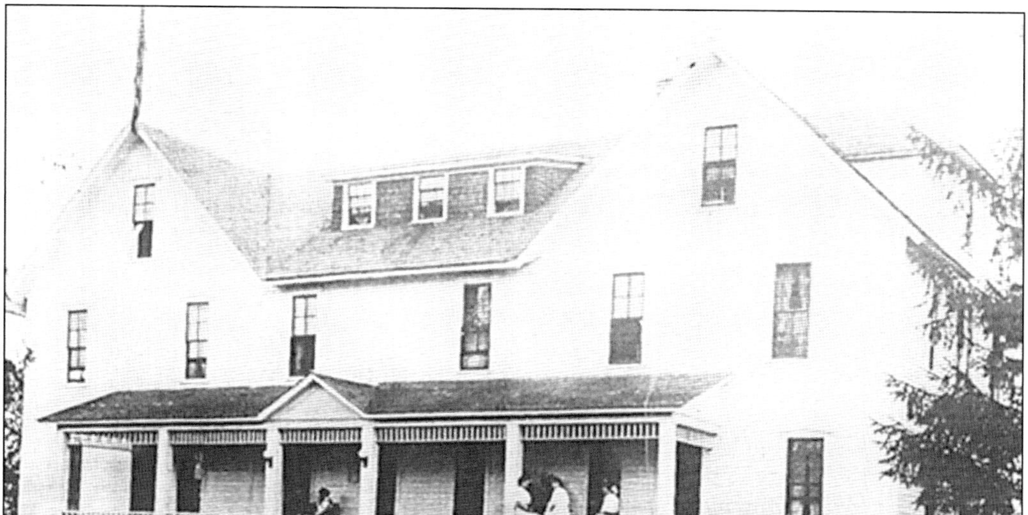

In the 1920s, the Folk School was revived on the grounds of the former Danish Folk High School, which had continued the voluntary school system founded in Denmark. Its aim was to provide higher education to men and women. It was a school free of stereotyped textbooks and examinations. Emphasis was placed on adult education, directed toward vocational, recreational, and civic problems. This method of education was believed to lead toward "directing the young people toward a high and noble life, thus enabling them to appreciate life indeed."

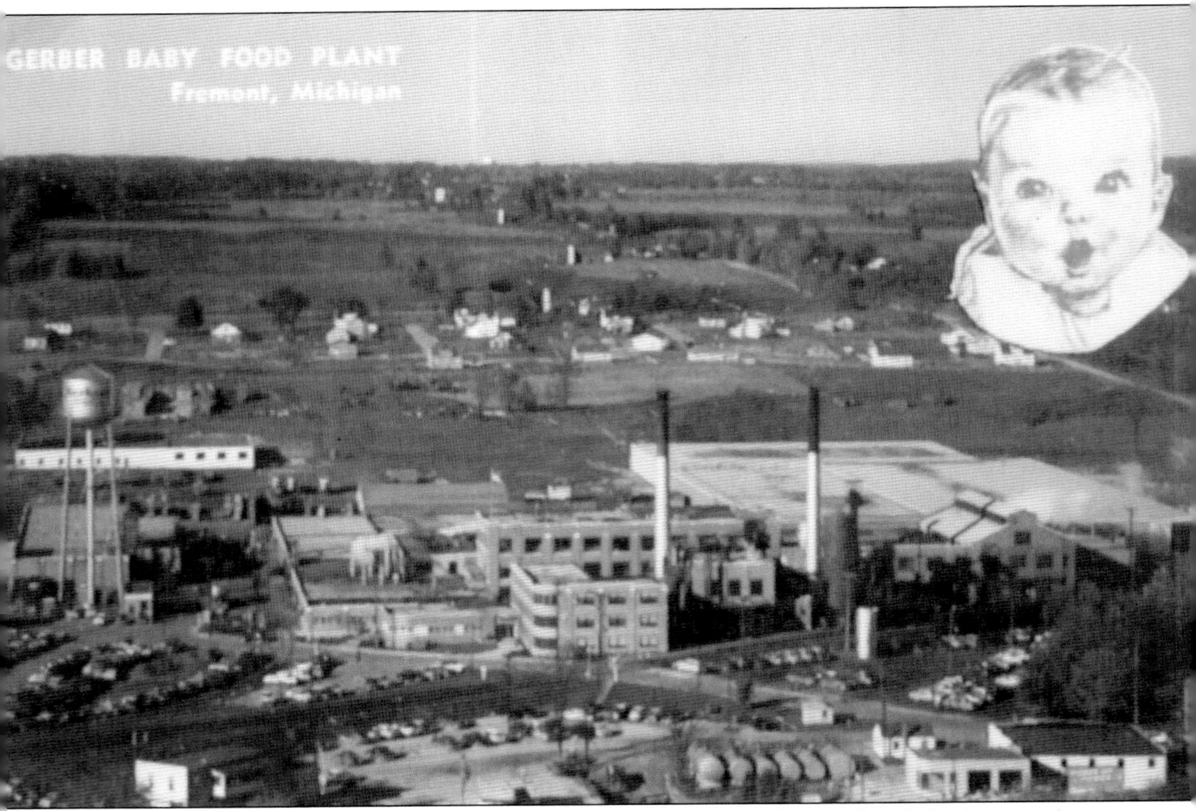

As the Gerber Baby Food Plant expanded and the logo of the Gerber Baby became known worldwide, many people took advantage of the plant tours that were offered. After completing the tour, visitors were given a packet with, among other things, recipes, a copy of the Gerber Baby picture, and a postcard featuring a photograph of the plant.

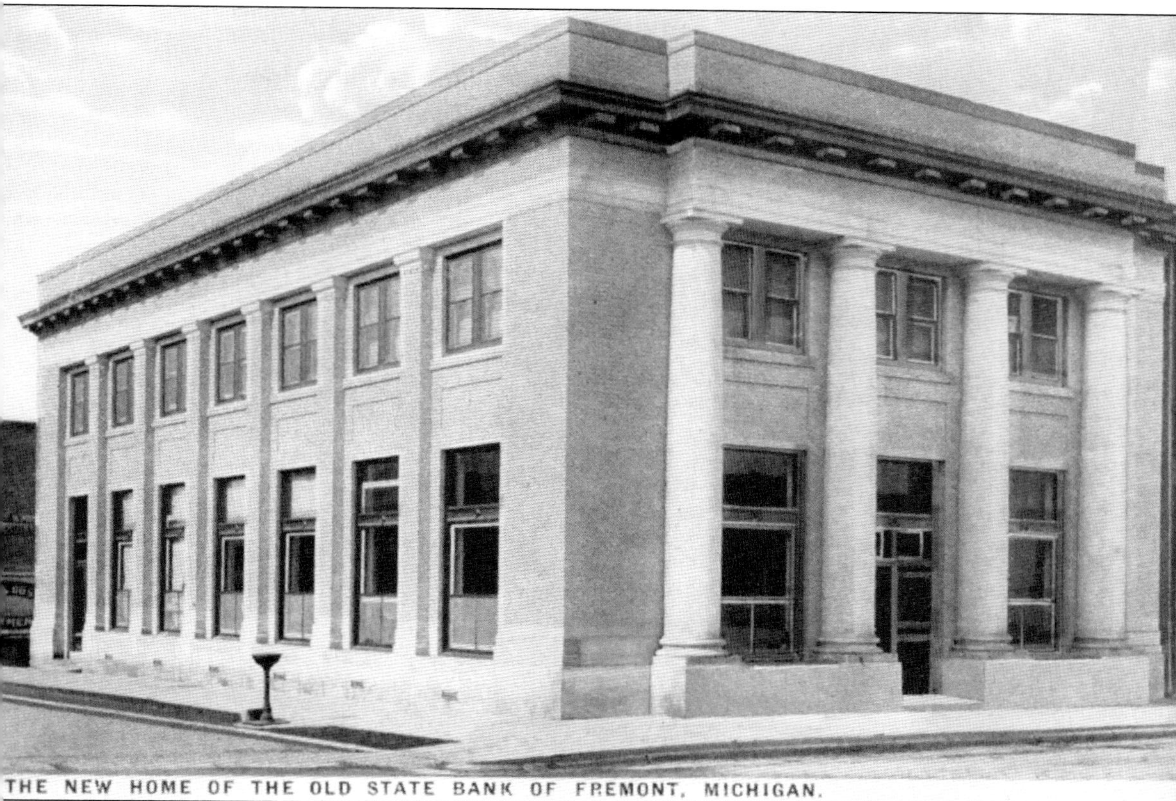

Old State Bank was established in Fremont, Michigan, in 1883 as a State Member Bank. In 1905, it was called First Bank of Michigan, and in 1906 it officially became Old State Bank. Now known as Huntington National Bank, it has long been located at 2 West Main Street in downtown Fremont. The present building, shown here, was constructed in 1915.

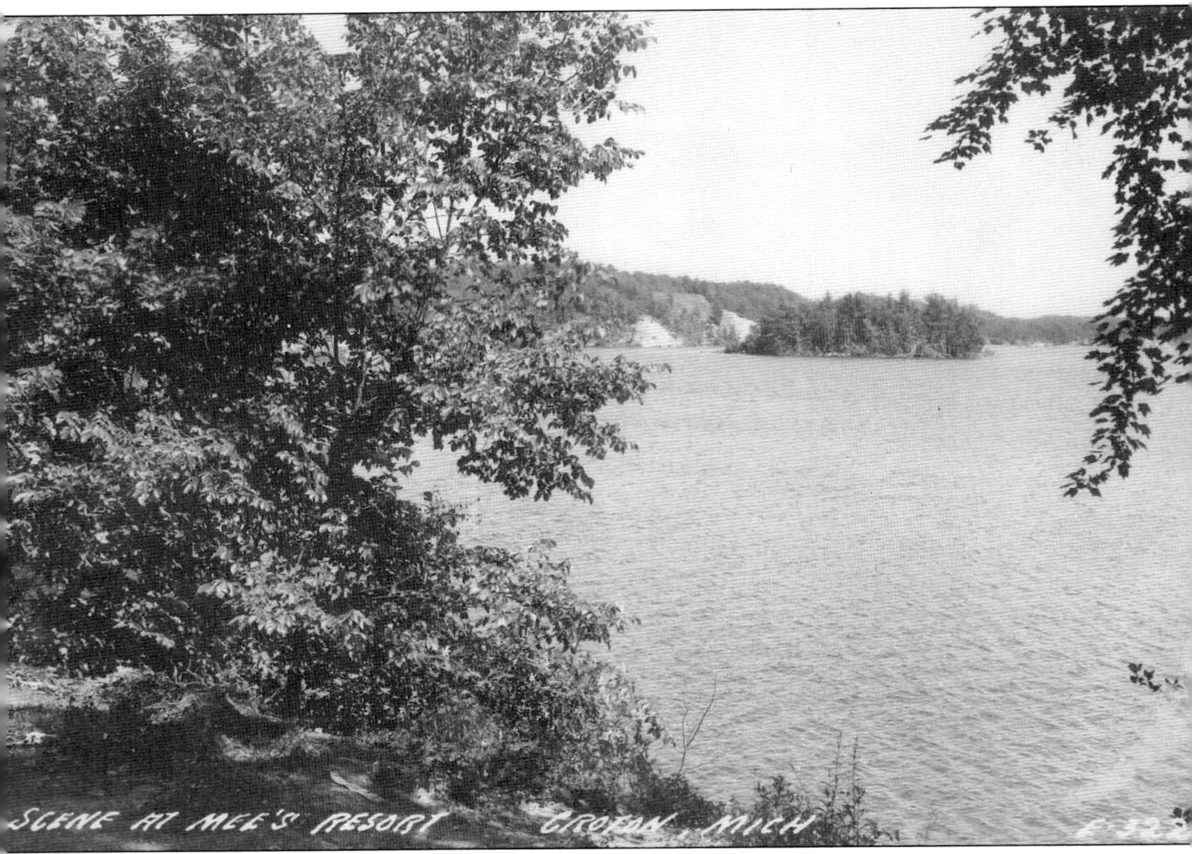

Mee's Pavilion and cottages in Croton, Michigan, was a busy place for tourists and visitors who came to Newaygo County to enjoy its streams, rivers, and lakes. Croton, the first place in Newaygo County to be established, in later years became well known as a relaxing resort, and today it is still a popular destination.

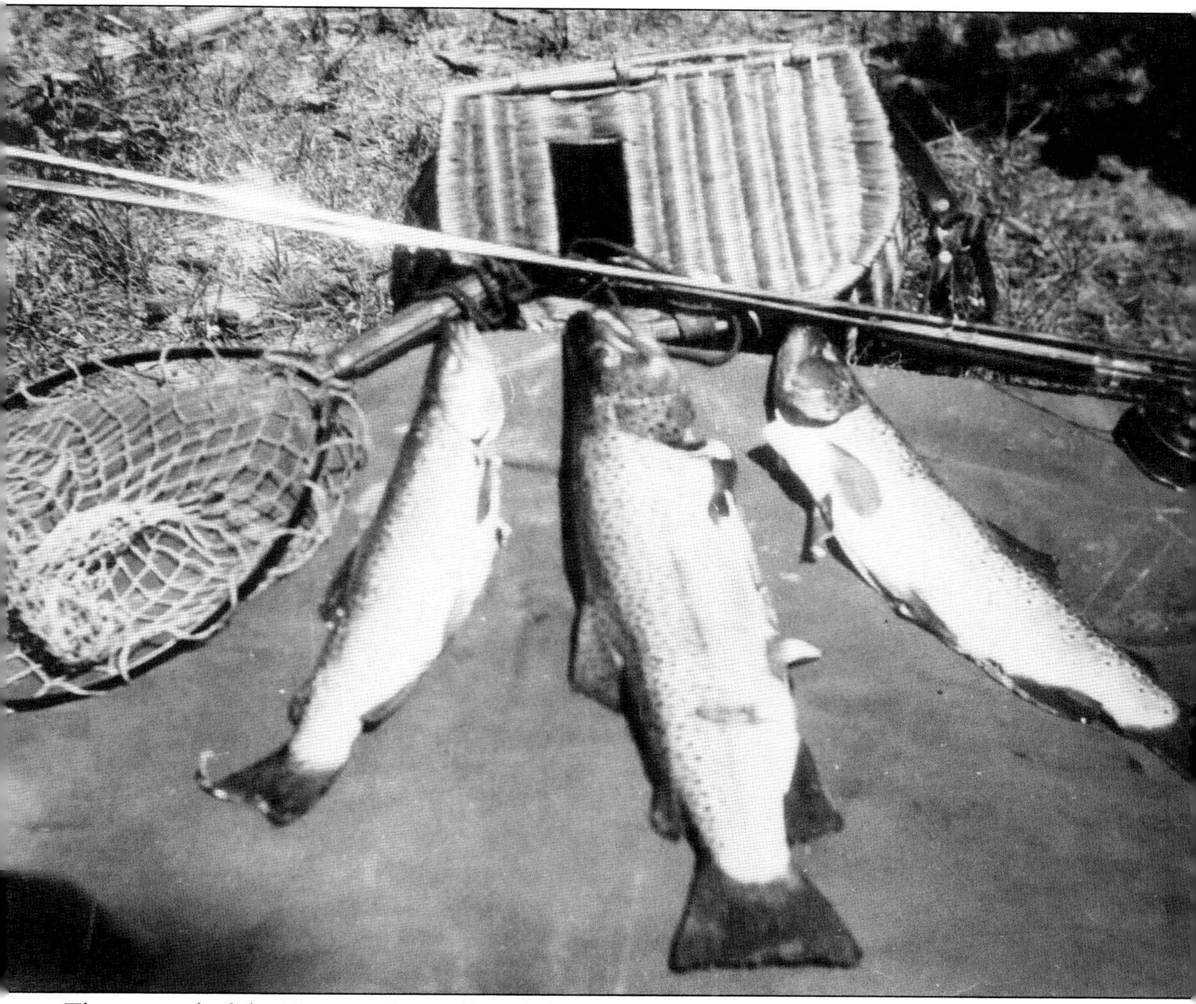

The removal of the Newaygo Dam allowed the river to be open for the passage of salmon and steelhead as far upstream as the Croton Dam. This provided natural spawning grounds for the fish, making anglers happy with the prospect of better angling opportunities.

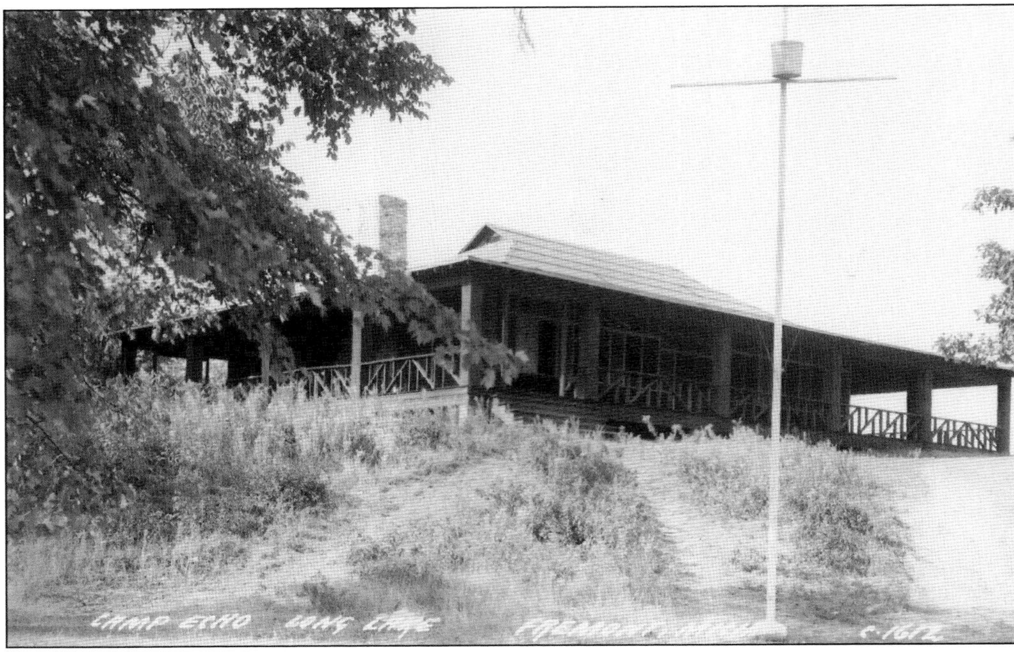

In the early 1920s, YMCA board member and Boys' Work Committee chairman F.P. Davis Sr., Boys Work secretary ? Freeman, general secretary James Bixby, and board and committee member Chester Cook began looking for a permanent home for Camp Echo. After rejecting sites at Town Line Lake and another nearby lake, they arrived at the south end of Ryerson Long Lake. The men, according to camp archives, were "electrified by what they saw—a beautiful lake with a peninsula in the middle cleared except for trees around the edge and a real forest of trees in the distance." They negotiated the purchase of the property, and Camp Echo moved to the site in 1924.

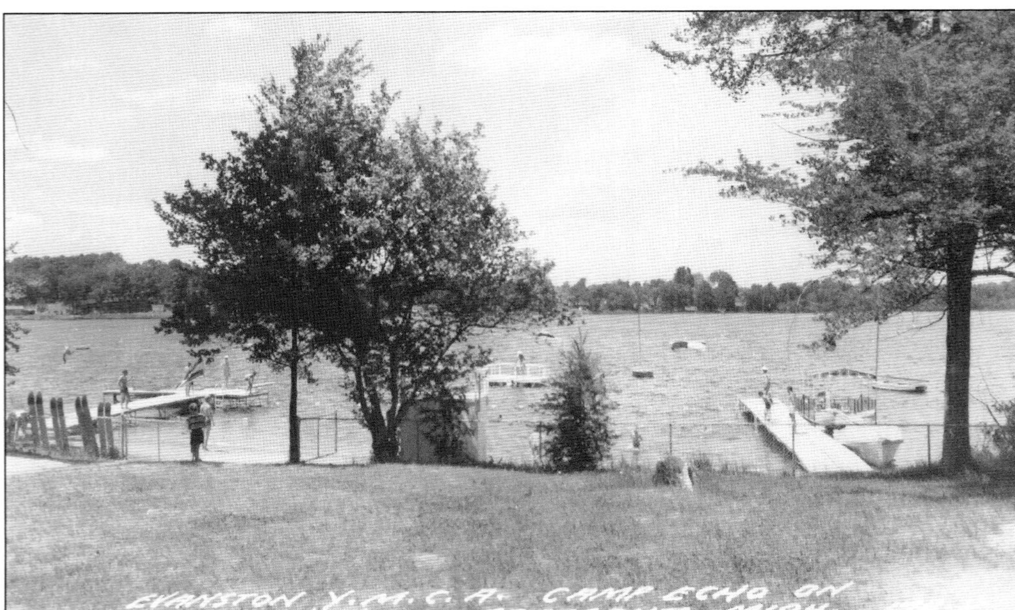

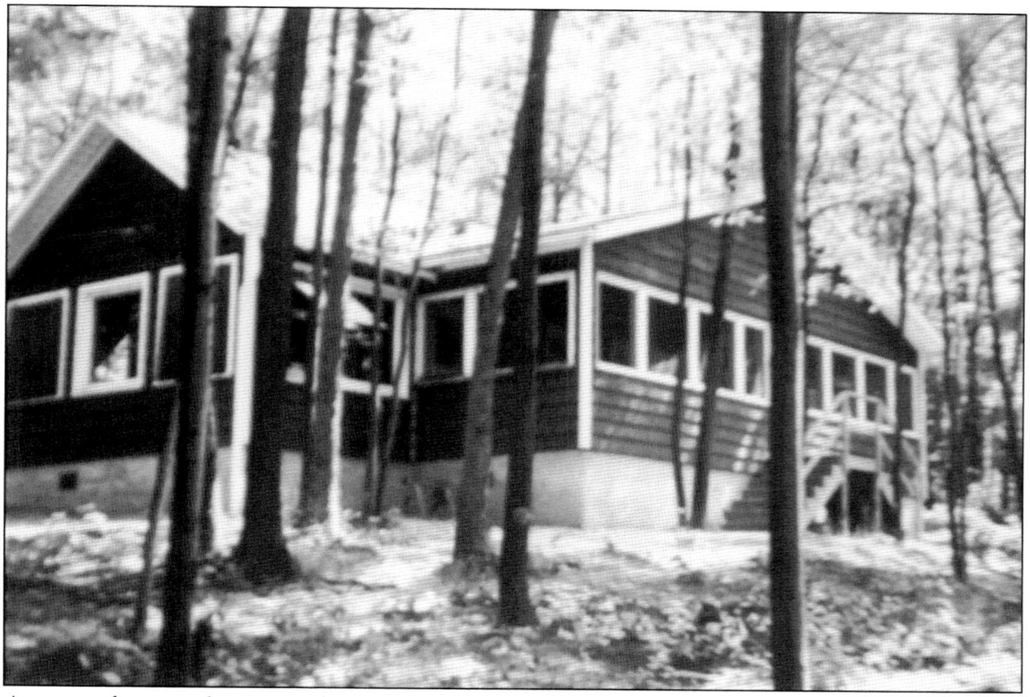

A group of women from Grand Rapids purchased 40 acres of pristine wooded property on Pickerel Lake for young women and girls. The money was raised to purchase the land by conducting a door-to-door fundraiser. The camp took its name from the nearby town of Newaygo. Camp Newaygo was established in 1926 under the direction of Florence A. Foster. (Courtesy of Camp Newaygo.)

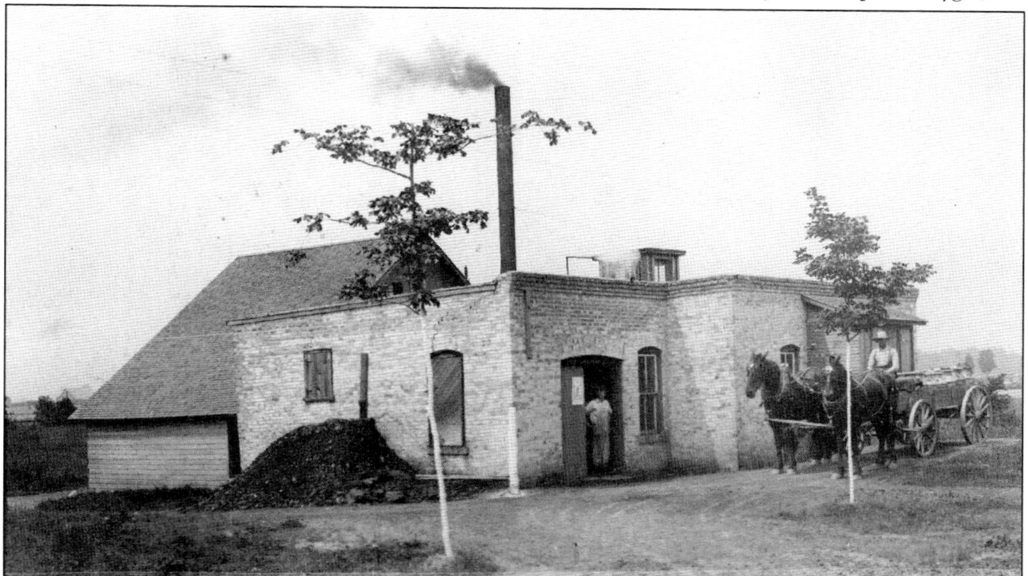

Crystal Lake Creamery in Wooster was a thriving business in the 1920s, but with a failing economy it eventually closed down. Wooster, in Sherman Township, was a flag station for the Chicago & Northwestern Railroad. It was given a post office on November 14, 1882. The post office closed on October 22, 1891.

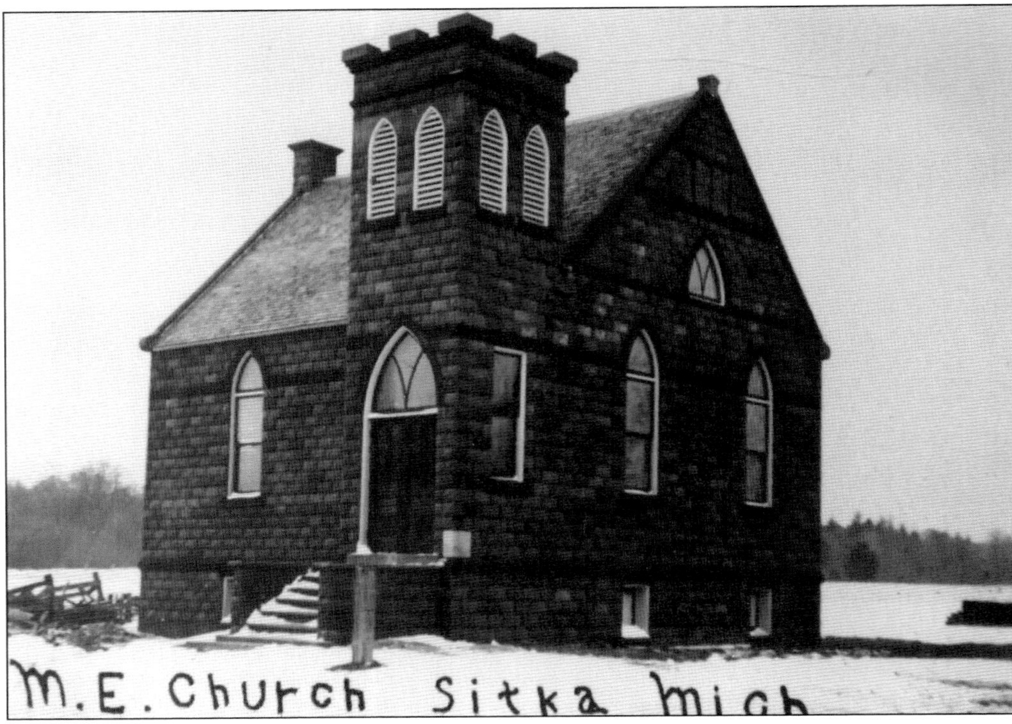

In Sheridan Township, the town of Sitka was a growing community in the 1920s, consisting mostly of farmland. It was named after Sitka, Alaska, which the United States had just purchased from Russia. Local citizens built the new Methodist church (shown here), which rapidly became, along with the community hall, the focal point for the town.

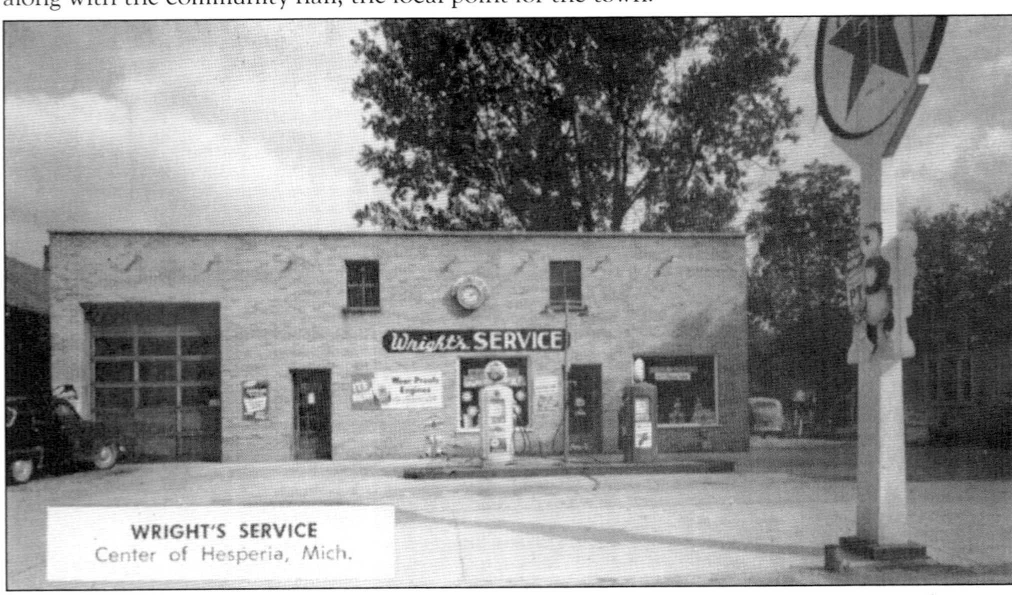

Wright's Service in Hesperia, Michigan, was in the center of town. It sold Texaco products and Montgomery Ward tires and batteries, and it offered "Cross Sight" wheel alignment and general service. The station's phone number was 2295. With the growing number of automobile owners in the 1920s, service stations started popping up all over the county.

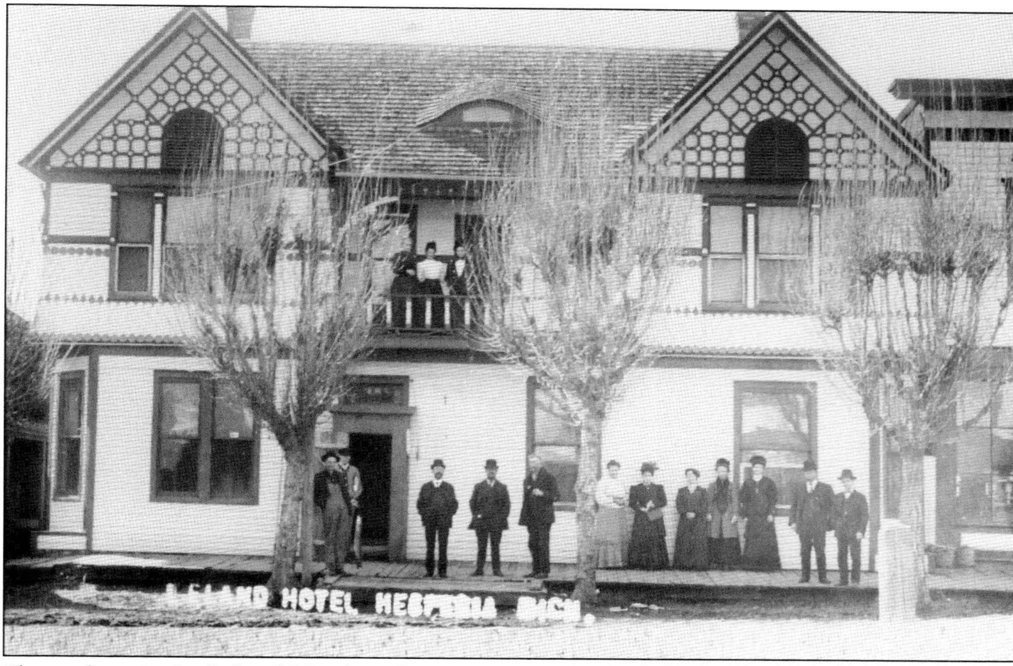

Shown here is the Leland Hotel in downtown Hesperia. A very stylish hotel in its day, it was also known as the Saint Charles Hotel. Other hotels in Hesperia were the Hesperia House and the Nichols Hotel.

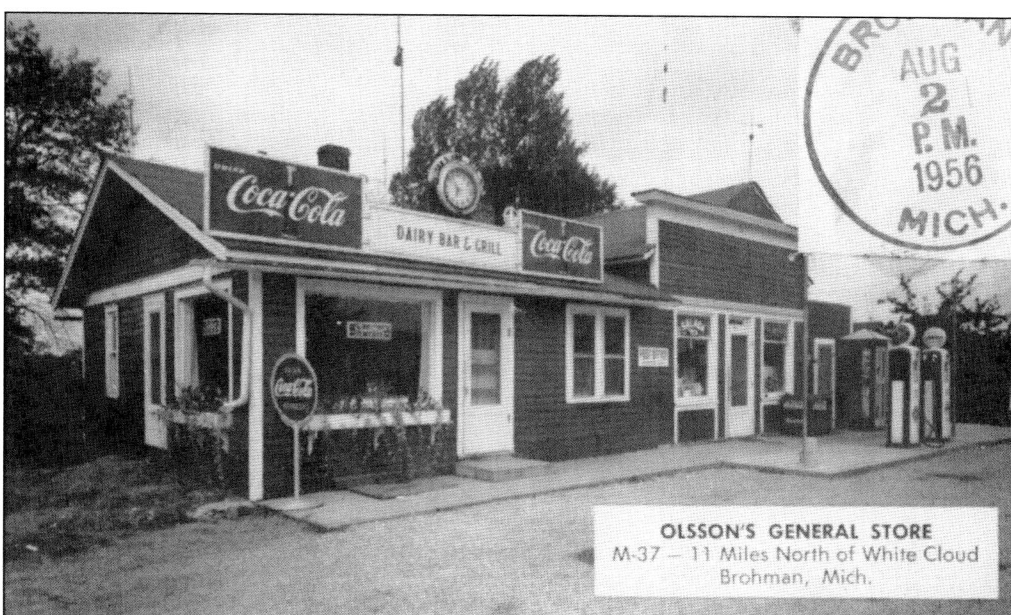

Olsson's General Store is located 11 miles north of White Cloud in Broham, Michigan. Known as a sportsman's paradise, Broham was a destination of many outdoorsmen. The store offered quality meats, general merchandise, and a post office. One could also get a quick snack in the Dairy Bar and Grill.

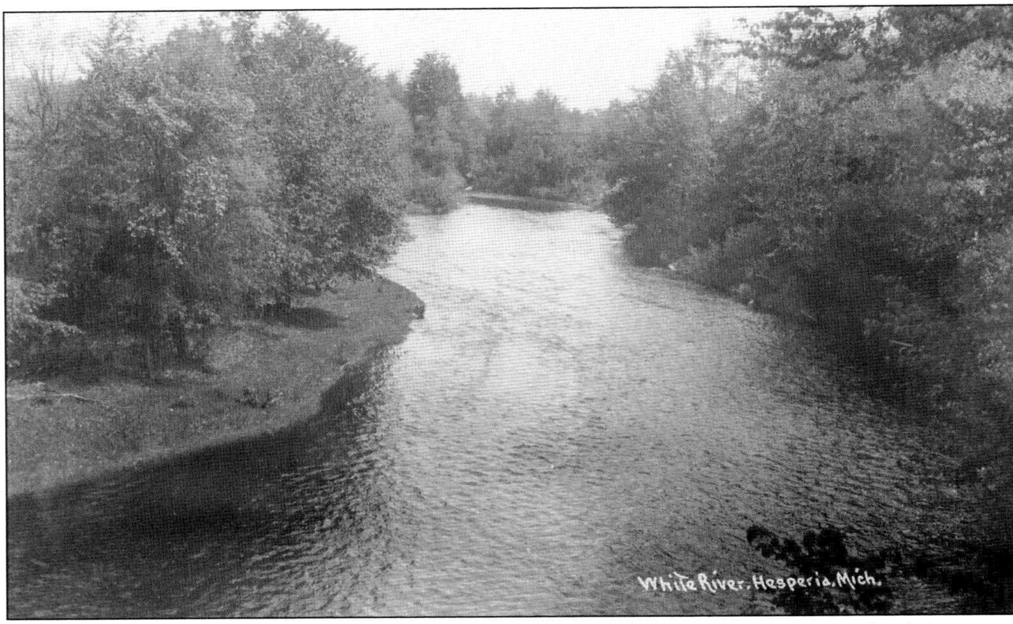

The White River meanders through Hesperia, making the town a great spot for fishing and boating. Through the years, many people have enjoyed swimming along the river as it flows past Hesperia's many parks.

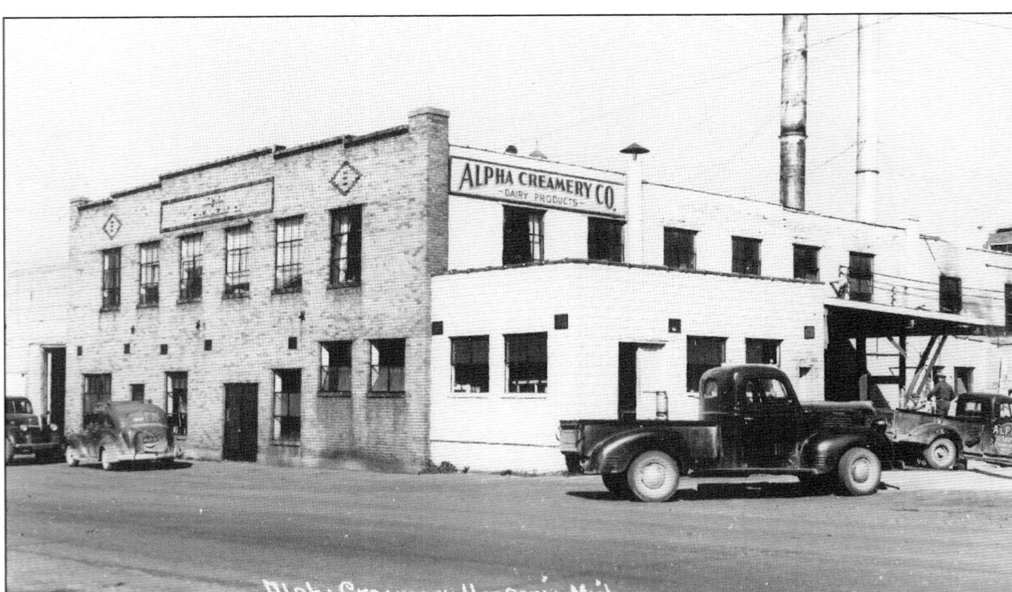

Over 2.25 million pounds of Alfa butter were sold between October 1919 and December 1924. This fact was reported in a full-page advertisement in the *Hesperia Union* on June 19, 1925. The Alfa Dairy was owned and operated by E.L. LeFevre and Edward and Ralph Bekkering.

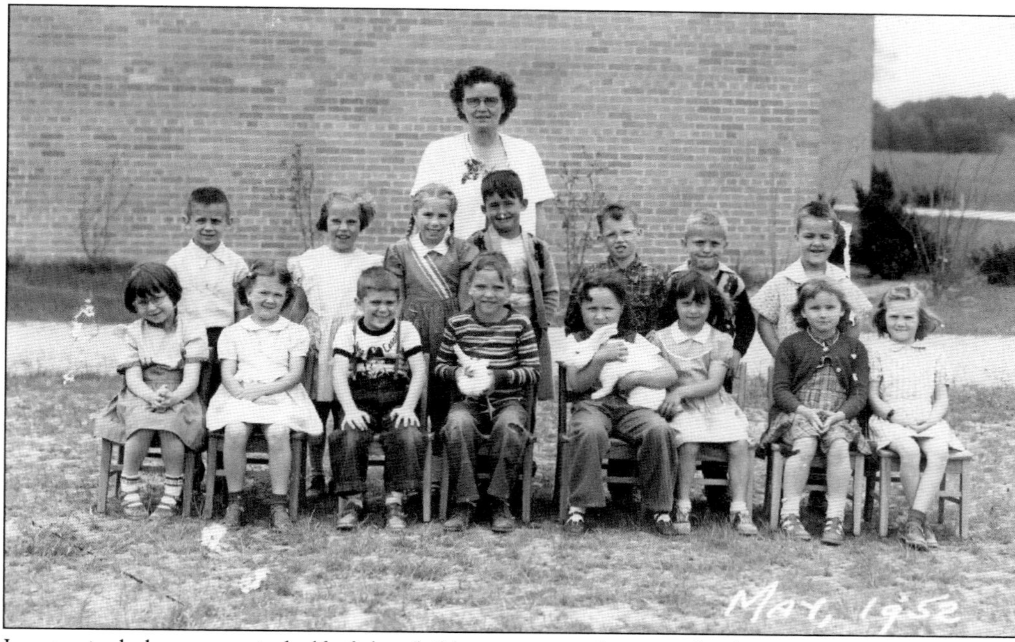

In a typical class portrait, half of the children are seated on small school chairs, and the rest of the students stand behind them with the teacher. In this May 1952 photograph, taken in front of an unnamed school, the class bunny and chicken are being held by children in the front row.

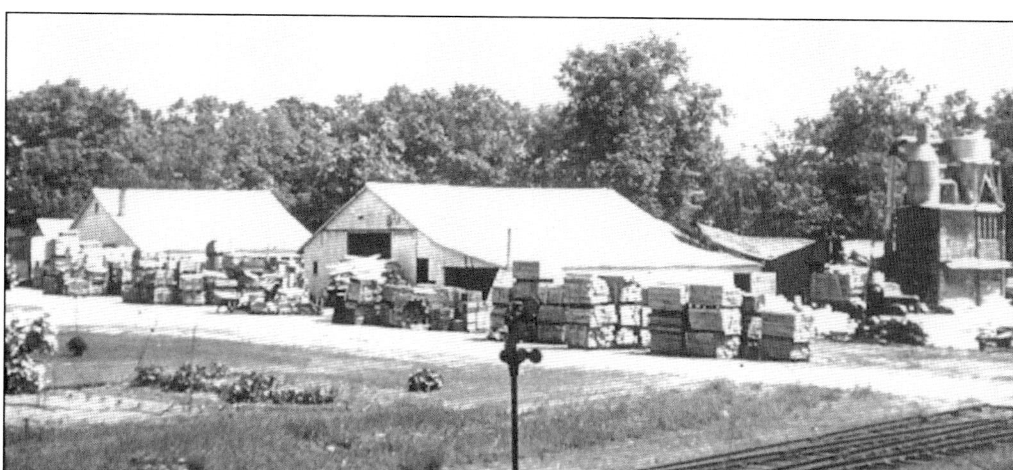

In 1913, Orlie Briggs started a mill in White Cloud, which was still operating in 1946. In 1943, there were several mills still in operation. The largest of these was the Briggs Lumber Company, shown here. Other mills in operation at that time were owned and operated by Stanley Forwood in White Cloud, a group of local businessmen for the Grant Crate Mill in Grant, Herbert Scott in Bridgeton, Stanley Purcell in Newaygo, Thomas Spence and Jack Underwood in Bitely, Scott Bridges in White Cloud, Charles Harrison in Sand Lake, Lloyd Murphy in Troy, and Gerald Spencer in Newaygo.

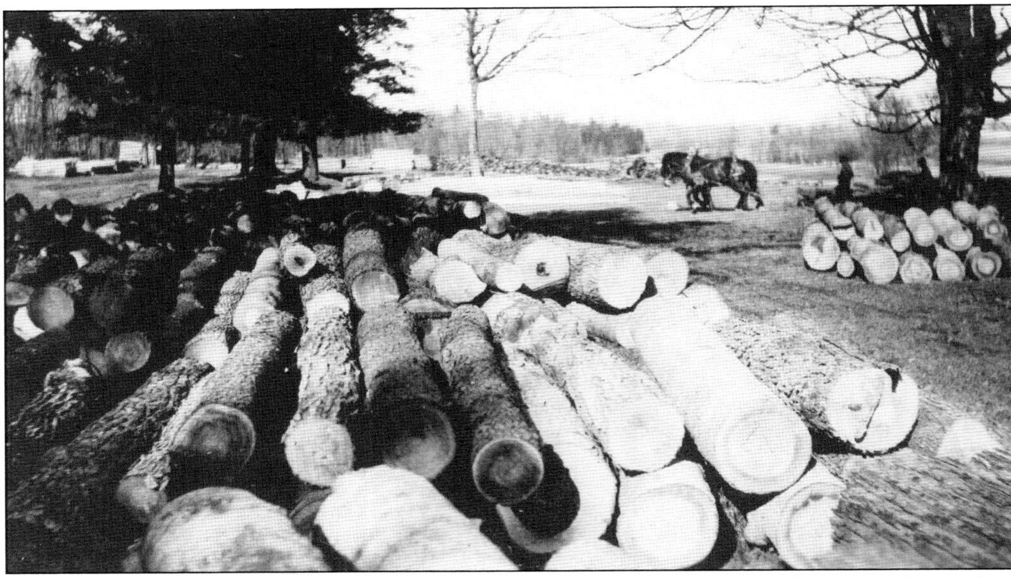

In 1931, forest rangers looking for mature hardwood for military use found a giant white oak on a far lot east of Fremont. The foresters estimated that the tree had approximately 2,000 board feet and would cut into 18-foot logs. It measured approximately four feet through the trunk at the height of a man's chest.

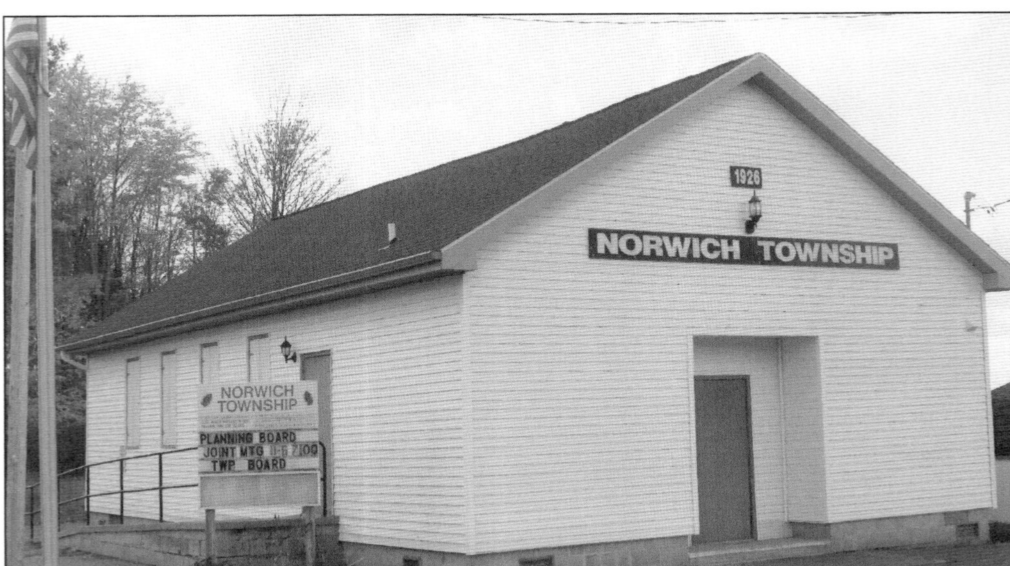

Norwich Township Hall was located in the town of Hungerford. Today, it is centrally located in the township on the corner of North Cypress Road and Eight Mile Road. Built in 1926, it was wired by O&A Electric Cooperative in 1938. Today, it is used as a meeting hall and a place for civic events and parties by residents of Norwich Township.

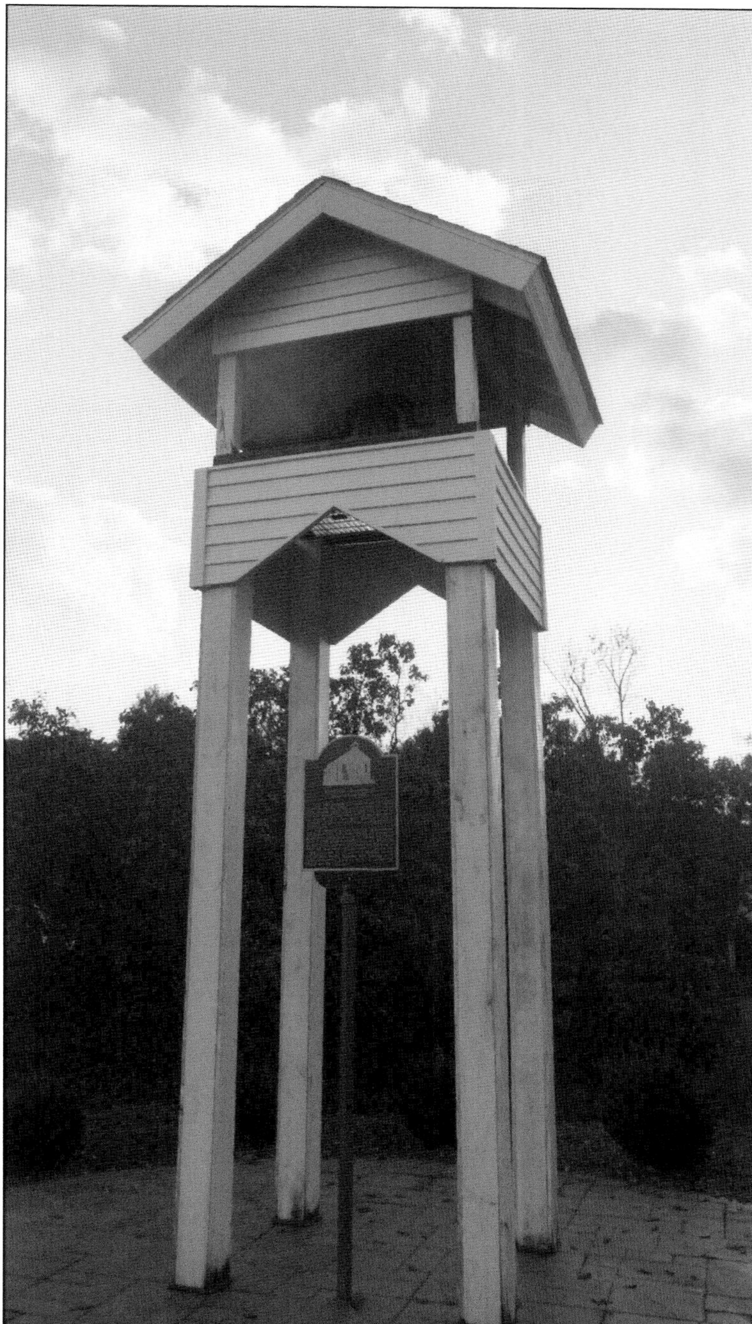

Woodville is a small crossroads now, with only a gas station, a church, and a few homes. The Woodville School closed in 1959. Today, a memorial, including the original school bell, stands in dedication to the students who attended from 1883 to 1959. The Woodville Ladies Aid Society purchased the school in 1960 and held bake sales to help the community. The school no longer stands, but through the generous workers who gave their time, money, and expertise, a memorial stands to remind residents of what once was.

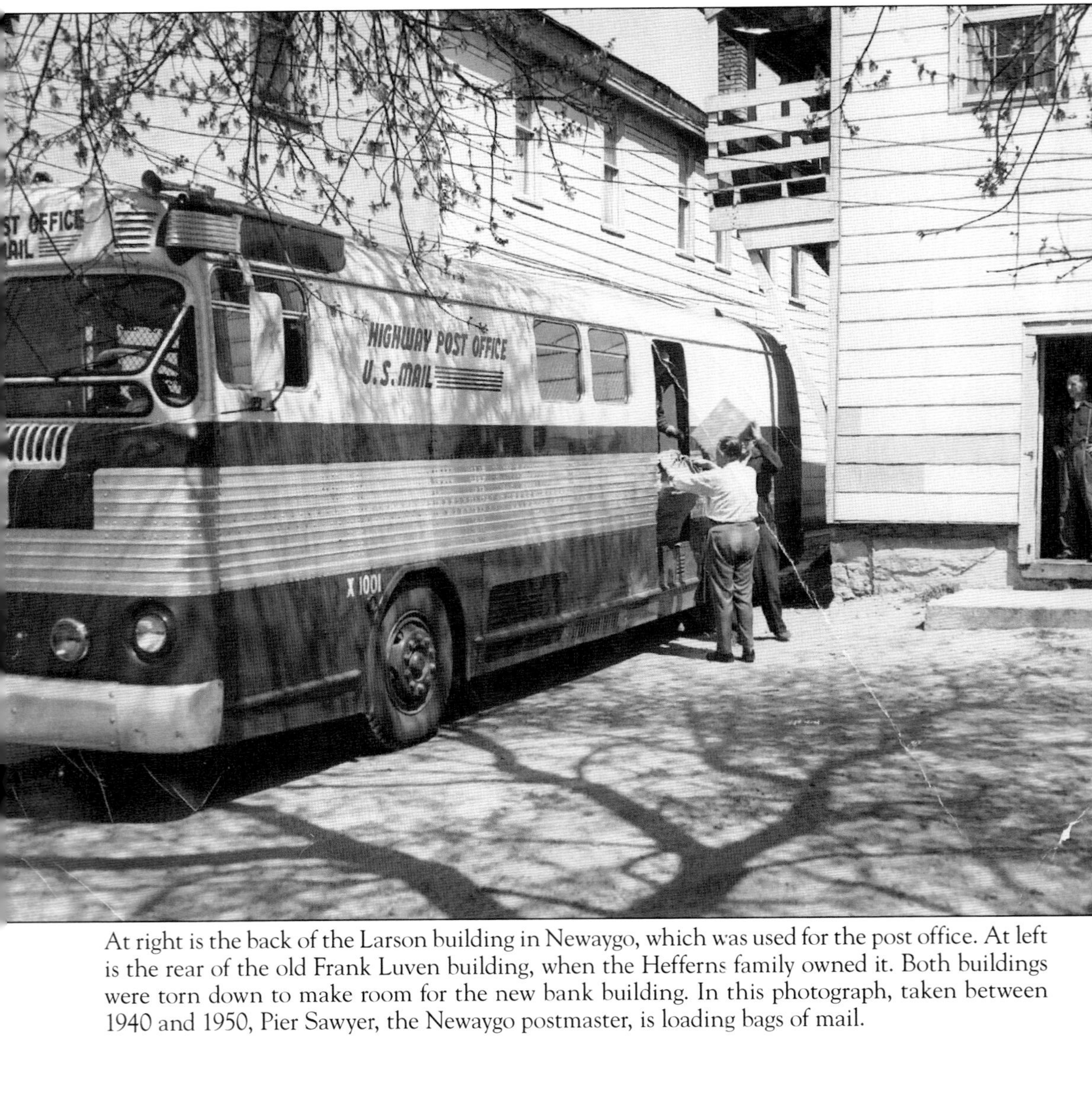

At right is the back of the Larson building in Newaygo, which was used for the post office. At left is the rear of the old Frank Luven building, when the Hefferns family owned it. Both buildings were torn down to make room for the new bank building. In this photograph, taken between 1940 and 1950, Pier Sawyer, the Newaygo postmaster, is loading bags of mail.

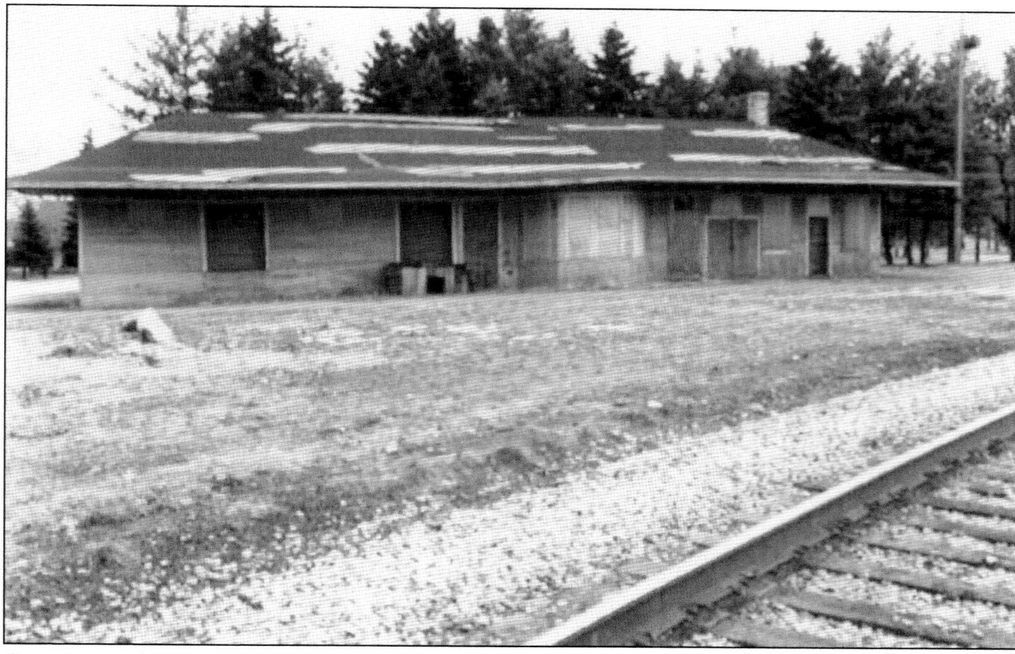

On a sunny day in July 1979, the old White Cloud train depot was moved to its new home at the Peavey Resort on West One Mile Road amid much fanfare. It had stood on its original ground in the town of White Cloud for nearly 100 years. Then, for several years, it had fallen into disrepair. When the depot was offered for sale, the City of White Cloud was not in a position to purchase it. The Kenneth Peavey family bought it and, with much work, restored it, thus keeping a part of White Cloud history safe for future generations.

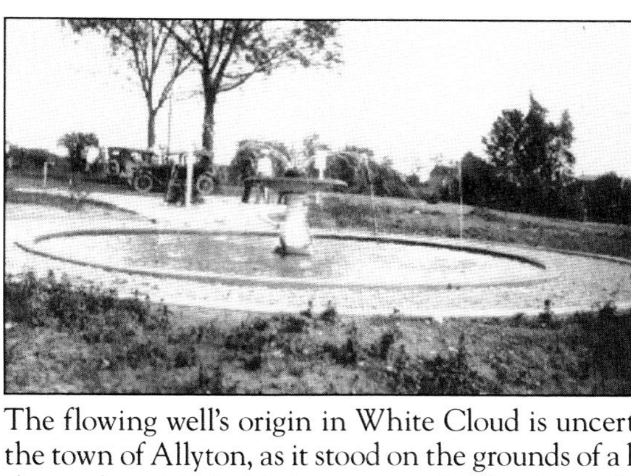

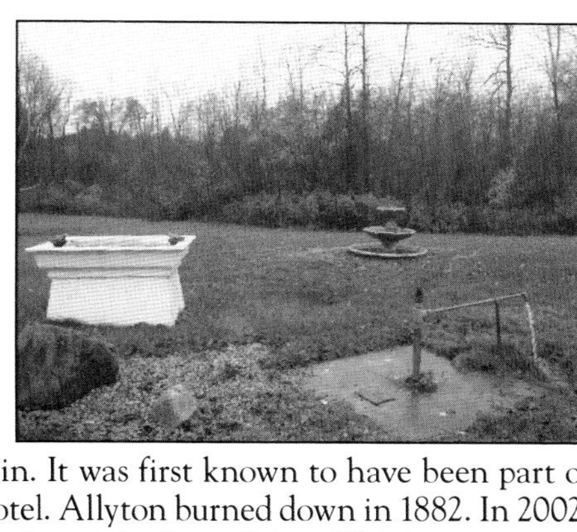

The flowing well's origin in White Cloud is uncertain. It was first known to have been part of the town of Allyton, as it stood on the grounds of a hotel. Allyton burned down in 1882. In 2002, the garden club decided to restore the flowing well to its original condition. This is an ongoing project, and more restoration is being planned.

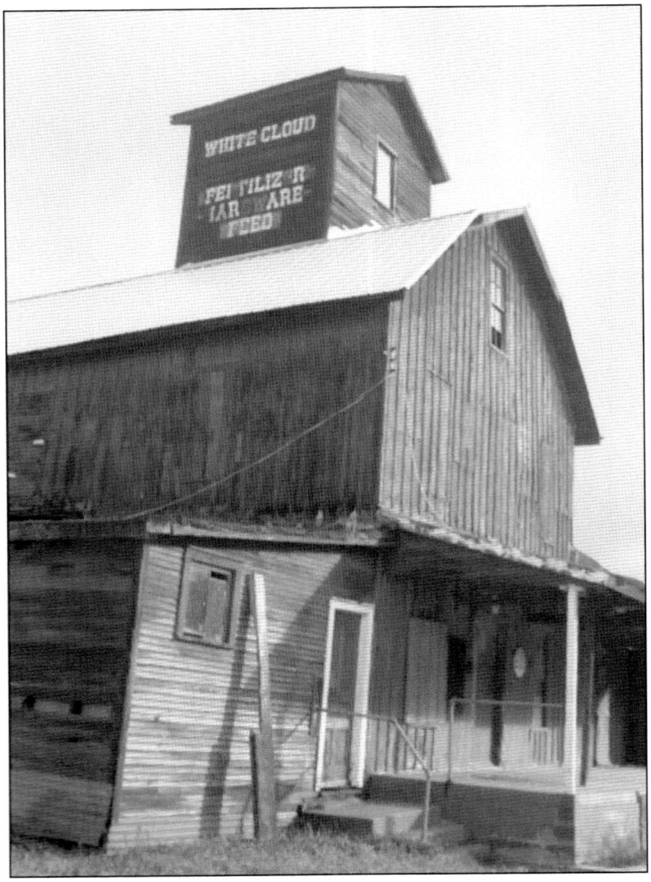

In 1917, Bert Johnson, Jake Allers, Jim Twillegar, Fred Anderson, and Voight Godfrey got together to bring the railroad to White Cloud so they could sell their produce. They formed the White Cloud Co-Operative. In 1937 and 1938, when O&A brought electricity to rural areas, there was a need to purchase new merchandise. So, it bought the "Old Potato House" just east of the railroad tracks on East Wilcox Avenue. This photograph is of the White Cloud Co-Op building.

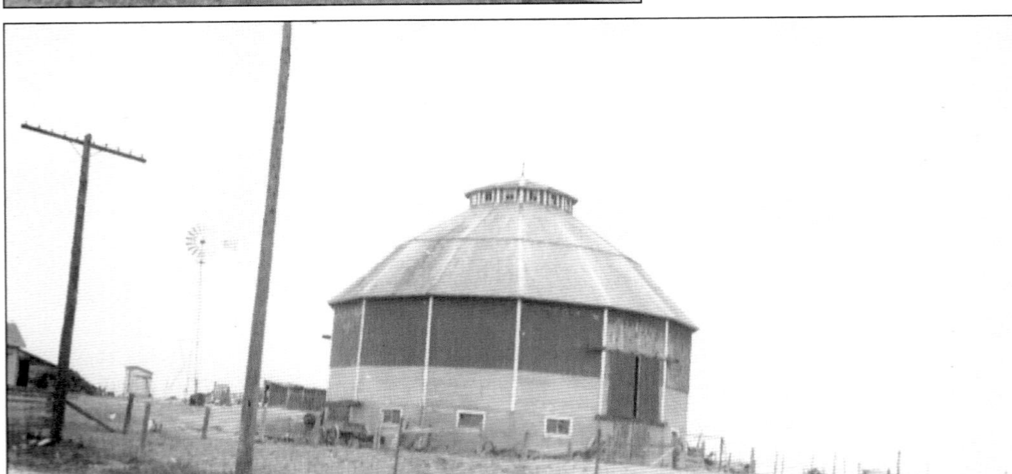

Newaygo has an active farming heritage that continues today. There are many wonderful barns in the county reflective of that heritage. One of the most picturesque of these was the round barn of Nels Jensen. For many years, this large barn was a landmark in the Grant community.

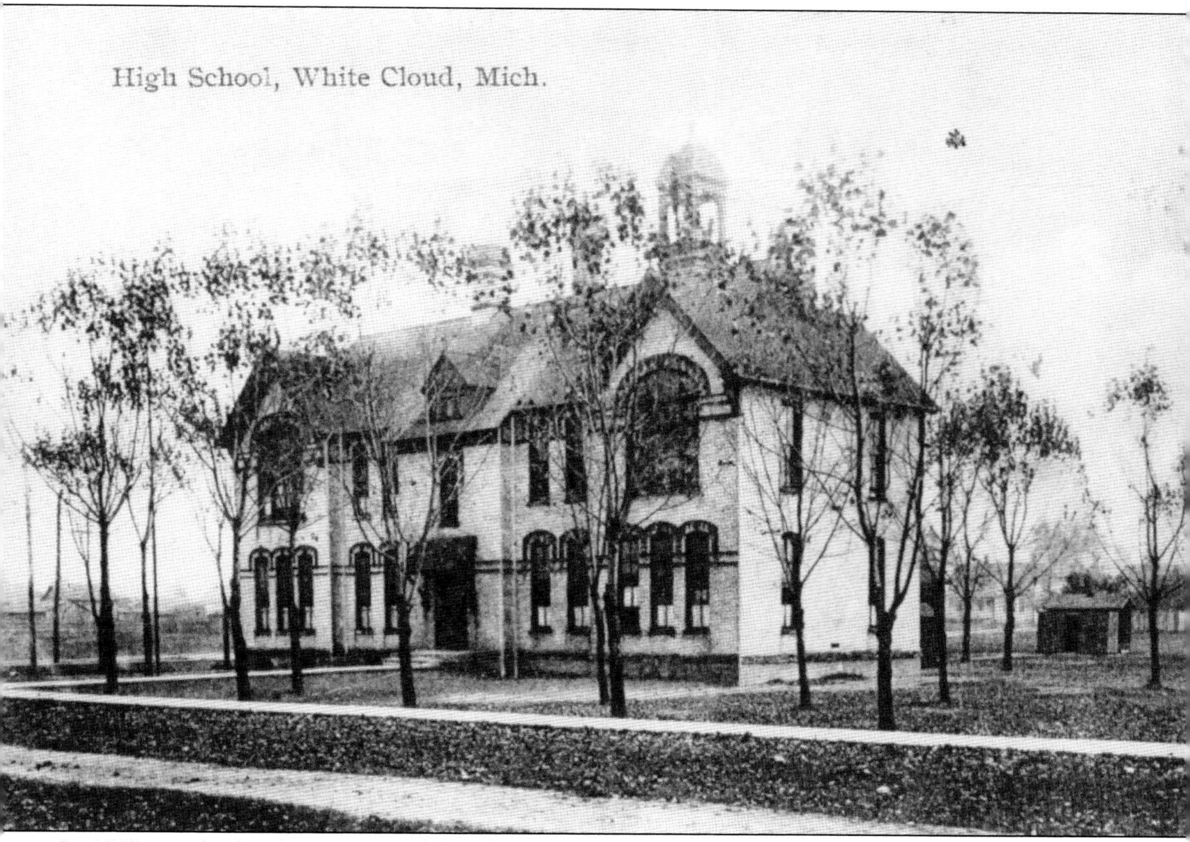

In 1947, rural schools were consolidated into the White Cloud school system. This brought a need for more space to accommodate the extra students, as this old school was too small. The city built a new elementary school on West Wilcox Avenue in 1954 to provide space for the influx of students. A new high school building was constructed in 1992.

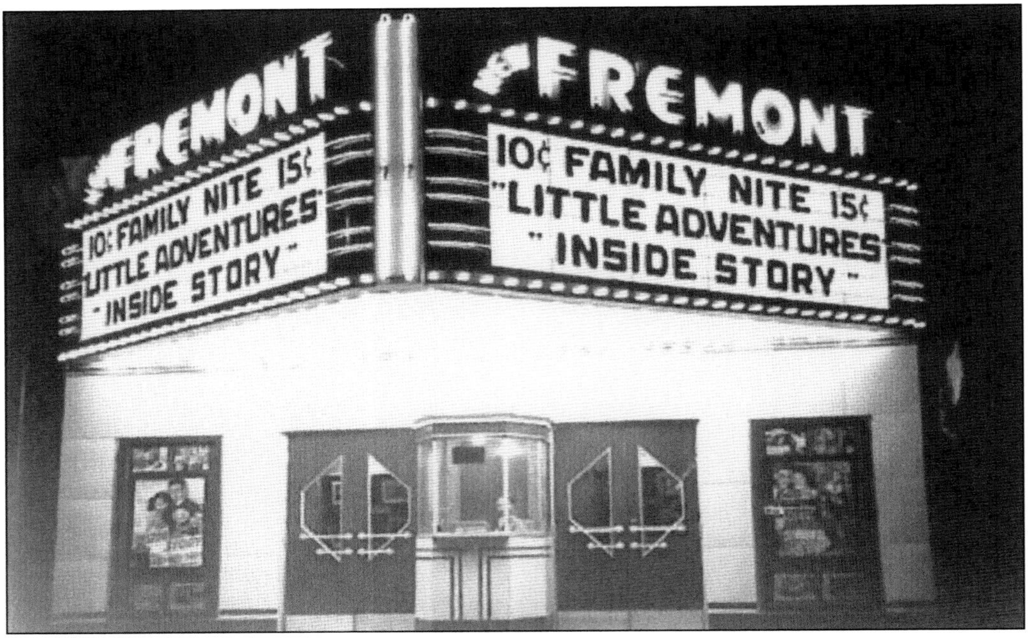

There have been several movie theaters in the town of Fremont. For many years, the Oz Theatre (below) was the favorite hangout on movie nights. It was located on the north side of West Main Street. After the movie, it was a quick walk across the street to Caruso's Confectionery for an ice-cream sundae.

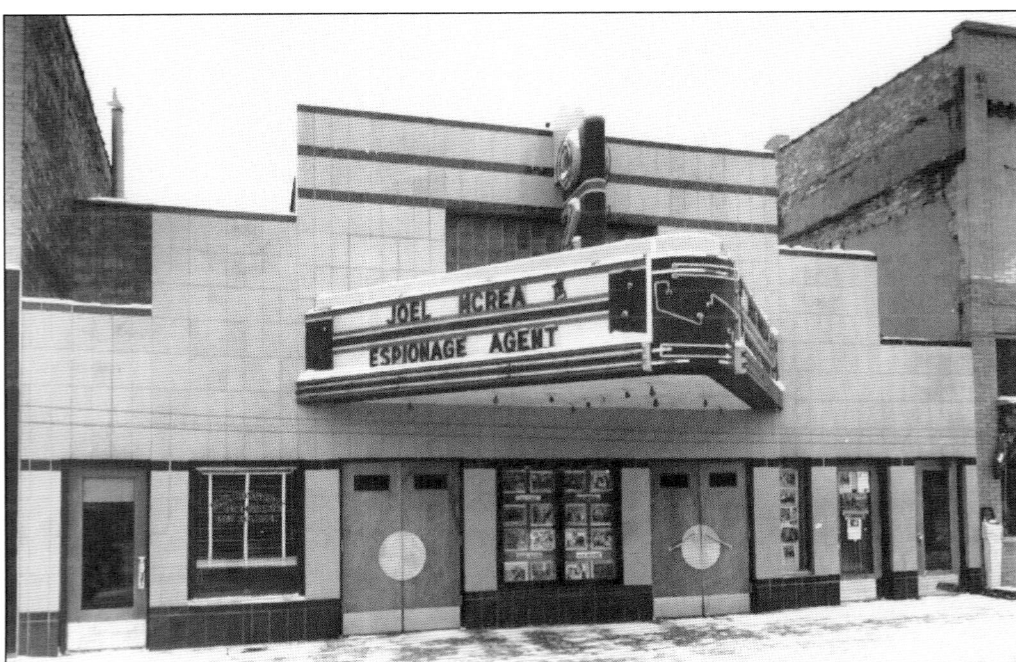

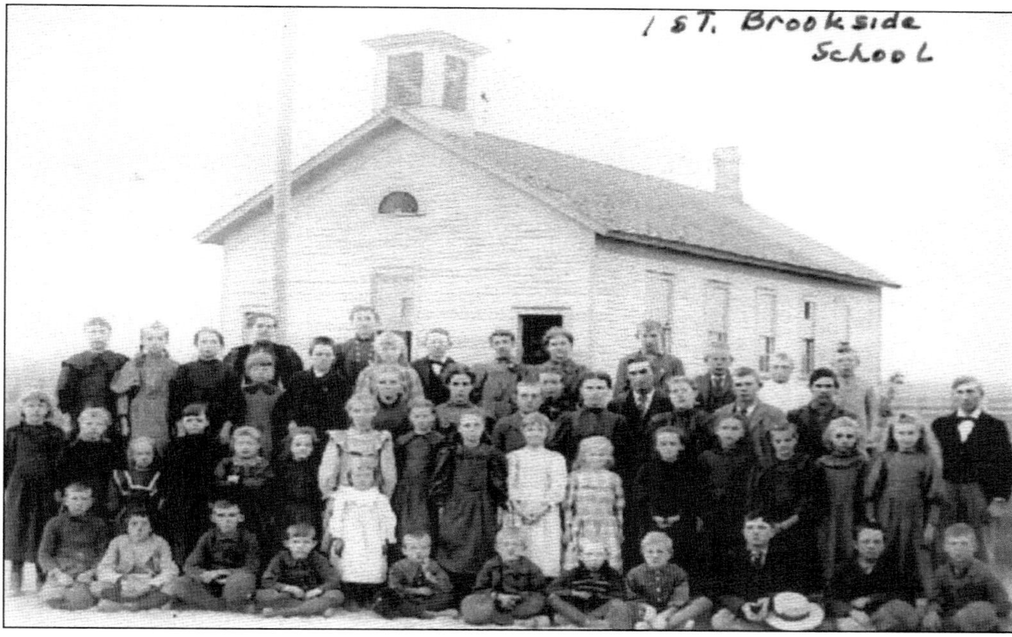

The most recent Brookside school (still standing) is the one seen below. It stands on the northwest corner of Green Avenue and Seventy-second Street. It was a much larger school and remained in operation until it was consolidated into Fremont Public Schools.

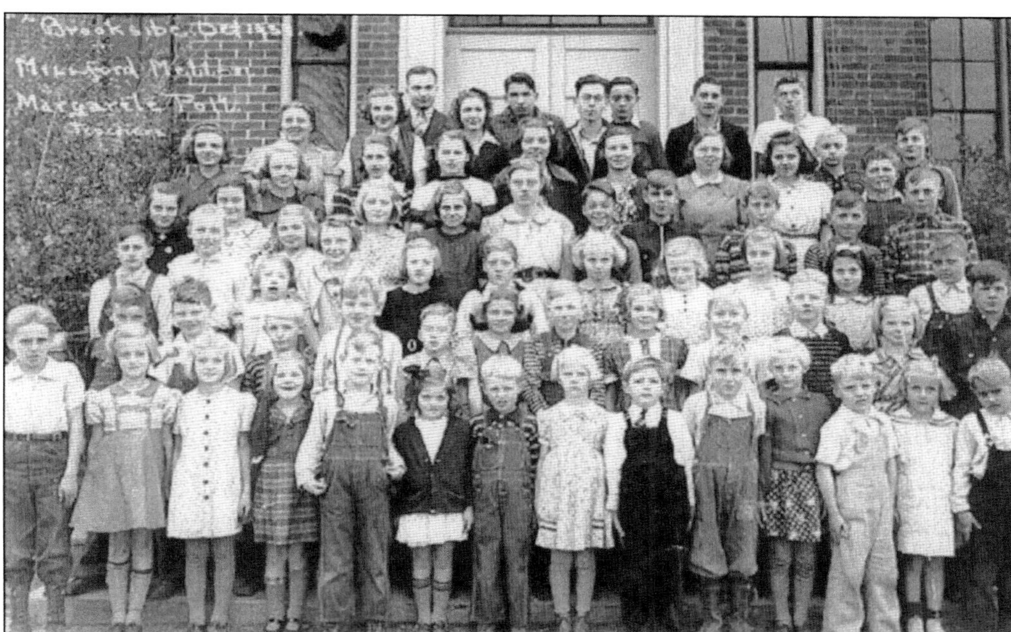

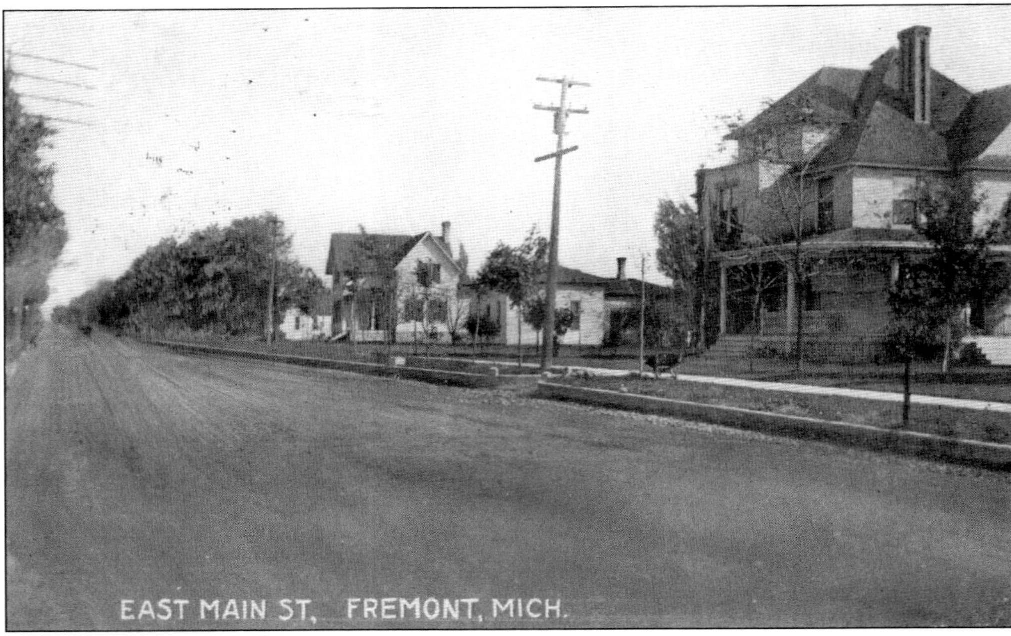

Dial telephone service started in August 1963. Most of the rural areas around Fremont did not have phone service from the large companies, so they had to form their own. Rural communities would sell stock in the company, set up the poles, string the wires, install the phones, and then connect to the lines belonging to the large companies.

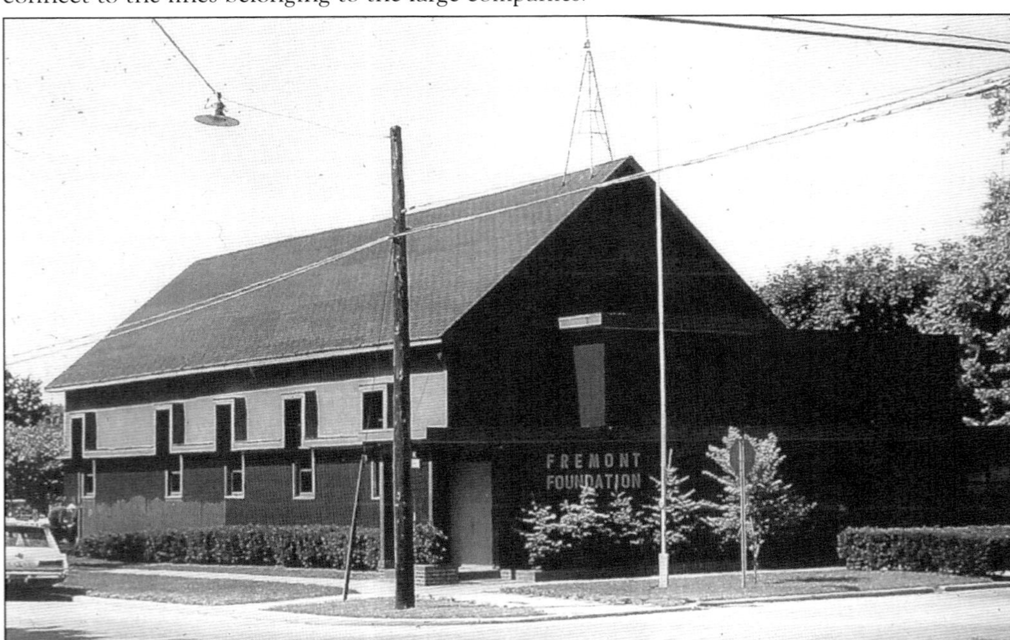

The Fremont Area Community Foundation (FACF) dates to the 1930s, when a few visionary philanthropists created charitable trusts to benefit their community. These funds were incorporated in 1951, forming the private Fremont Foundation. FACF was reorganized 21 years later into its current structure as a community foundation.

GILLILAND TRUCKING SERVICE

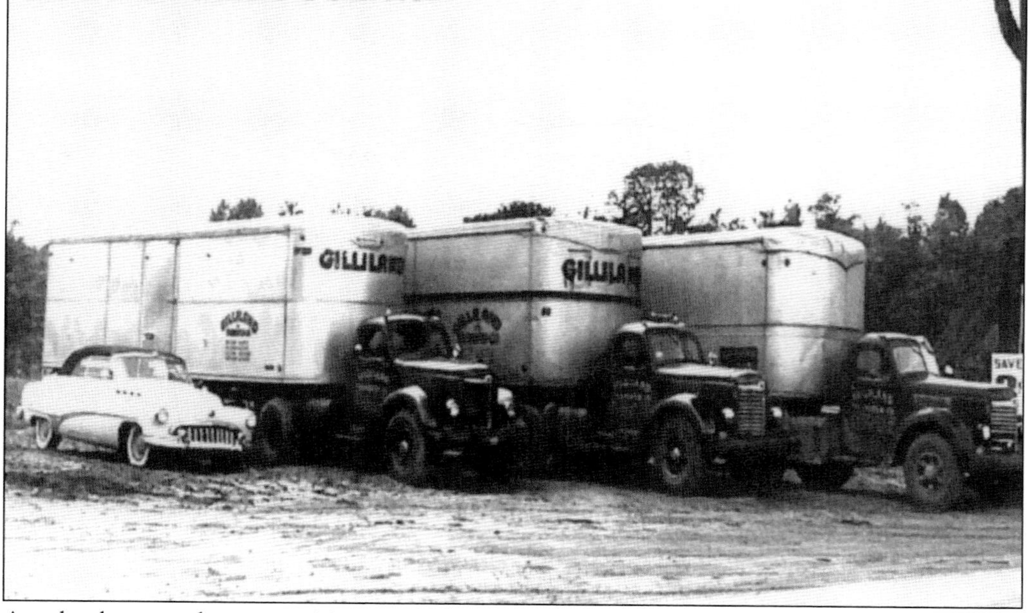

Another longtime business in Newaygo County was Gilliland Trucking Service, based in Fremont. With all of the farms in the area, the company quickly became essential in the transportation of produce to stores and processing plants. Now known as Michigan Produce Haulers, it continues to serve area farms and canning facilities.

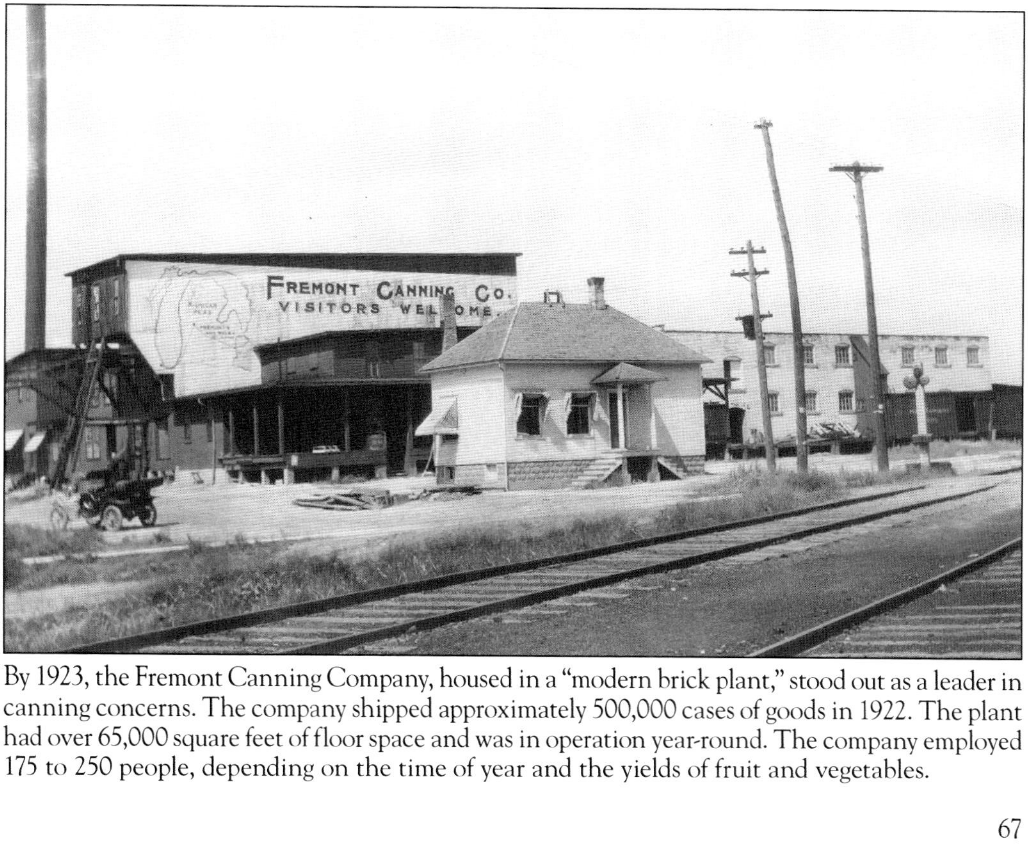

By 1923, the Fremont Canning Company, housed in a "modern brick plant," stood out as a leader in canning concerns. The company shipped approximately 500,000 cases of goods in 1922. The plant had over 65,000 square feet of floor space and was in operation year-round. The company employed 175 to 250 people, depending on the time of year and the yields of fruit and vegetables.

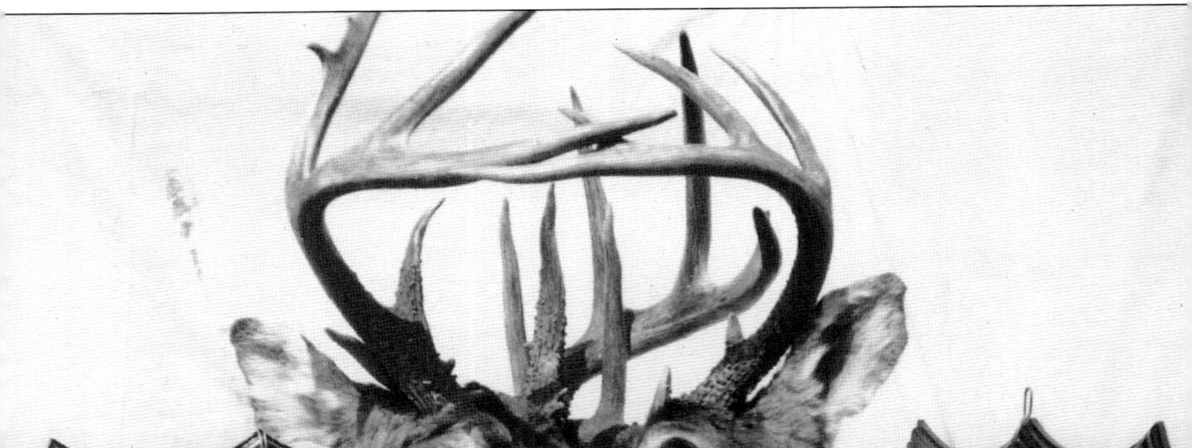

These two deer, their heads mounted with horns locked together, were found near Big Star Lake. They died of starvation after becoming intertwined. L.D. Puff displayed the mounts in his hardware store for many years. Newaygo County is a popular hunting area, attracting adventurers from all over.

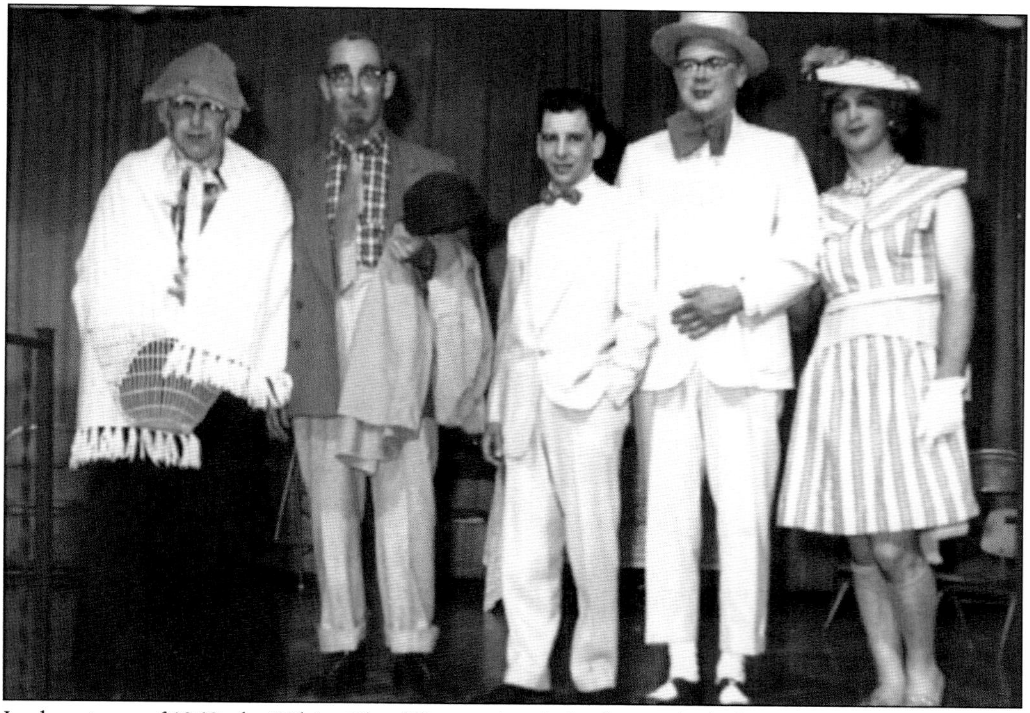

In the winter of 1968, the White Cloud Rotary decided to have a little fun, stir up some civic pride, and raise money for its general fund. Accordingly, it employed Iva Keefer, a professional director, to put on a show. Talent was drawn from throughout the community, and props and costumes were mostly provided by Keefer. Rehearsals were brief but intense, lasting about two weeks. To generate interest, Walt Sowles's role as the bride was promoted in advertising, but the identity of the groom remained a mystery, even to the rest of the cast. Secrecy was maintained right up to curtain time. When he did appear, many cast members did not recognize M.L. Barkley, a man old enough to be the bride's grandfather. All but a few audience members were stumped, even though the Barkleys had lived in the area for years. The program went over well and proved to be a good moneymaker. Many people attended both shows. Among the cast members were Harold Branch, Fred Foodle, Roger Mallett, Mac Slade, Gordon Sowles, Kenneth DeBlake, Elmer May, Barney Fowler, George Rosenberg, Jack Jones, Don Rudert, Bill Bird, Donald Cruzan, Ed Green, and Gorden Alger.

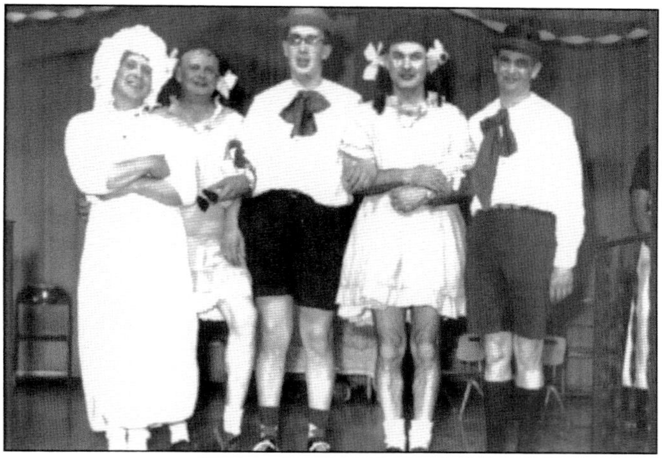

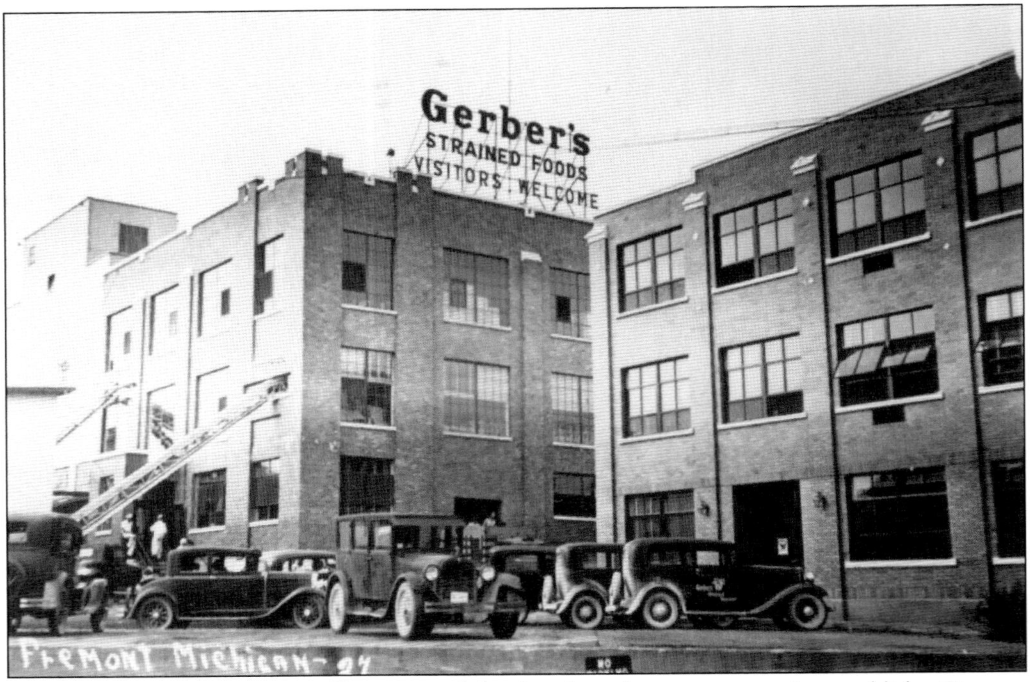

In early March 1944, the City of Fremont and the chamber of commerce voted to establish a German prisoner-of-war camp in the vicinity of Fremont. The plan had been previously presented to Gerber employees through departmental meetings, and endorsements were given by both local unions, about prisoner labor. On May 16, the first prisoners arrived; there were 25 German POWs and 12 US military police. On July 8, three prisoners escaped the encampment but were soon found in a barn two miles north of Hart, Michigan. At the time of the camp's closing in October 1945, it housed 250 German POWs. The labor prisoners provided was a necessity because many local men were in the armed forces at the time, causing a severe shortage of able-bodied men at the Gerber plant and on area farms. Through the aid of this labor, it was possible to keep Gerber's production at a fairly high level, thus preserving jobs for Fremont-area residents and returning military men. Many of the German POWs returned to Fremont to stay, or just to visit, after the war.

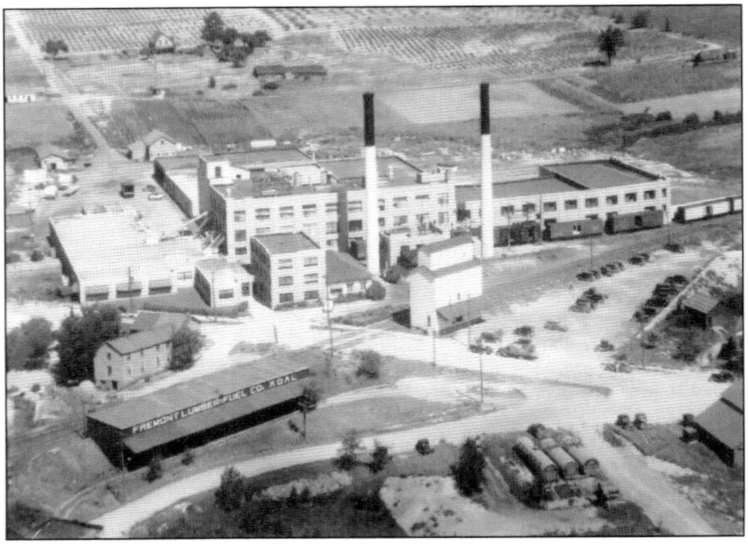

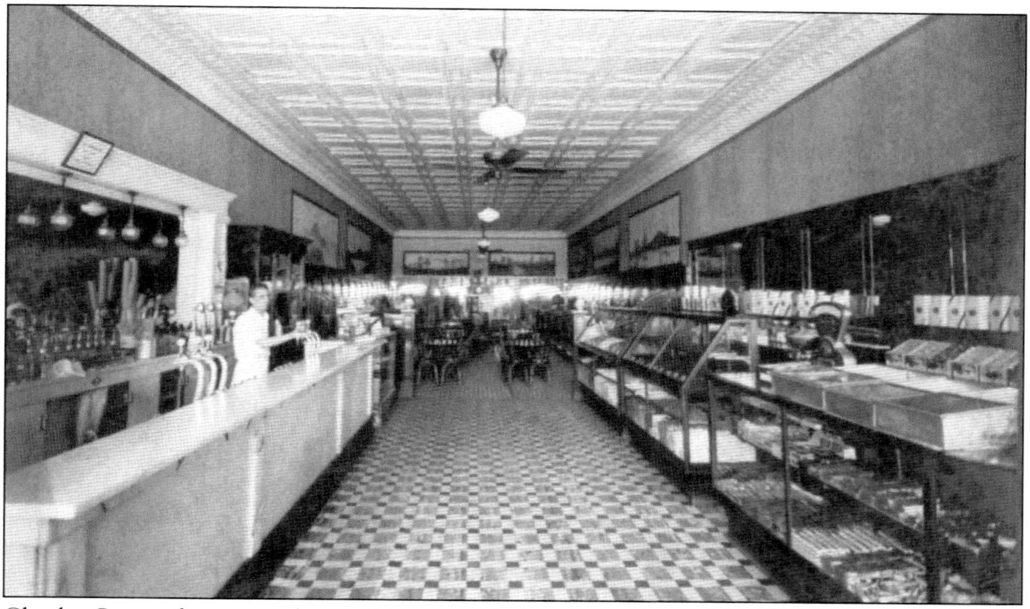

Charles Caruso first opened a small fruit stand where the offices of the *Times Indicator* are today on Main Street. He then purchased the store at 10 West Main Street in 1919. Shortly after, in 1920, he sent for his wife and three children in Italy. Later, when Charles neared retirement, the two older boys took over the West Main Street store. In 1935, Charles's wife, Risolia, died. The store was then sold to daughter Mary and her husband, Michael Spadafore. When Michael died in 1964, the store was sold outside of the family. In 2012, it became the home of the Terry Wantz Historical Research Center.

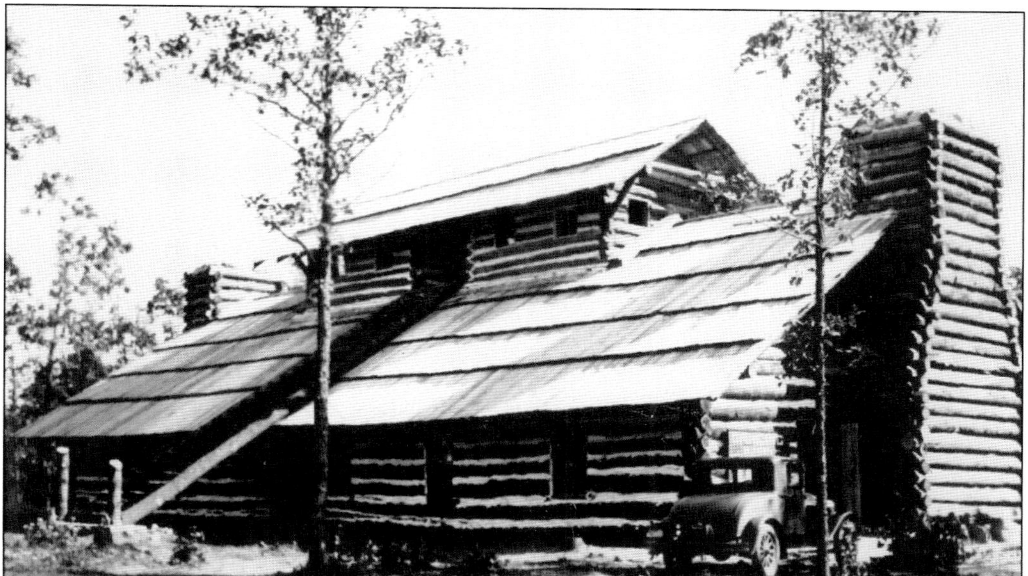

The big pavilion located at Big Bend Park in Croton, later to be known as Oxbow Park, was built by Elmore Westgate in 1929–1930. Dances and parties were held every weekend, with people coming from all around. The logs became infested with worms, damaging the logs. The pavilion was in use for only a year or two before it collapsed due to poor construction.

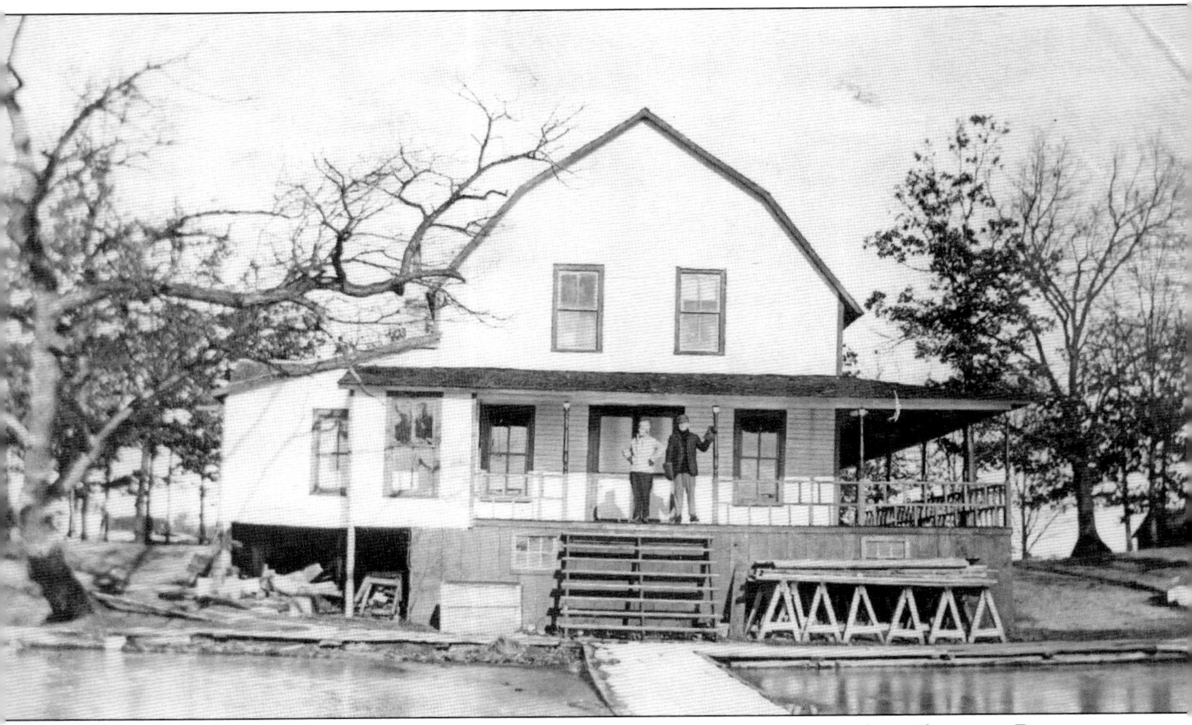

The Whitmore Pavilion on Hess Lake is seen here in the wintertime. The Whitmore Resort was home to many parties, potlucks, and visitors from all over the world. Vacationers could purchase ice cream and sodas at the pavilion, as well as rent boats and arrange for room and board. It was a do-it-yourself amusement center.

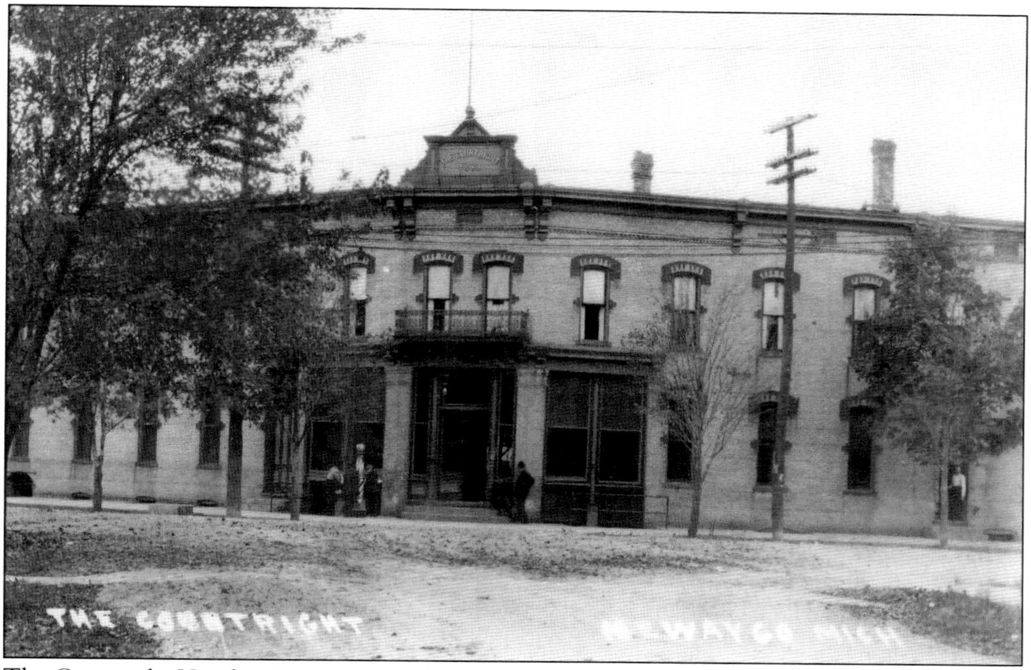

The Courtright Hotel was a century-old landmark that burned down in April 1991. It saw visits by personalities such as Henry Ford and mobsters George "Baby Face" Nelson and Al Capone. The hotel reached its peak in the 1920s and 1930s. It was purchased just a year prior to the fire by a person who was looking forward to bringing it back to its historic luster.

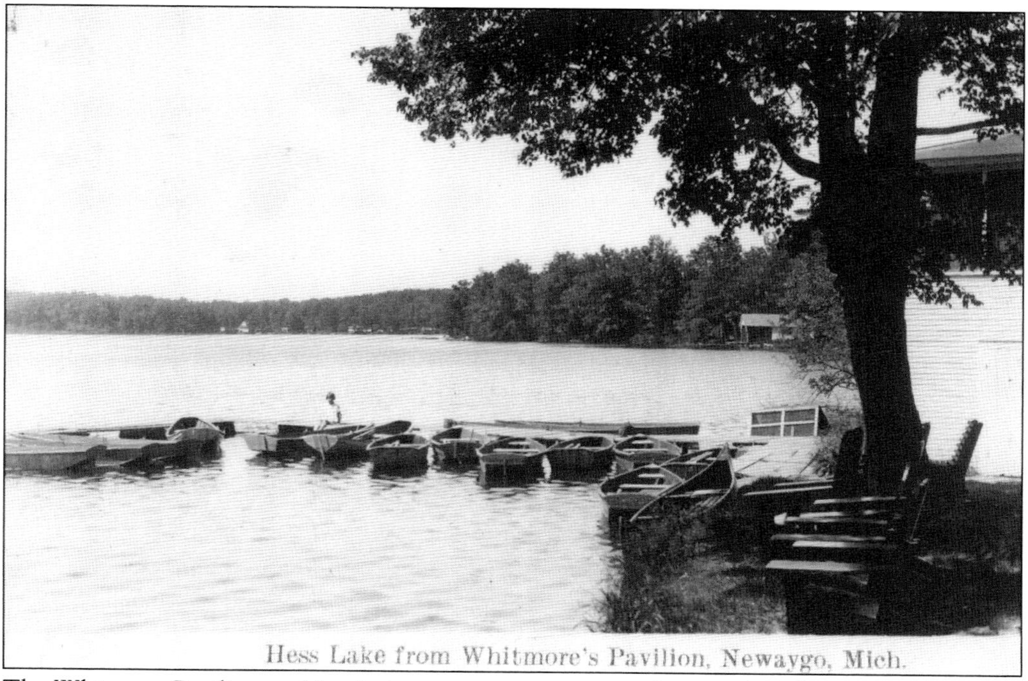

The Whitmore Pavilion on Hess Lake was a summertime gathering place for many people. The lake is an 1,125-acre body of water known for its swimming, boating, and fishing opportunities. Hess Lake is home to many resorts and summer cottages.

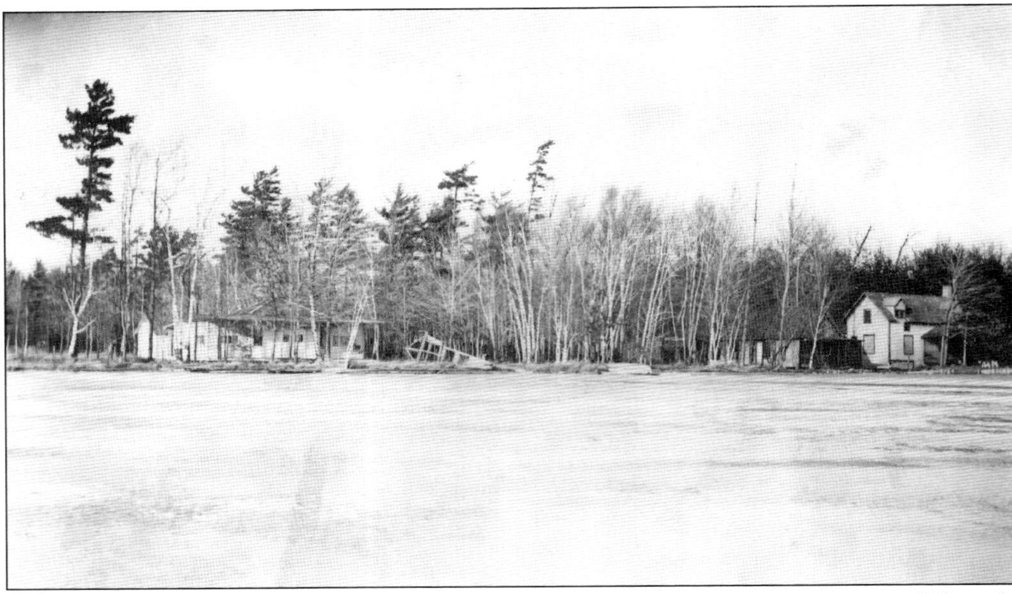

This is the Riblet–Thompson point on the north side of Hess Lake in the wintertime. When the tourists left at the end of summer, a few people still lived on the lake during the winter, enjoying the quiet.

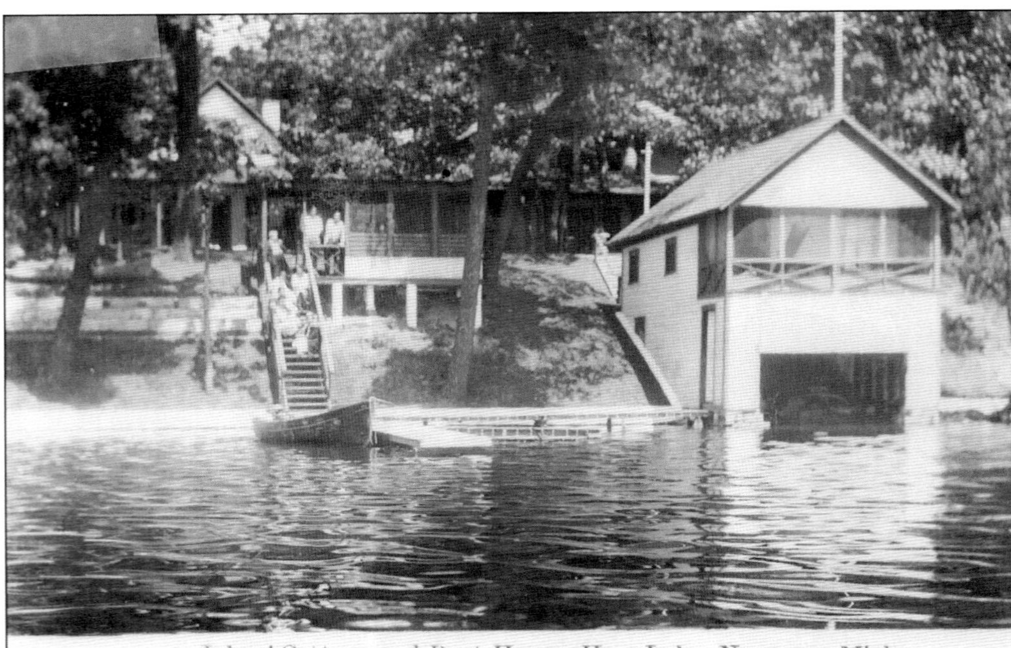

Shown here is John's Cottage and Boat House on Hess Lake. This cottage was originally owned by C.A. Day, an executive of Marshall Field's in Chicago. Many people from Detroit, Chicago, and Grand Rapids, among other cities, came to Newaygo County to enjoy its lakes and natural beauty, often renting cottages for weekends and vacations.

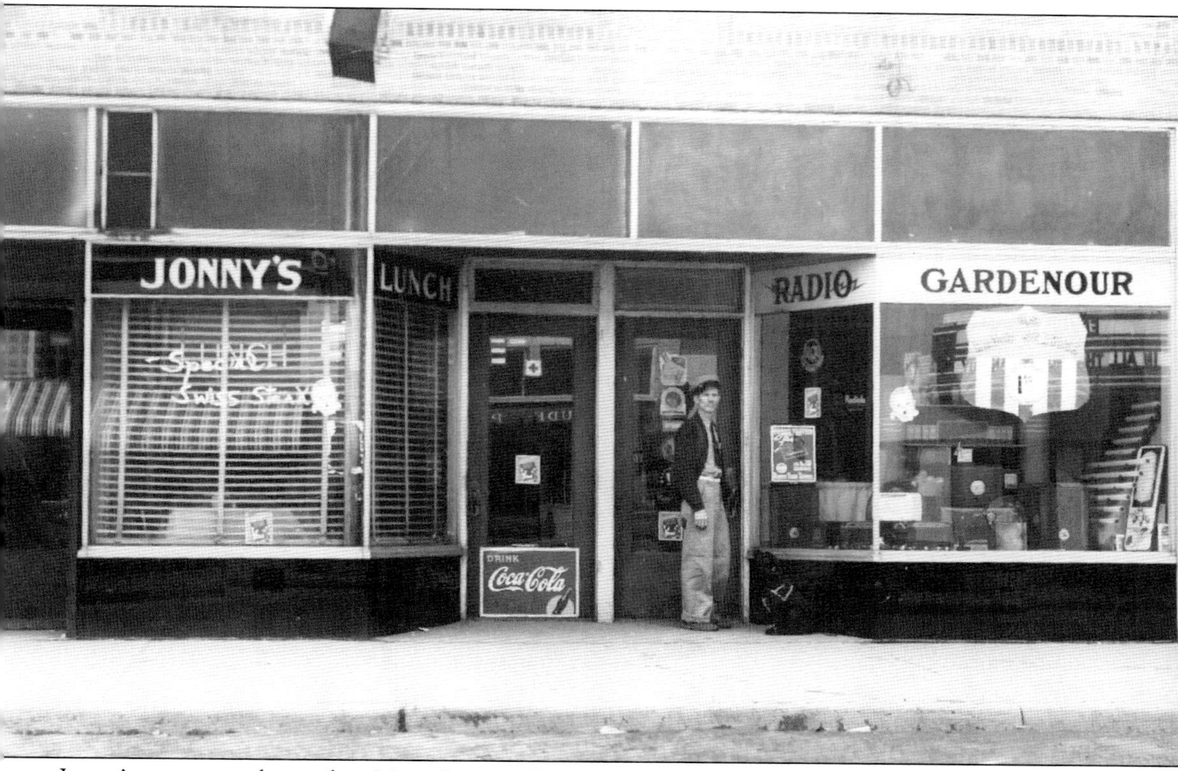

Jonny's restaurant, located on Main Street in Fremont, was a diner located in a building owned by the Caruso family. When Jonny's went out of business, an establishment was run in the building for a short time. Then, Jack Kartus opened an eatery known as J&J's Diner, which later became Jane's. The diner, a favorite of residents, had many regulars.

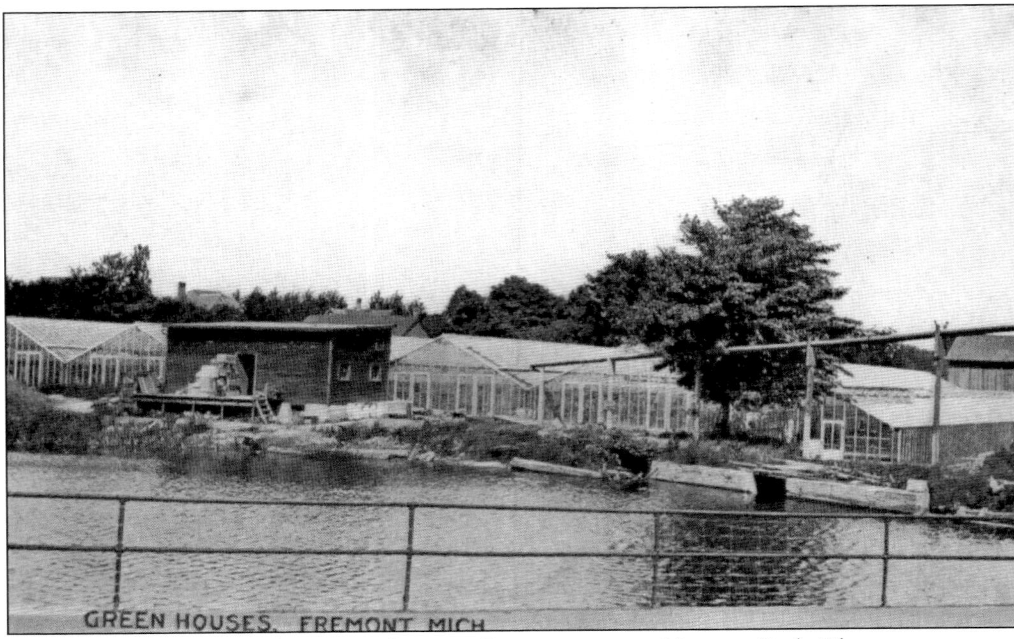

Greenhouses were located on Main Street in Fremont, next to Veterans Park. They were operated for many years using the creek and millpond as a water source for irrigation.

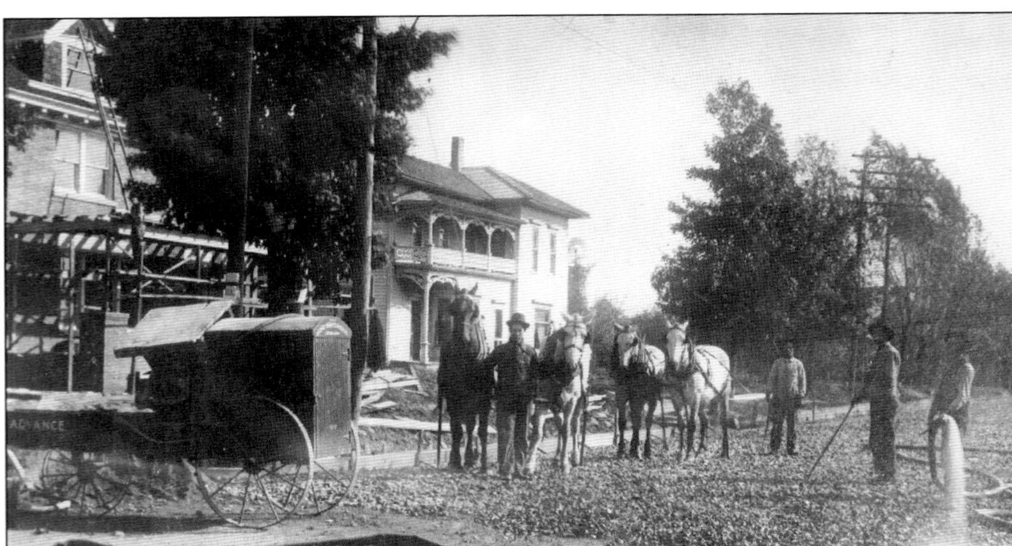

In this west-facing photograph, workers create new streets on the corner of Main and Stewart Streets in Fremont. The Kempf home is visible on the far left. Earl Maynard is holding the horses in front, and the person holding the hose is George Dickinson.

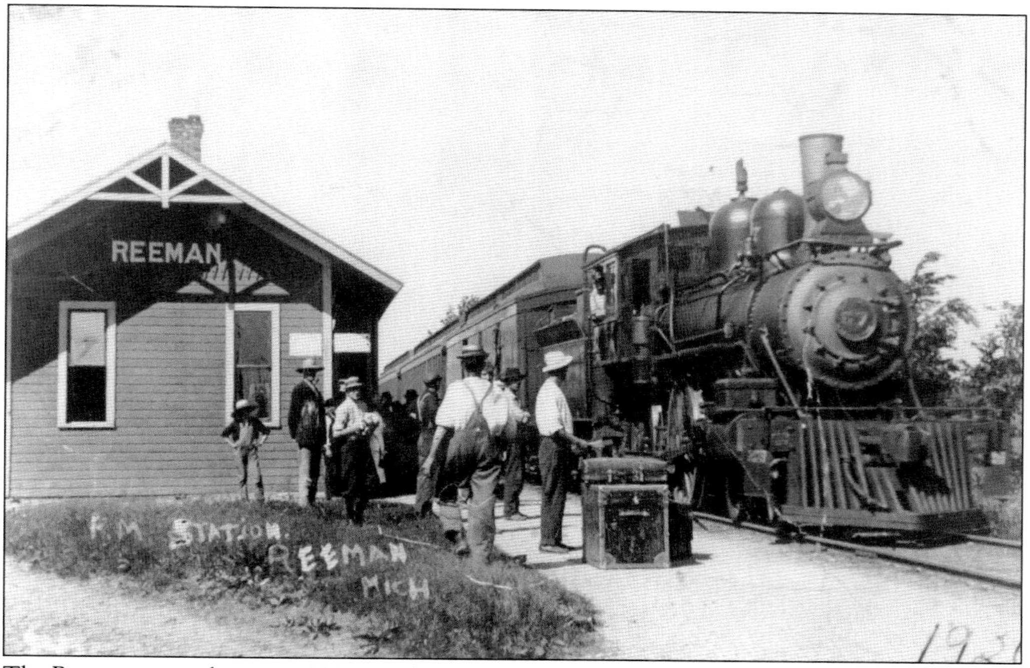

The Reeman train depot in 1920 was a busy station. The train was part of the Chicago & Western Michigan Railway (later Pere Marquette). Frank Reed built a flour mill, and John Brinkman constructed a general store in the vicinity. Combining their two names, they came up with the name Reeman. Sheridan Township was founded by Jarred McQueen in 1865.

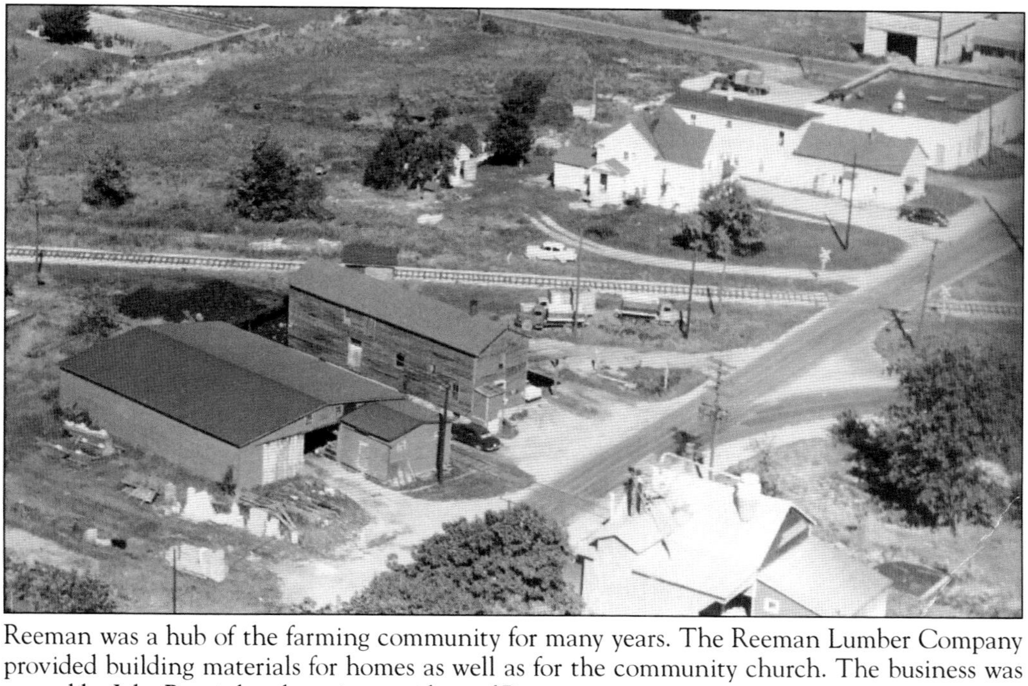

Reeman was a hub of the farming community for many years. The Reeman Lumber Company provided building materials for homes as well as for the community church. The business was owned by Jake Remink, a longtime resident of Reeman.

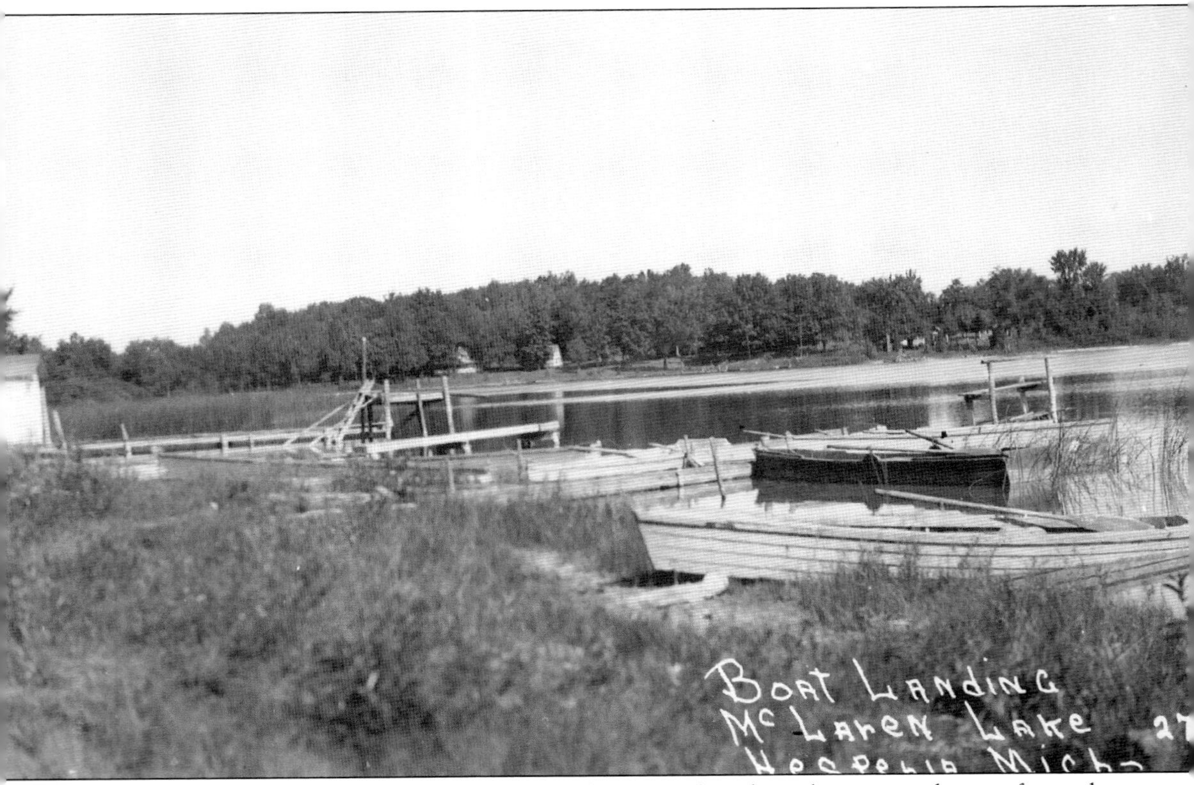

McLaren Lake, located four miles northwest of Hesperia, has always been a popular spot for outdoor sporting activities. The lake has a shoreline of 4.95 miles and has a surface area of 271 acres and a depth of 70 feet. This is a 1927 photograph of the boat landing on the lake.

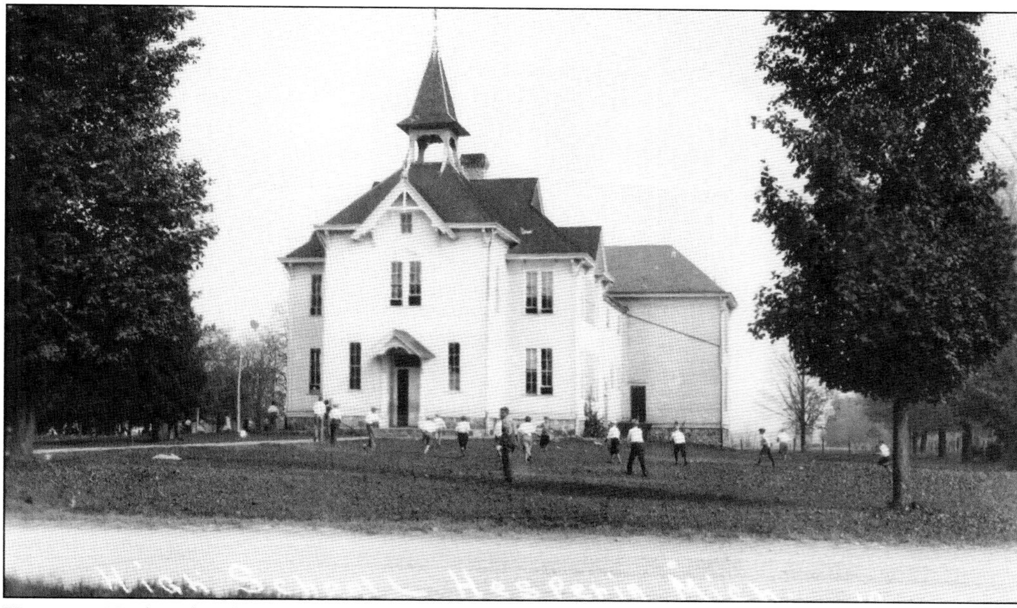

Hesperia High School was built by 1882, answering the need for a growing community. At that time, there were 184 students attending classes. In April 1932, the wooden structure burned down. The Community Building then housed the students until a new school was constructed in 1964.

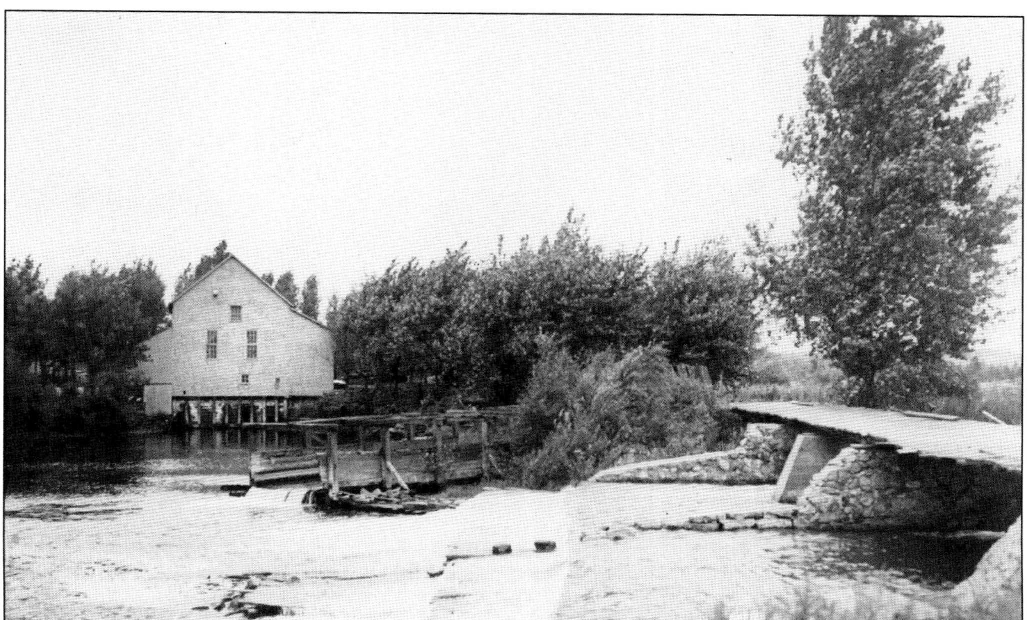

In Hesperia's early days, the millpond was used for the busy lumber industry. The dam was put in to help harness the water for electricity. Over the years, the millpond has been used for fishing and as a popular swimming spot for many generations on hot summer days.

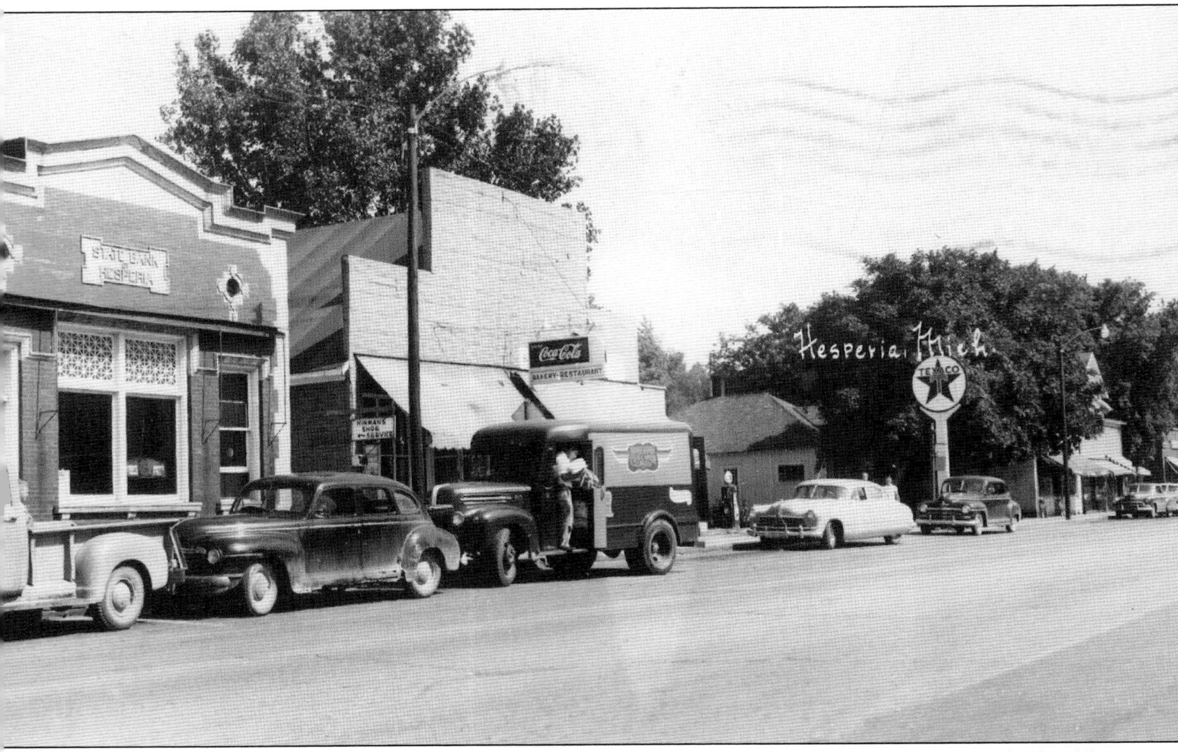

The 1950s was a busy time in Hesperia. This is the west side of downtown Hesperia. The building on the far left is the bank, which was started and originally owned by Frank J. Miller in April 1897. Earl Anderson was hired in 1914 as cashier and held that position for 44 years. Robert Bayle was assistant cashier from 1924 until 1958.

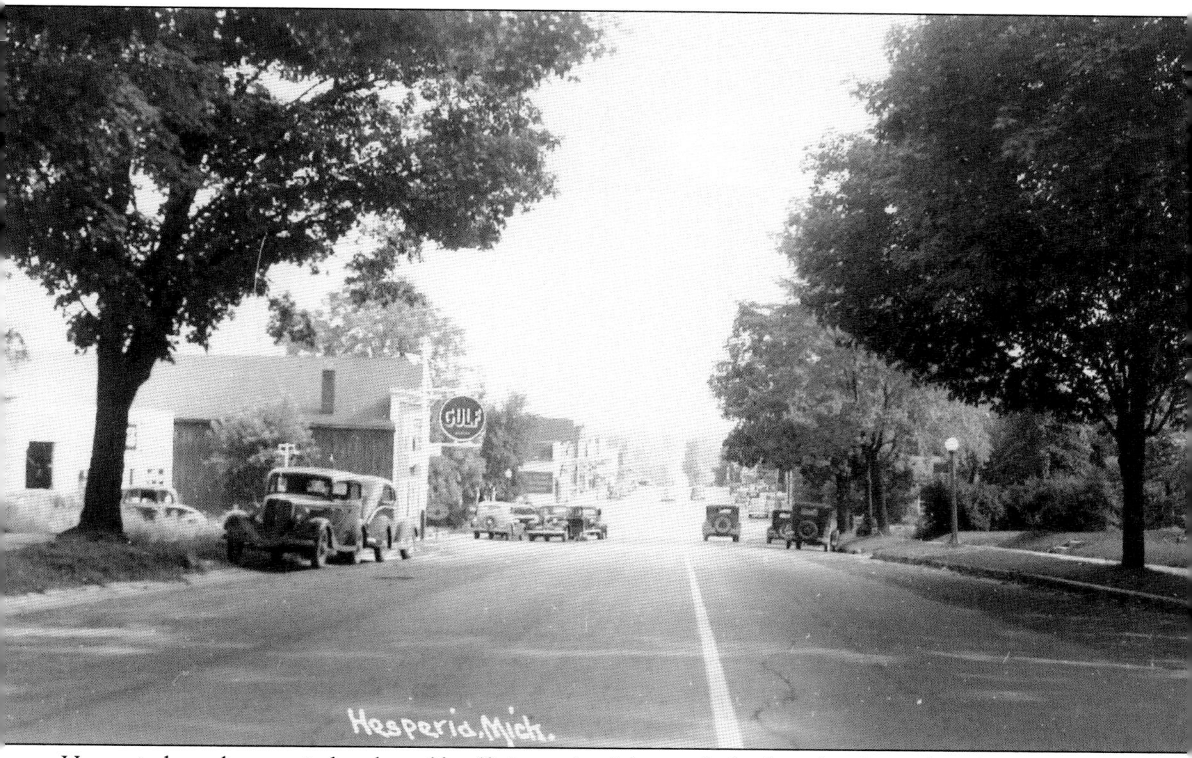

Hesperia has always tried to be self-sufficient. An "electric-light franchise" was hired by 1916. Telephone lines were put up by 1920, and the village streets were blacktopped around 1940. Sidewalks were modernized with concrete, water lines were put in, and the sewer lines were extended.

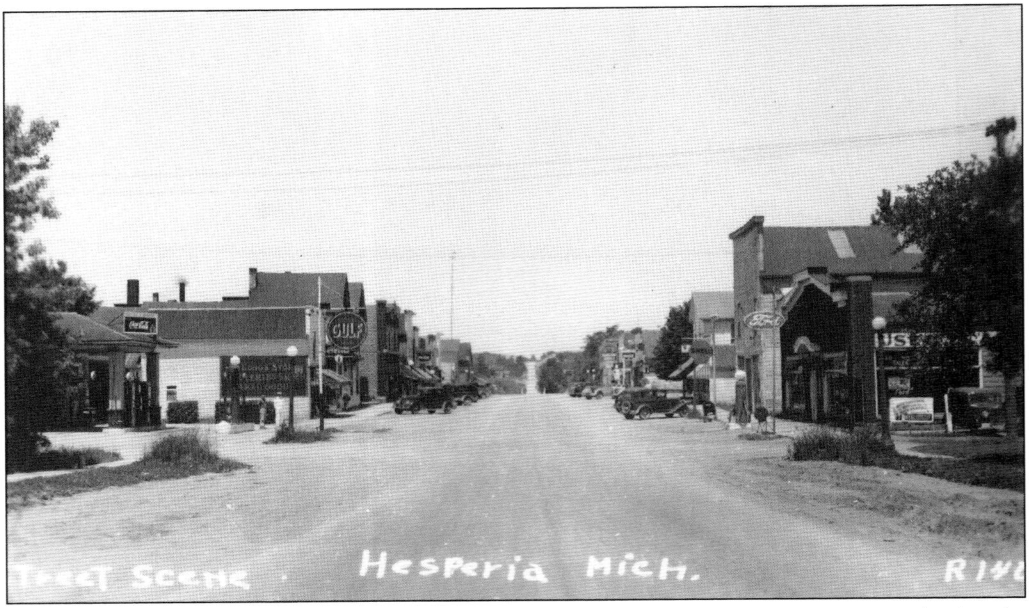

Hesperia Schools founded the Hesperia Movement, a community improvement organization, in 1901, and it continued into the 1920s. A "Big Meeting" was held every winter, bringing members of the towns and rural areas together. The meetings provided wholesome entertainment, as well as education and culture, to the Hesperia area, with the goal of building character and improving school conditions. In 1921, the Big Meeting was held in the new Husband & Turple Hardware store.

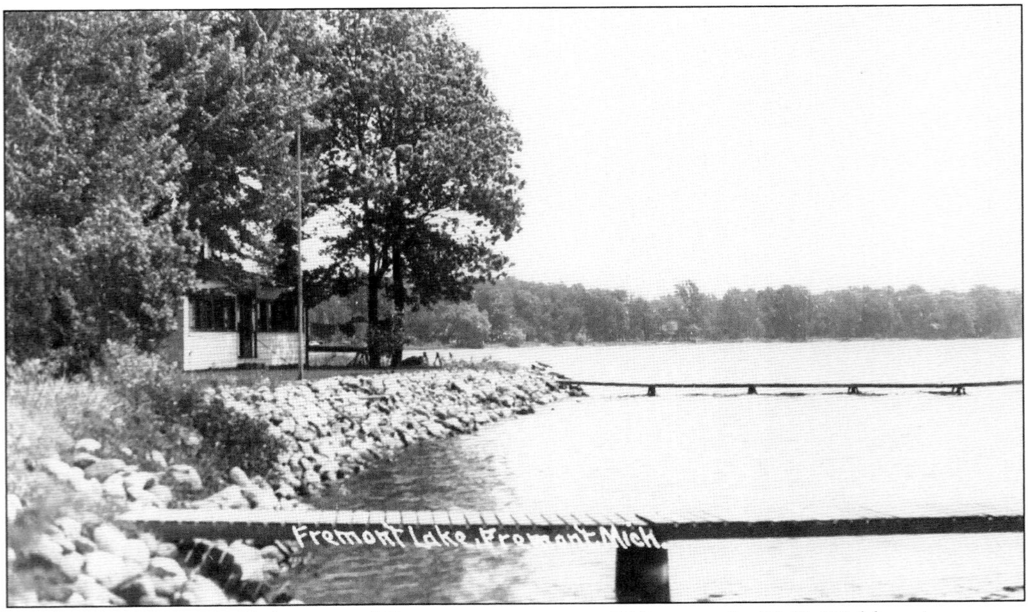

Fremont Lake, west of the city of Fremont, comprises 790 acres. In 1947, Hidden Acres was opened as a canoe livery that had a few cabins. It received its name because a visitor could not see it until he or she reached the top of a hill. There was another boat livery on the north side of the lake, owned by Rollo Martin and his wife. In addition, a livery named the Shack was owned by the Emmons family.

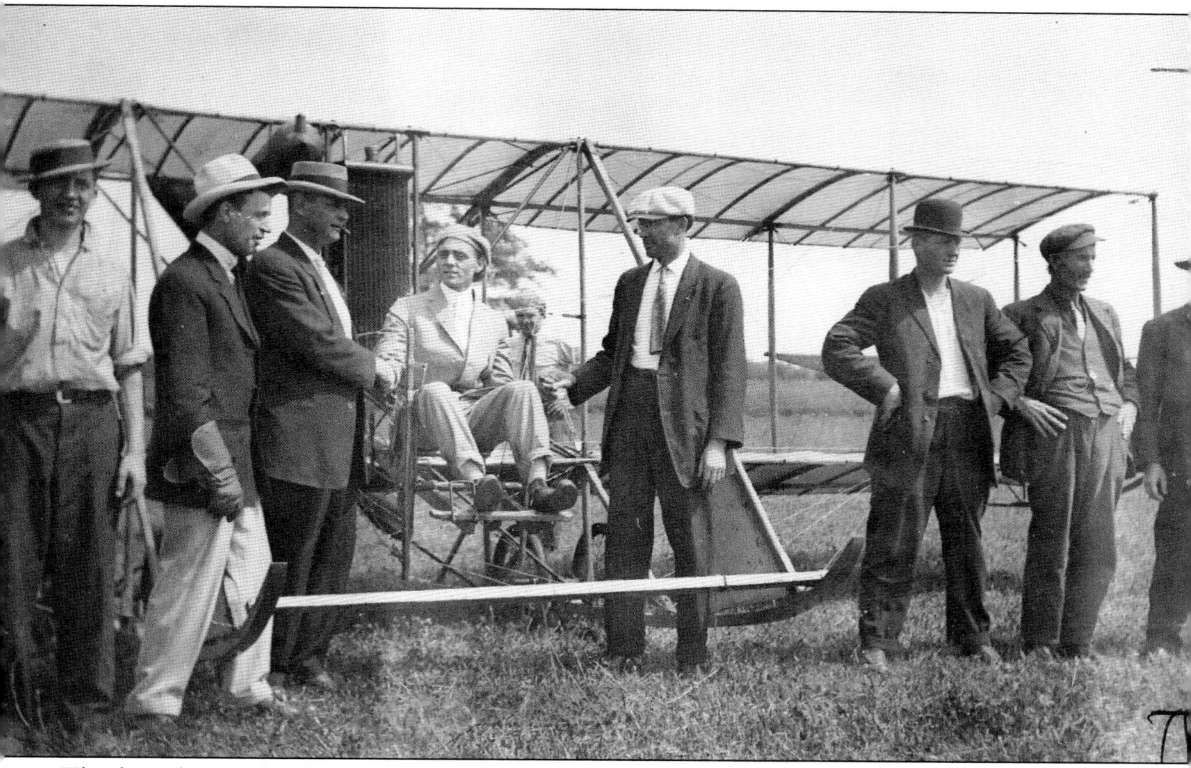

The first plane to land in Fremont caused quite a stir. In the following years, and with Gerber Products Company growing, the need for an airport became apparent. Today, the airport is one of the few remaining general aviation airports with the capacity to serve corporate needs in the region. The city-owned and -operated facility is located just 1.5 miles southwest of the Fremont Industrial Park. The airport is home to more than 50 aircraft.

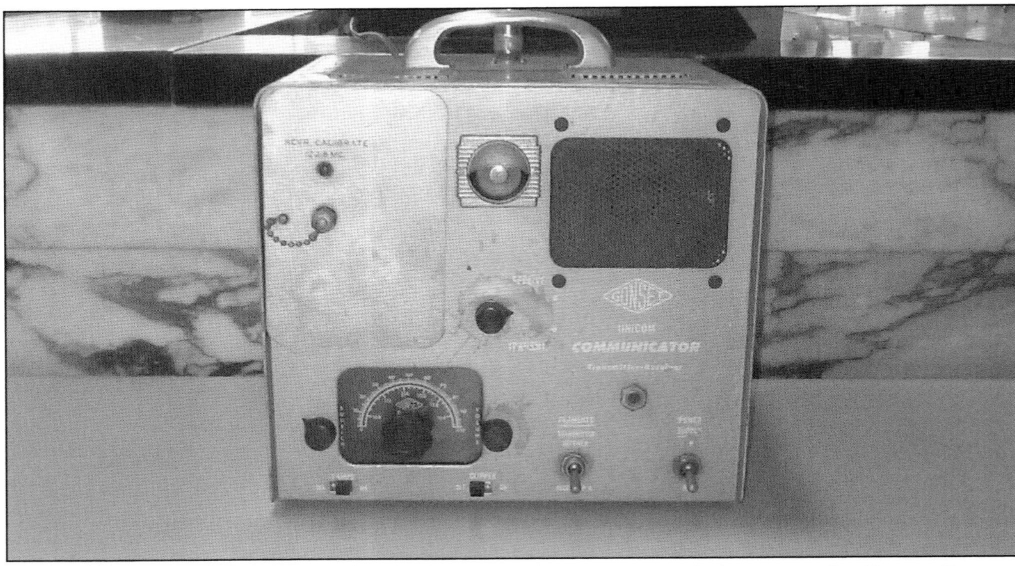

Kenneth Krapp, while visiting the Gerber aircraft crew, noticed this item: the first radio used at Fremont Airport. It had been sitting on a dusty shelf, neglected, having since been replaced. Krapp had, as a young lad, spent many hours hanging out around the airport, so he asked if he could have it. The crew checked with Gerber Products Company, and after it was removed from the company's inventory list, the radio was given to him. Doran Ditlow, a ham radio operator and person who repairs radios, saw it and asked if he could try to get it working—and he did. It now sits at the history center with the ability to pick up signals, but just not transmit them. It is a great addition to the center.

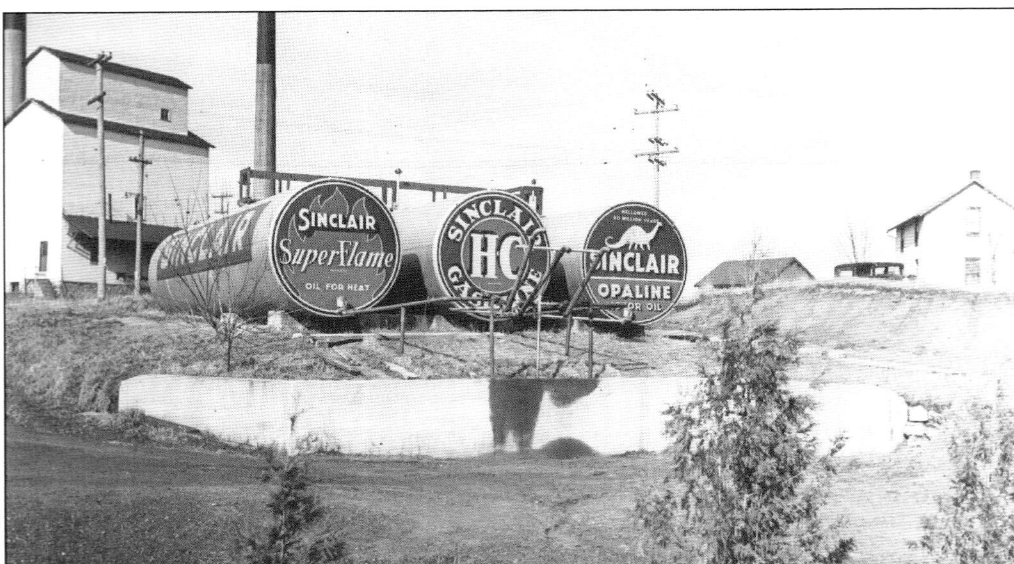

In the early days of gasoline-powered vehicles, gas tanks were not placed below ground as they are now. This photograph, from those days, shows an aboveground gasoline tank (center), a heating-oil tank (left), and a motor-oil tank.

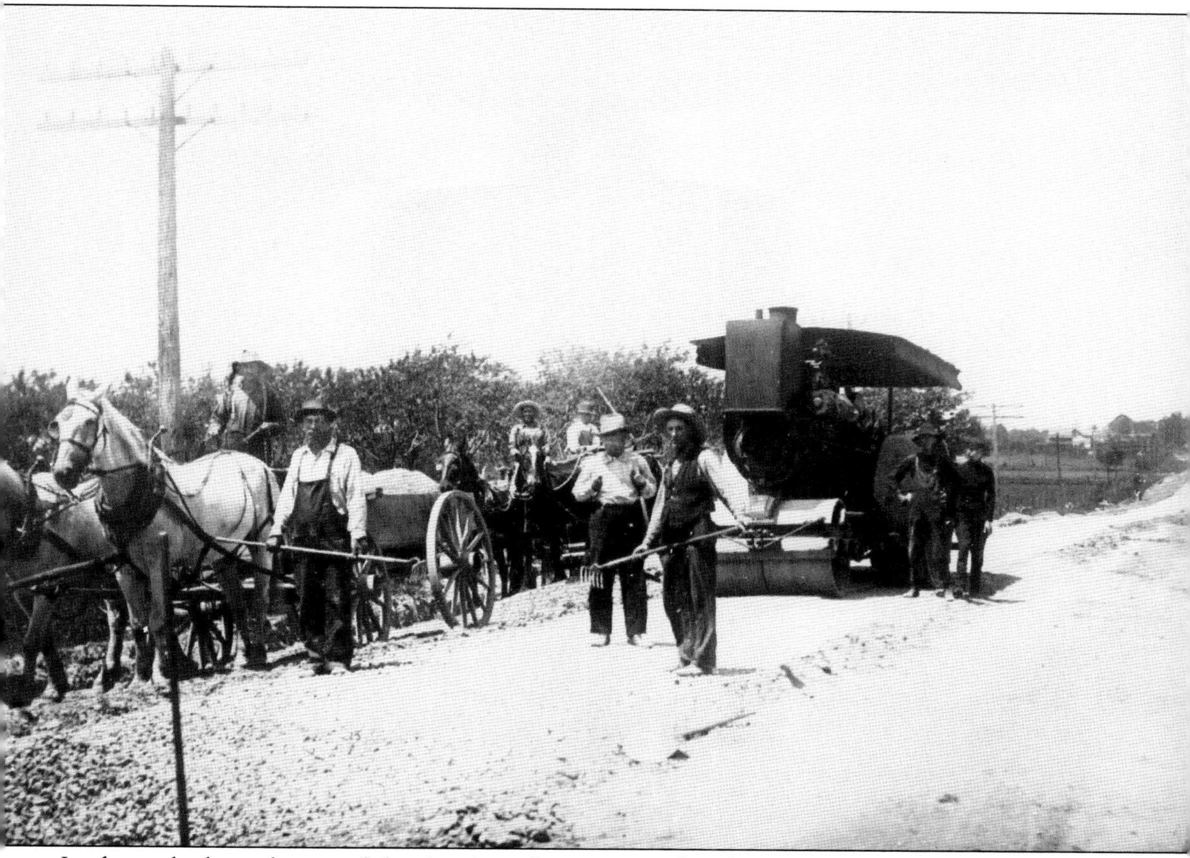

In the early days of automobiles, local residents prepared and maintained the roads. Farmers would spend the day working to grade and pack the road surfaces, often using their teams of horses. Here, the packer being used is self-propelled, operated probably by steam power, as were threshing machines of the same period.

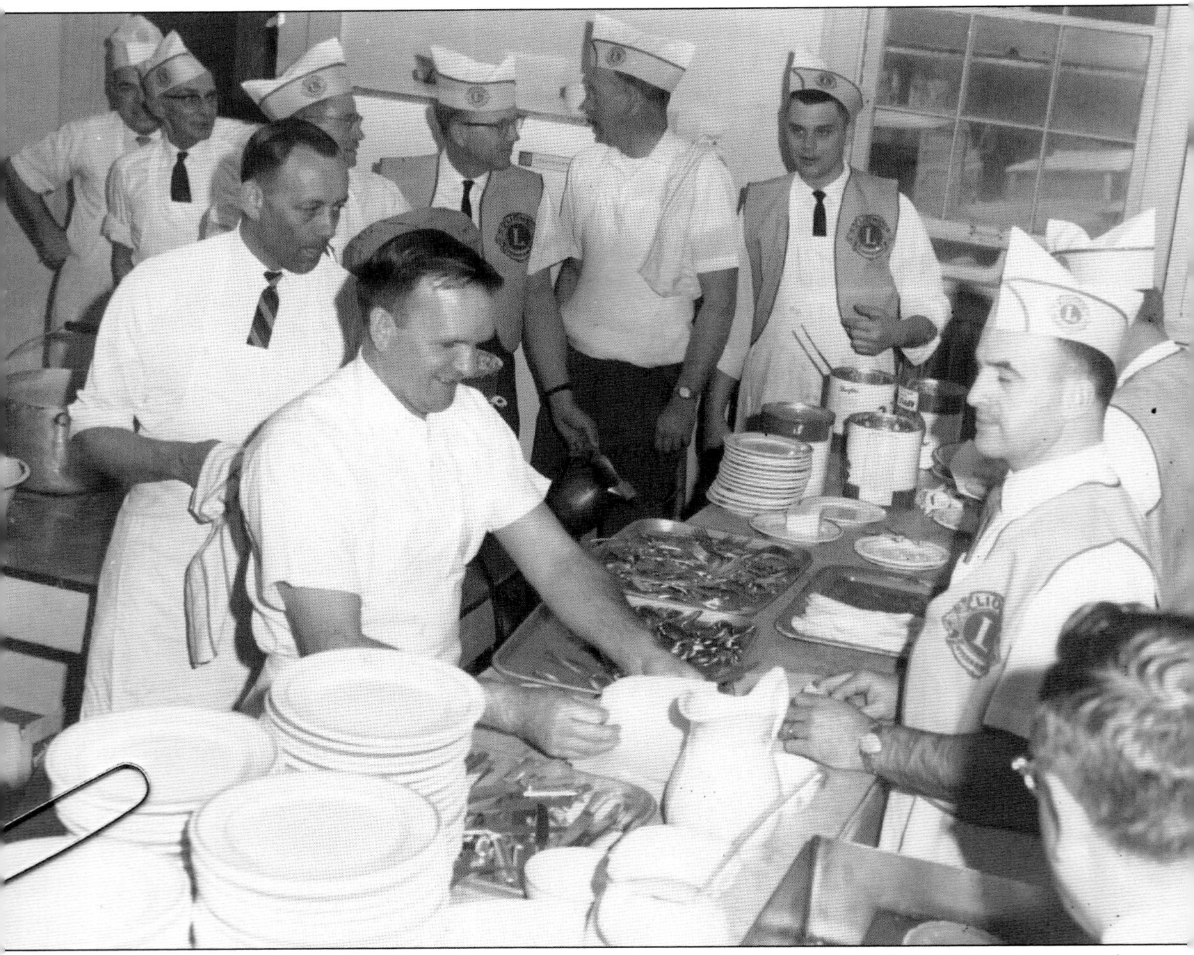

The Fremont Rotary has always been active in the area. This is an April 25, 1965, photograph of an annual pancake breakfast held in the community building. The Fremont Rotary Club was chartered in 1963 and has been an active group ever since. Other Newaygo County cities also have active Rotary clubs supporting their communities.

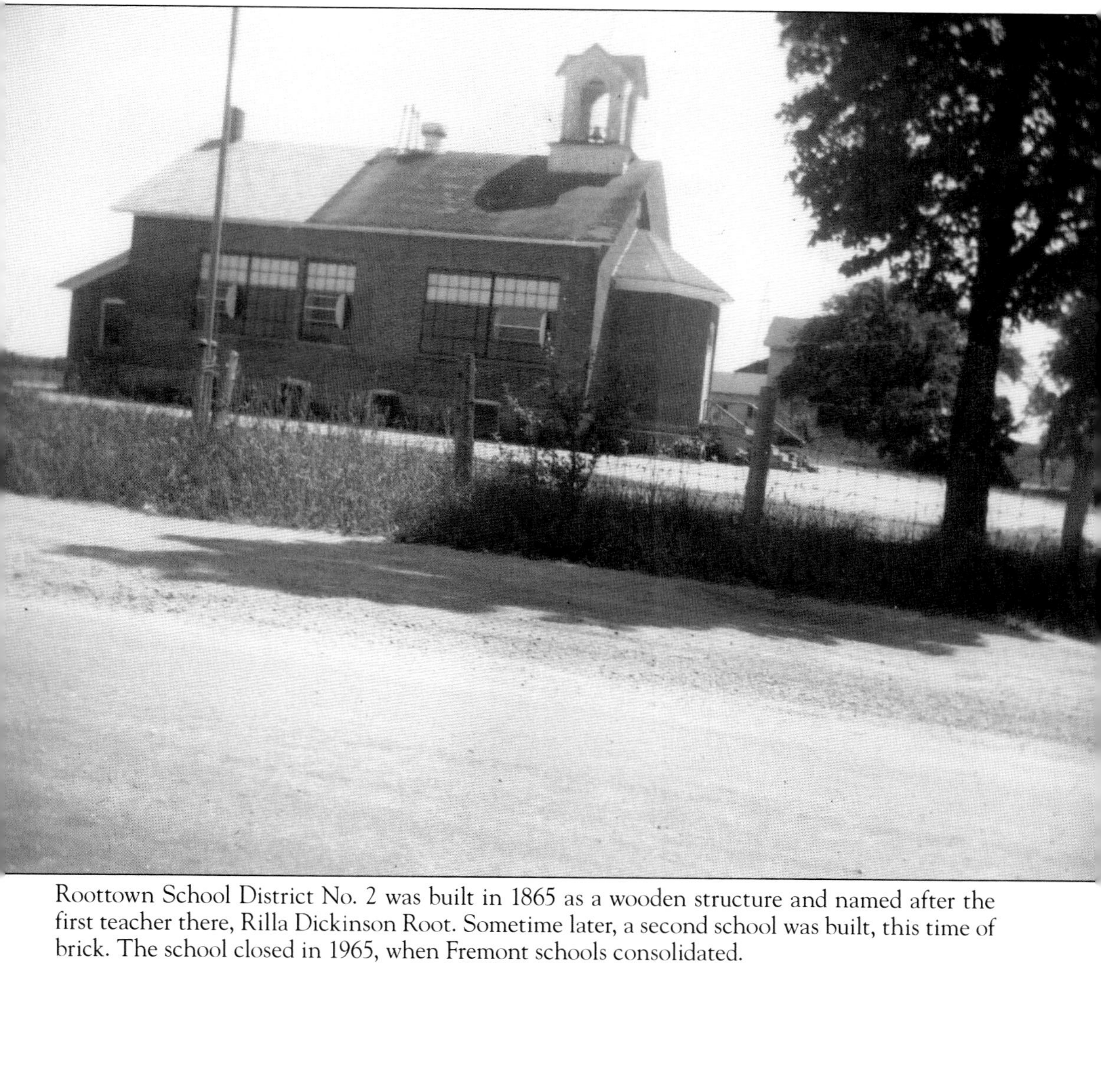

Roottown School District No. 2 was built in 1865 as a wooden structure and named after the first teacher there, Rilla Dickinson Root. Sometime later, a second school was built, this time of brick. The school closed in 1965, when Fremont schools consolidated.

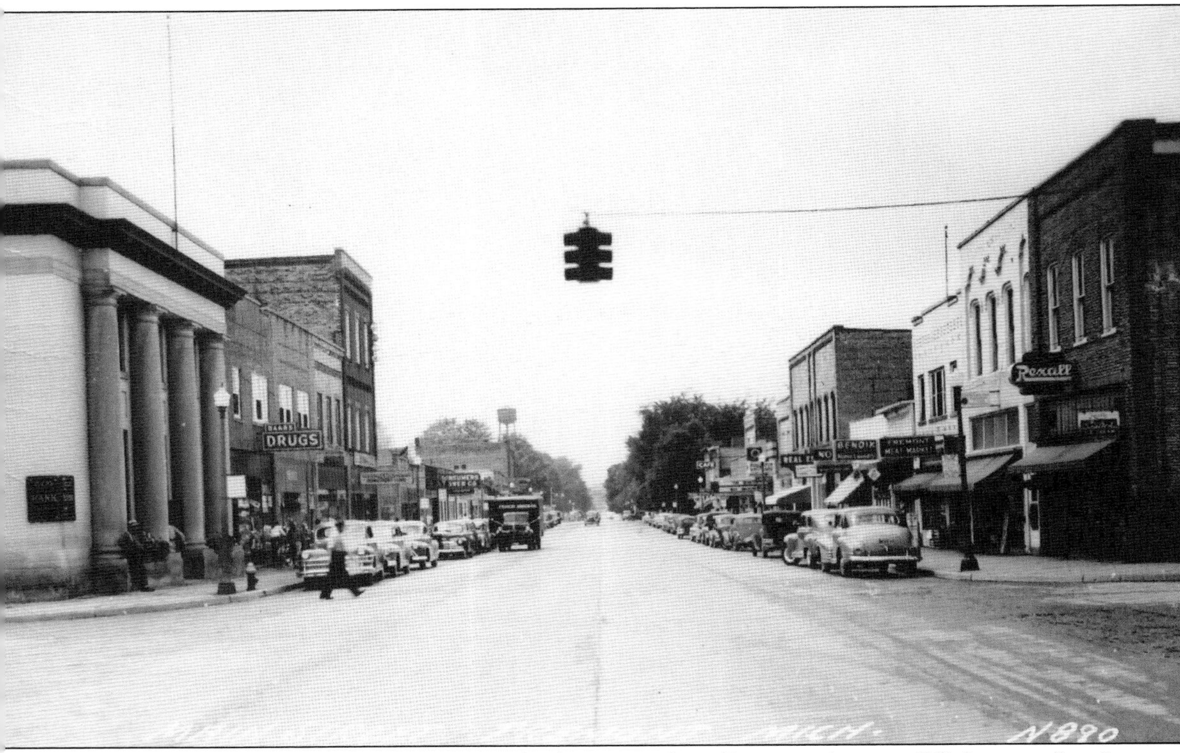

This is West Main Street in Fremont, looking west from Division Avenue. While some facades have changed, the large pillars of the bank on the corner remain. For many years, the traffic light on this corner was the only one in town. Farther down the street on the right are the trees of Veterans Park.

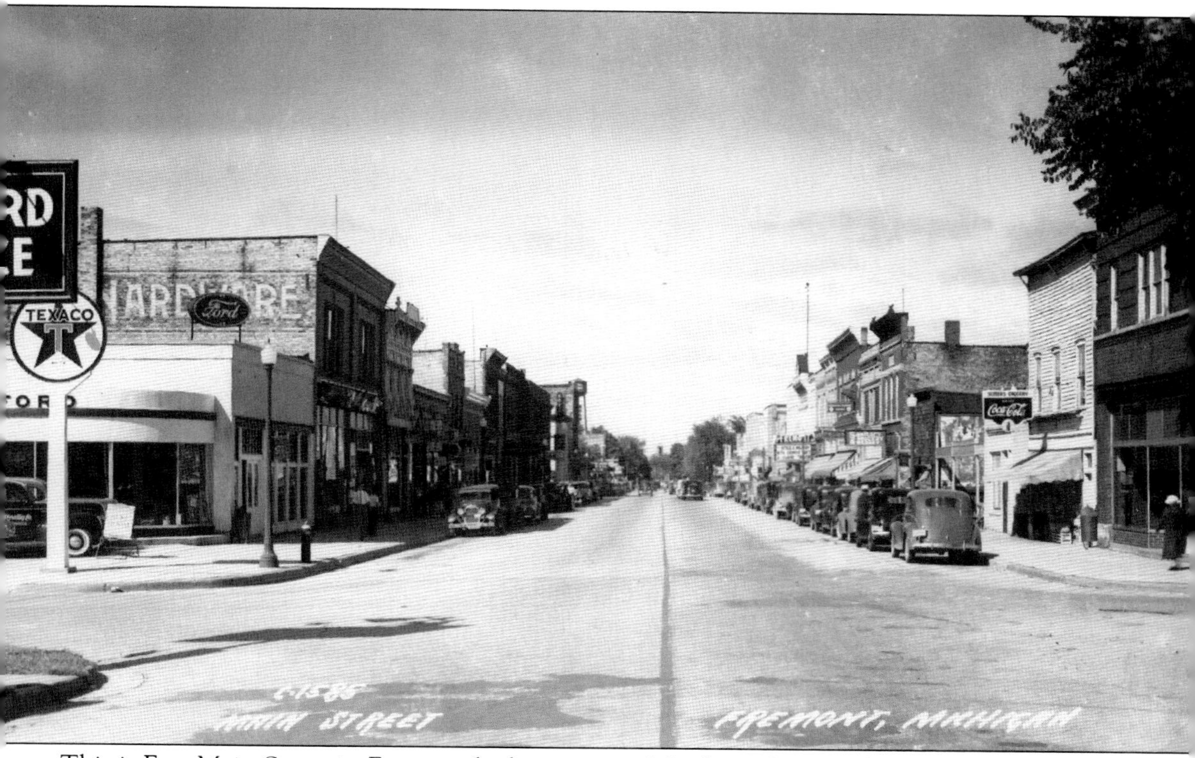

This is East Main Street in Fremont, looking west at Merchant Street. The Standard service station is now the library, and the Texaco-Ford dealer is a dry-cleaner operation, among other changes in small businesses. Many of these buildings are still standing, although repurposed. The tall building in the left foreground now has a pharmacy at street level and an archery range on the upper level.

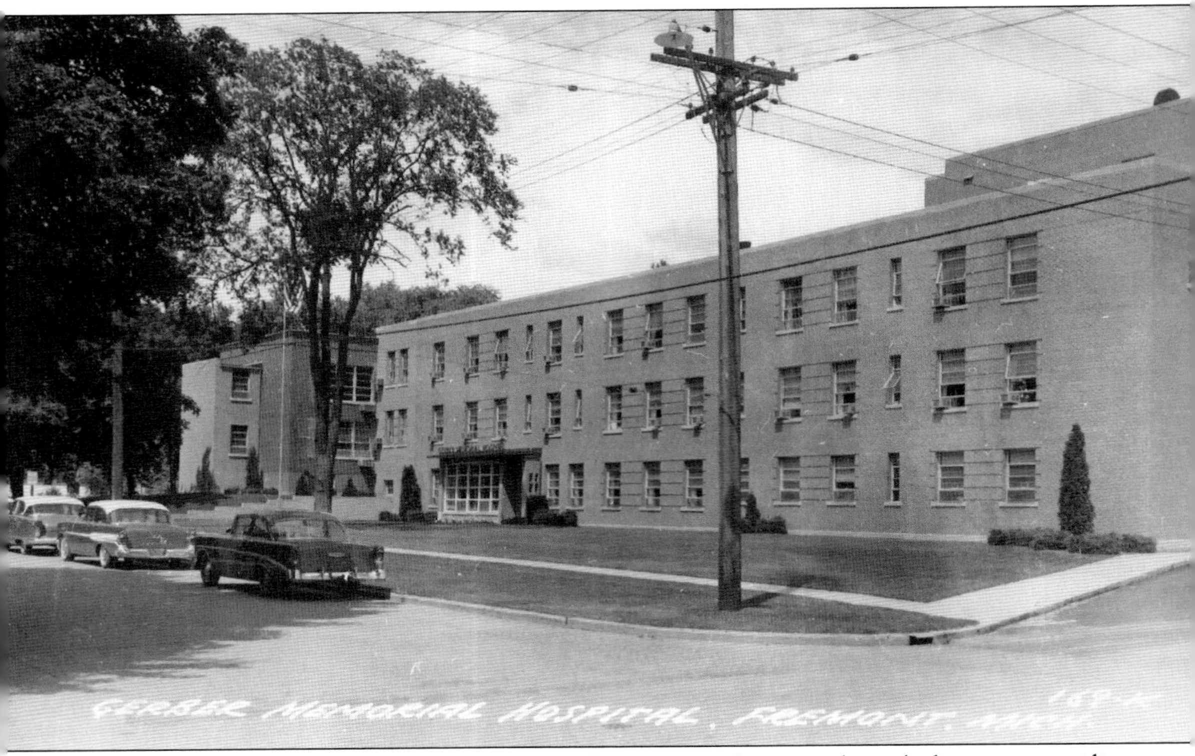

Spectrum Health Gerber Memorial Hospital has continued to grow through the years, providing the county with modern intensive care, cardiac care, and emergency room facilities. Many additions and renovations have been part of the growth of this facility, which serves all of Newaygo County. These expansions have enlarged the footprint of the hospital, expanding across Sullivan Street. This growth continues into the 21st century.

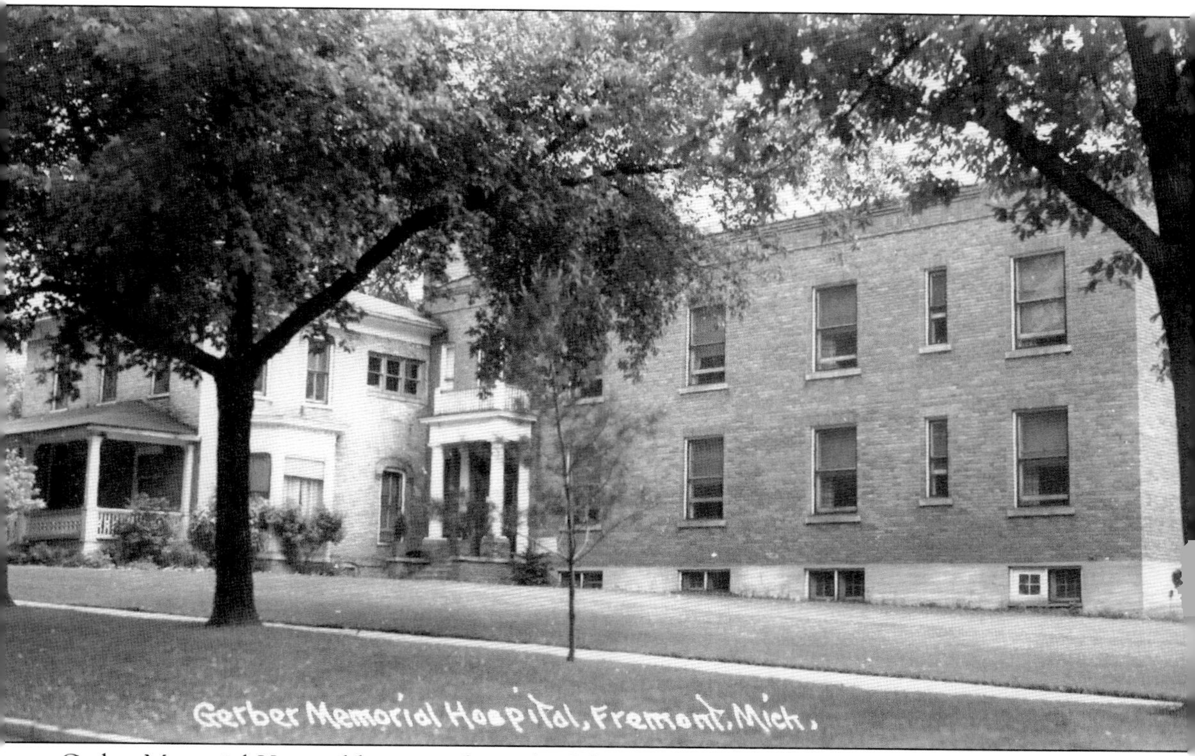

Gerber Memorial Hospital began with a gift of the Joseph and Agnes Gerber family home to the community of Fremont to be used for the relief of pain and suffering. The resulting hospital has been expanded several times off the side of the home, and in 1969 the original home was replaced with a new wing.

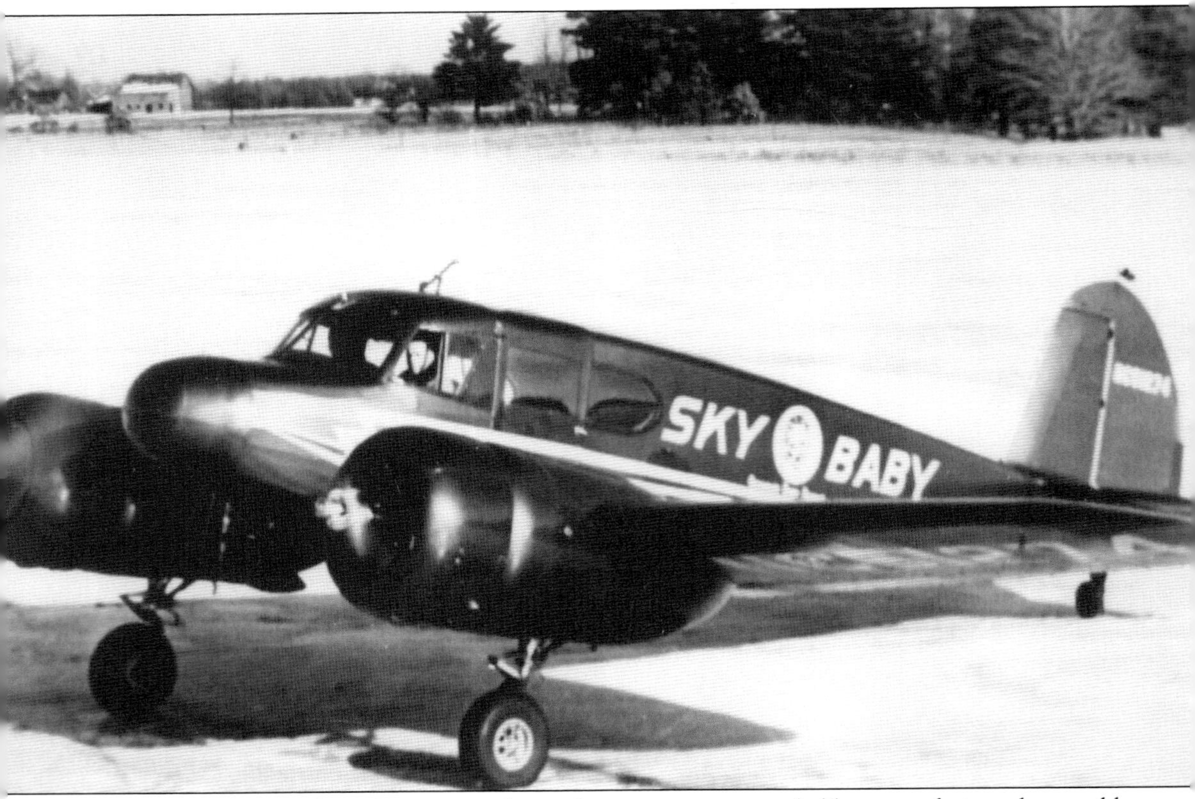

While Gerber Products Company is located in an area surrounded by many fruit and vegetable farms, it is some distance from Fremont to major airports in Grand Rapids or Chicago. Because of that, Gerber first branched into corporate aircraft in 1946. Its first plane was a four-seat, twin-engine Cessna, known as *Sky Baby*.

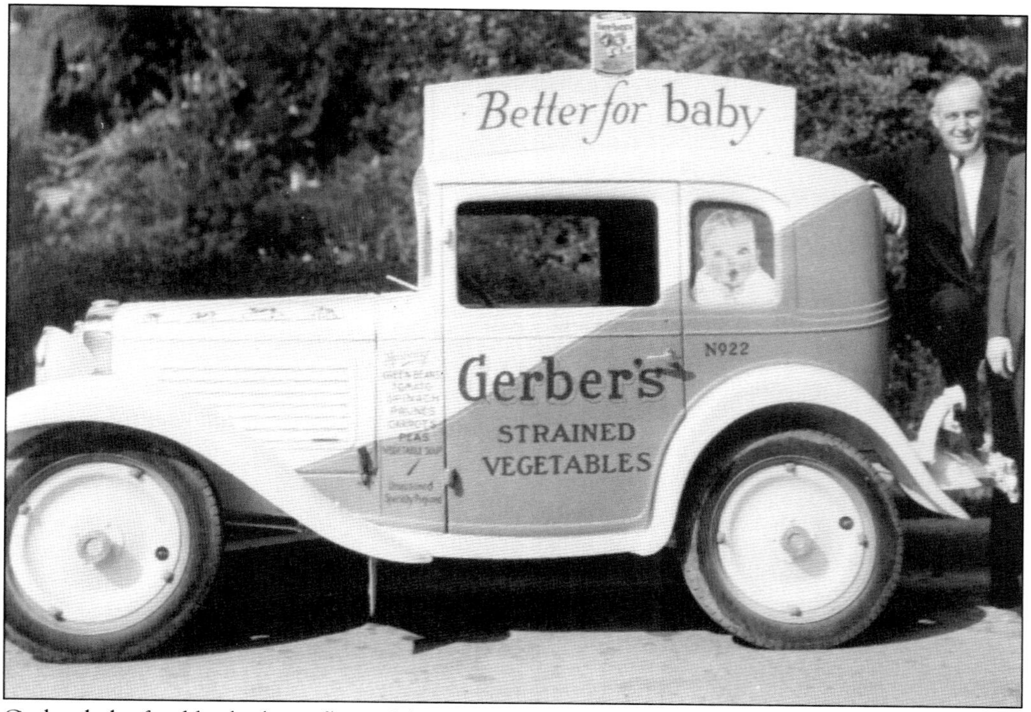

Gerber baby food had a large fleet of distinctive cars driven by its sales force. Promising to send six cans of baby food to mothers who sent in the names of their grocers, Gerber salesmen followed up by visiting the grocery store in these cars, with horns that played "Rock-a-Bye, Baby."

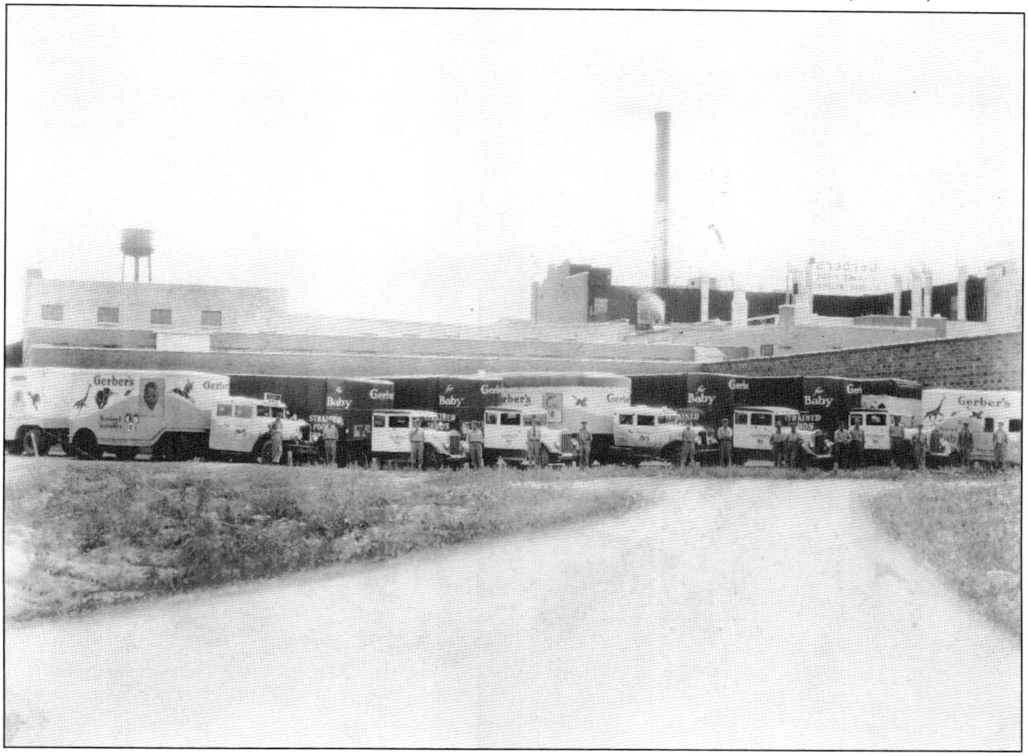

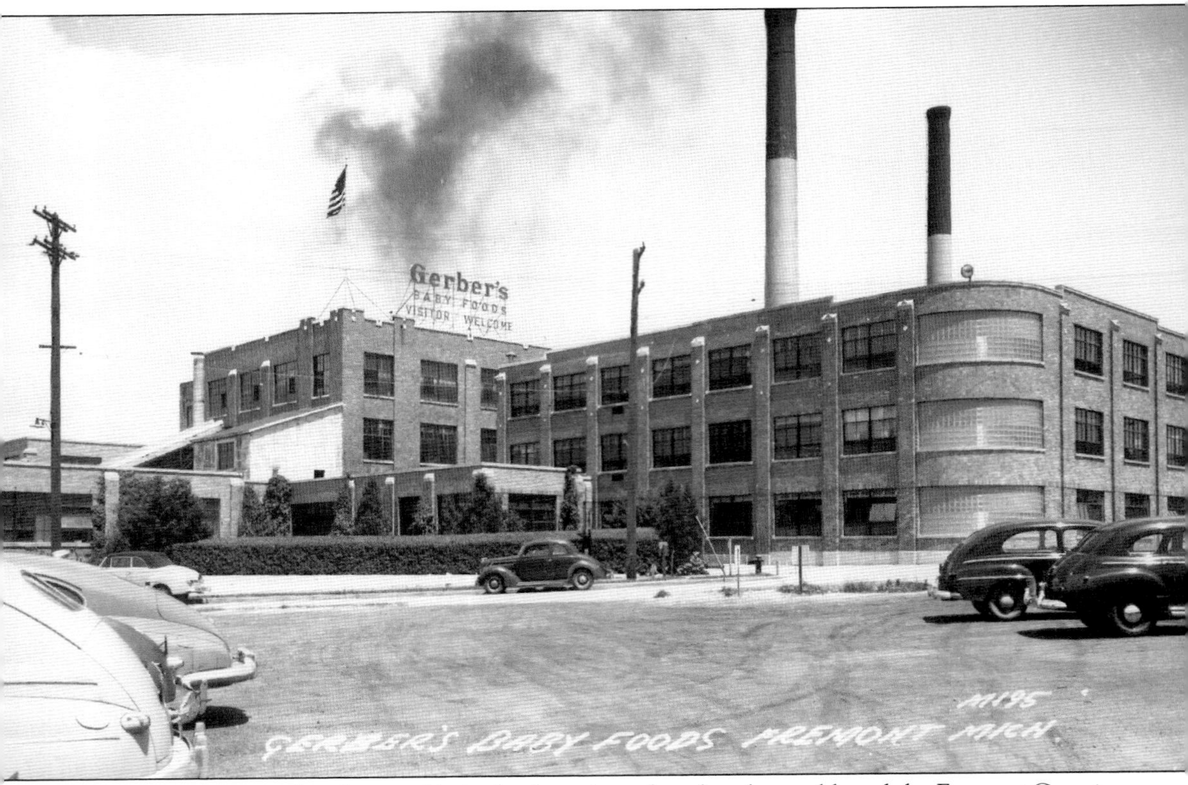

In 1928, processed and canned baby food was introduced to the world, and the Fremont Canning Company was transformed into Gerber Products Company. By the 1940s, it was a large company that even employed German POWs in 1944–1945. This photograph shows the Gerber office and factory in the 1940s.

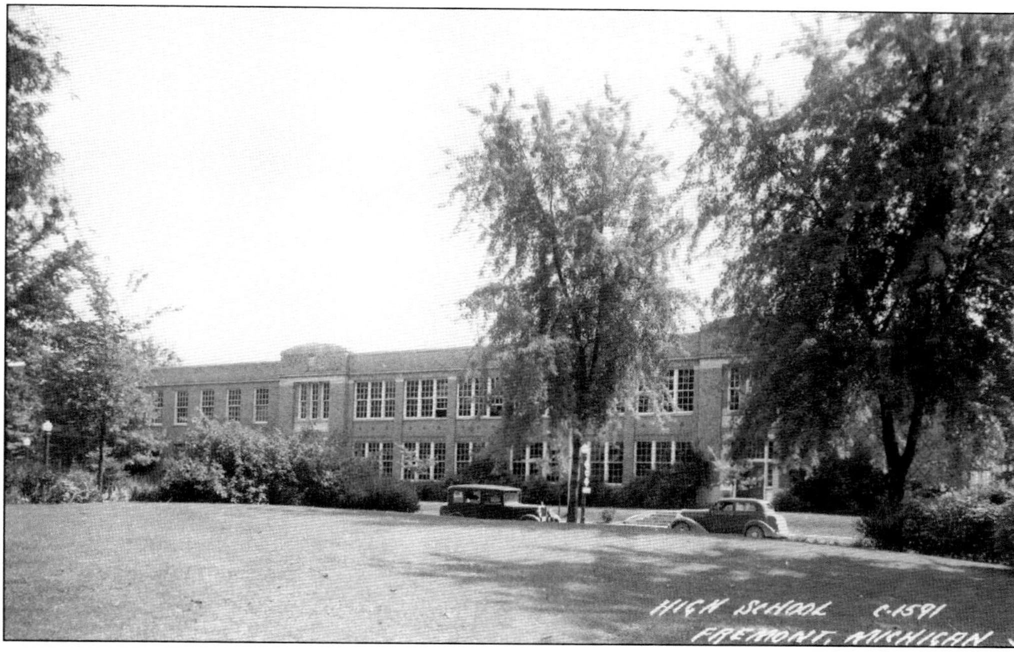

Even though the third addition on the previous Fremont High School (above), located on the corner of Main and Stewart Streets, was completed by 1910, in 1926 the older two-thirds of the school was replaced by a new brick high school. The third section of the old school (below, left) was replaced years later. Finally, in 2012, the entire school was superseded by an entirely new high school on the south side of town. That state-of-the-art building was the only new school to be completed that year in the state of Michigan.

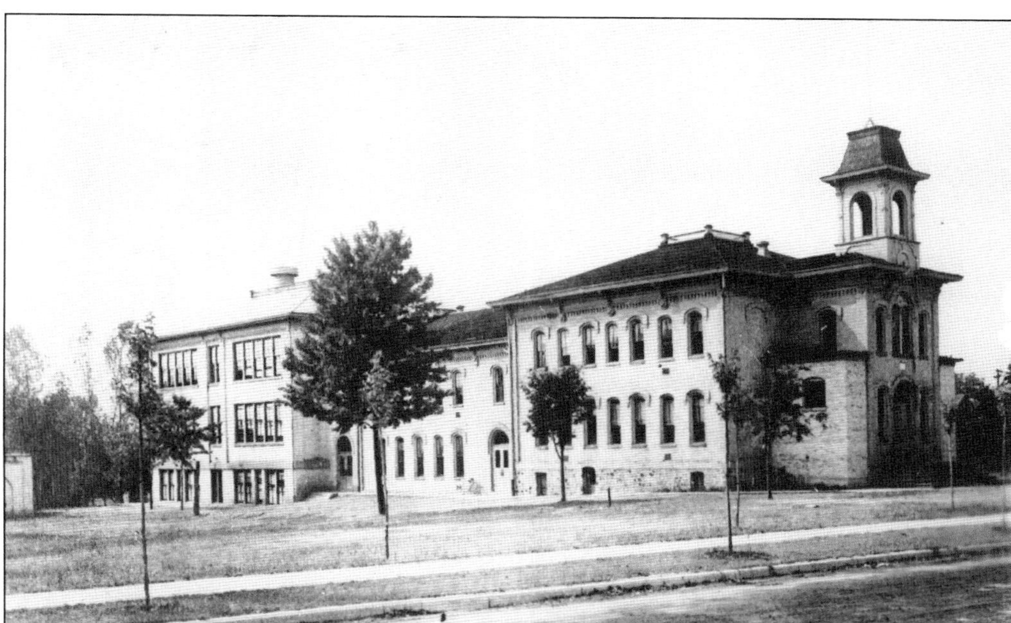

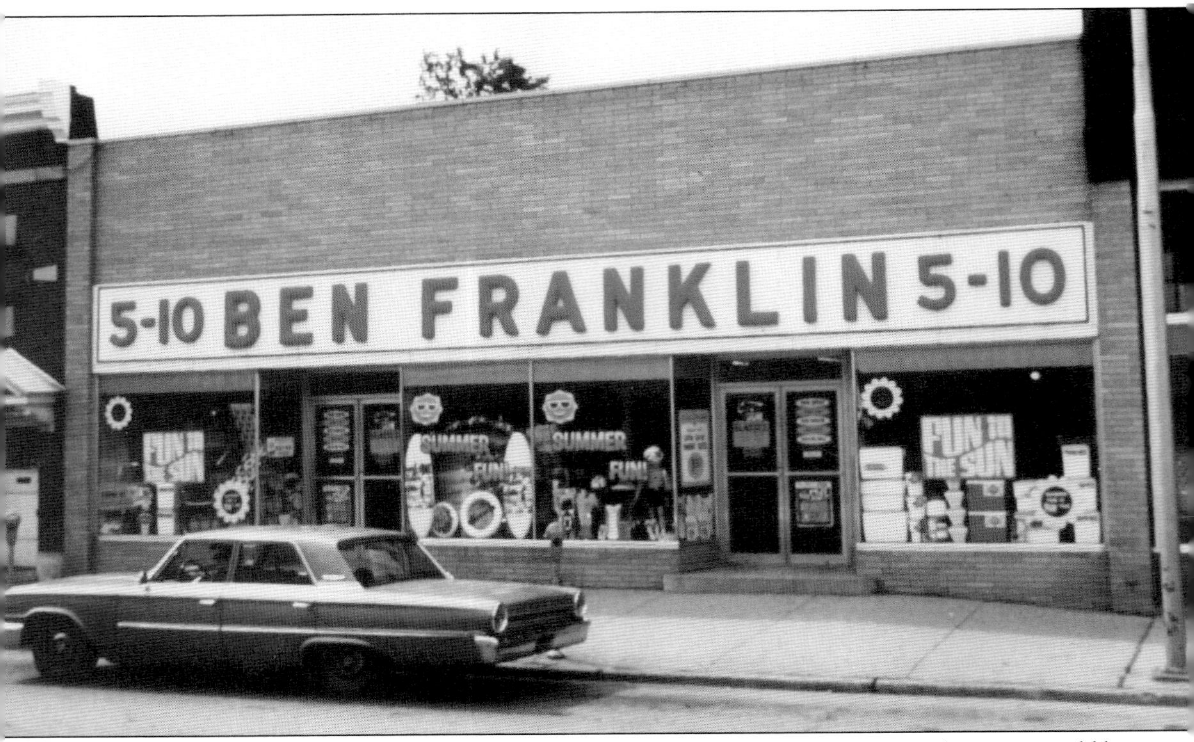

The Ben Franklin Store was a longtime institution in the Fremont area. Many bargains could be found there. Originally half the size shown here, the store doubled its frontage and expanded in the 1960s. Since closing, the building has been used as a furniture store and a secondhand store.

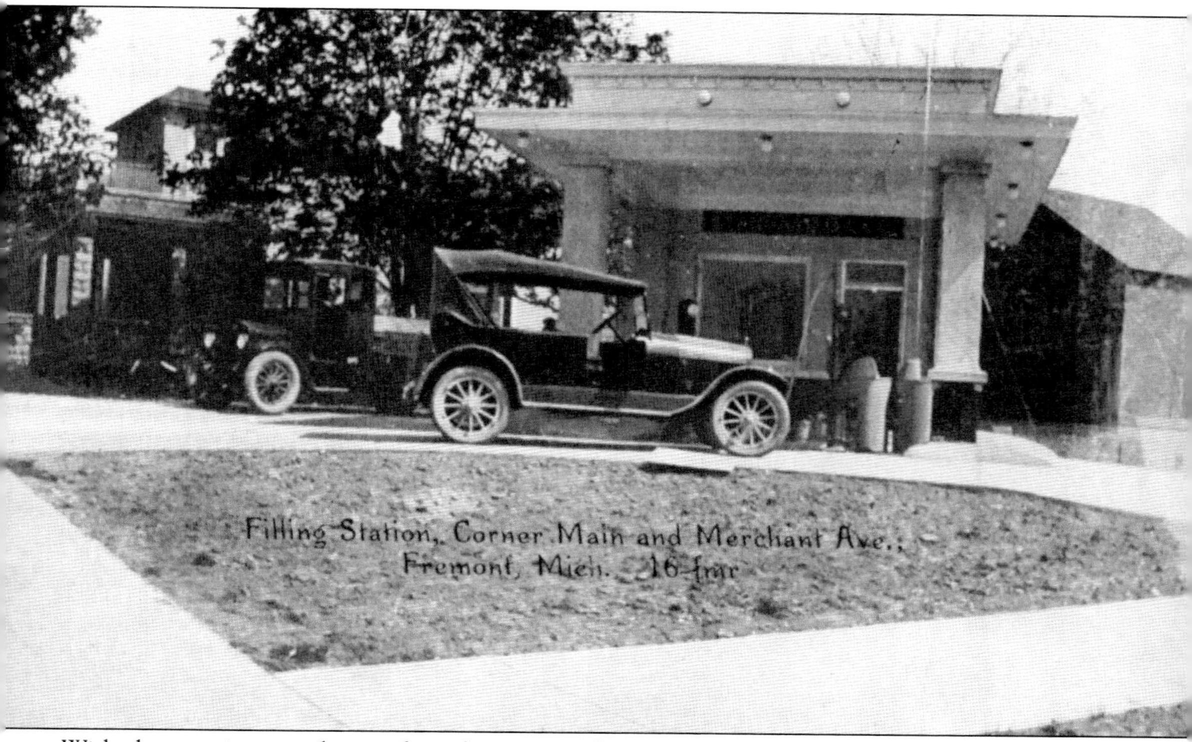

With the growing popularity of gasoline-powered transportation, filling stations soon started springing up around the county. This station was located in Fremont, on the corner of Main and Merchant Streets, near the current location of the library. Such stations in the early days of automobiles offered full service, such as cleaning the windshields and checking the oil for motorists.

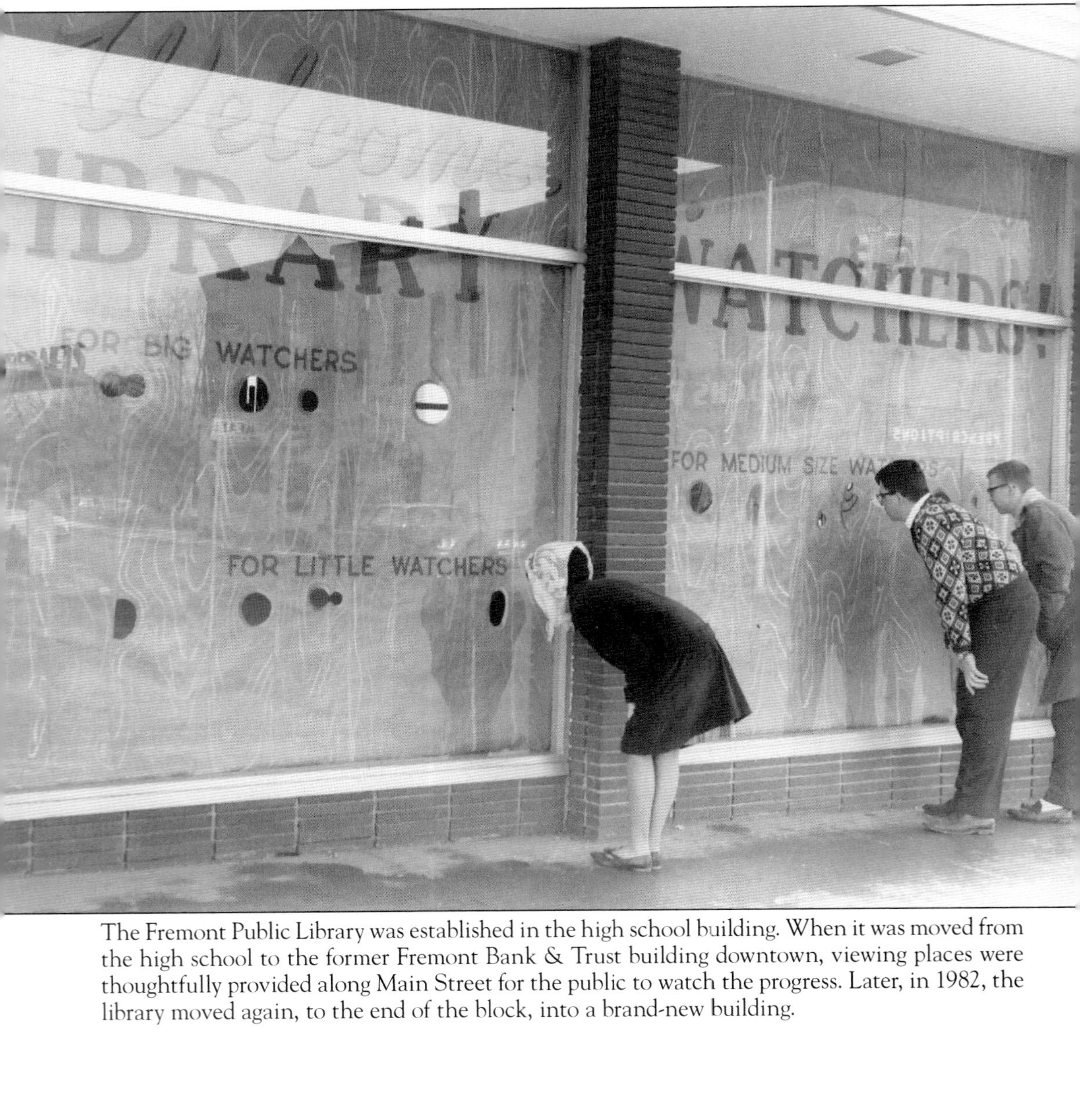

The Fremont Public Library was established in the high school building. When it was moved from the high school to the former Fremont Bank & Trust building downtown, viewing places were thoughtfully provided along Main Street for the public to watch the progress. Later, in 1982, the library moved again, to the end of the block, into a brand-new building.

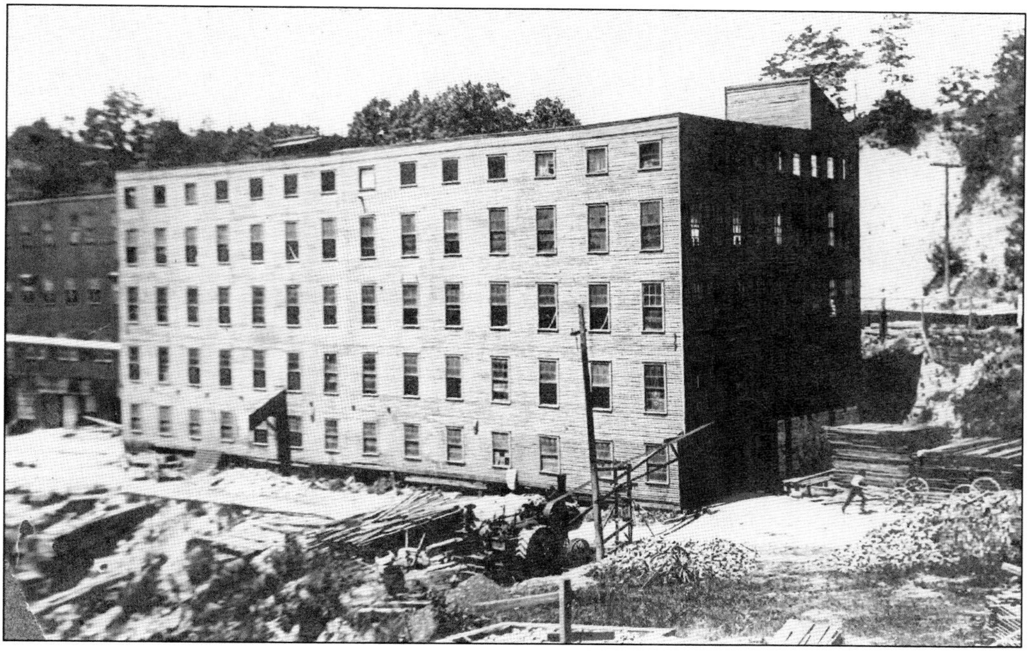

The Henry Rowe Manufacturing Company dates from 1926. Its catalog featured 40 pages of wood turnings, rosettes, drawer pulls, wood feet, and plugs. The catalog was used worldwide for furniture making, which was convenient, since the "Furniture City," Grand Rapids, was 45 miles to the south.

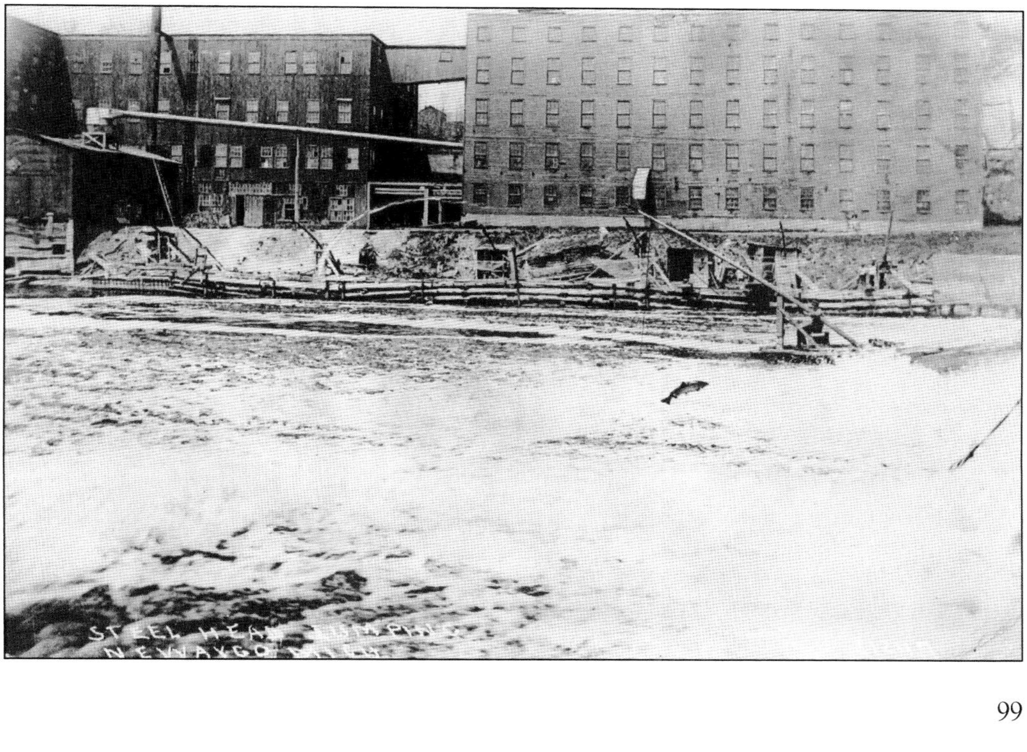

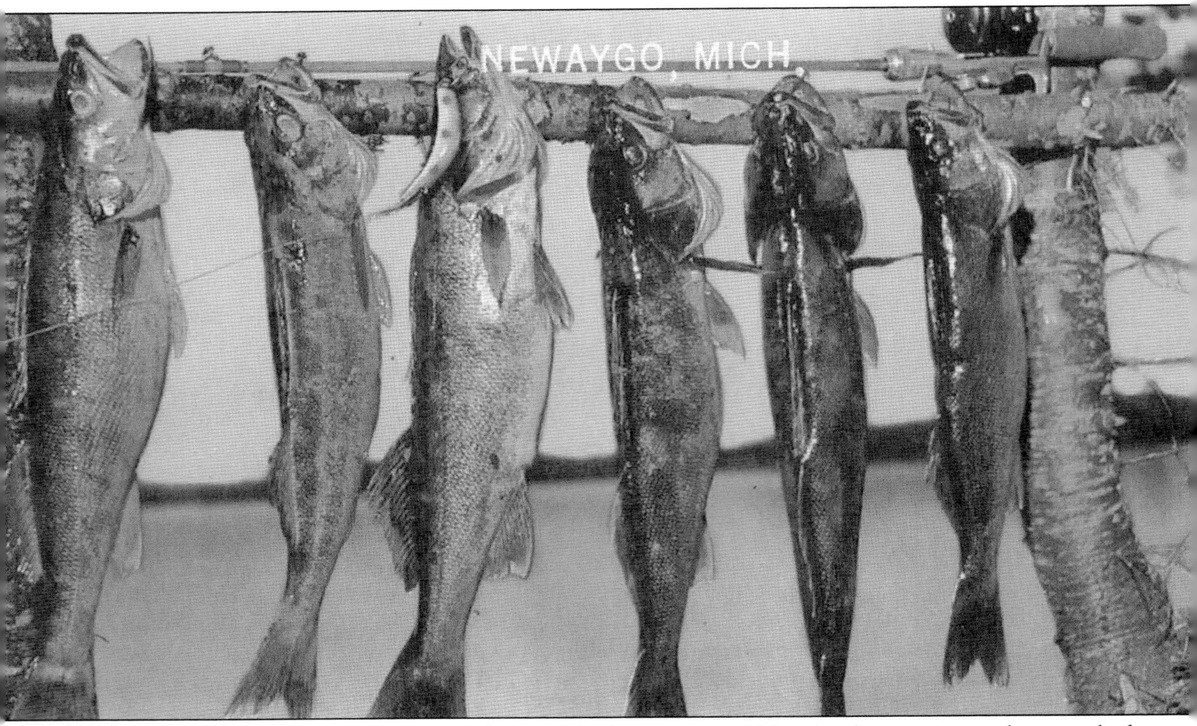

On October 17, 1968, in Lansing, Michigan, bids were opened for the destruction and removal of the Newaygo Dam. Although some salmon were going over the dam, more would go upstream if it was removed. The removal would also open up the river for the passage of walleye and steelhead farther upstream, as far as the Croton Dam, and provide a fishery and natural spawning ground for salmon and steelhead. In November 1968, engineers at the Michigan Department of Natural Resources gave a Grand Rapids contractor the green light to start battering down the Muskegon River's Newaygo Dam to clear the way for extending upstream fish runs in 1969. The $34,000 demolition project was completed in February 1969, with the final cleanup in September.

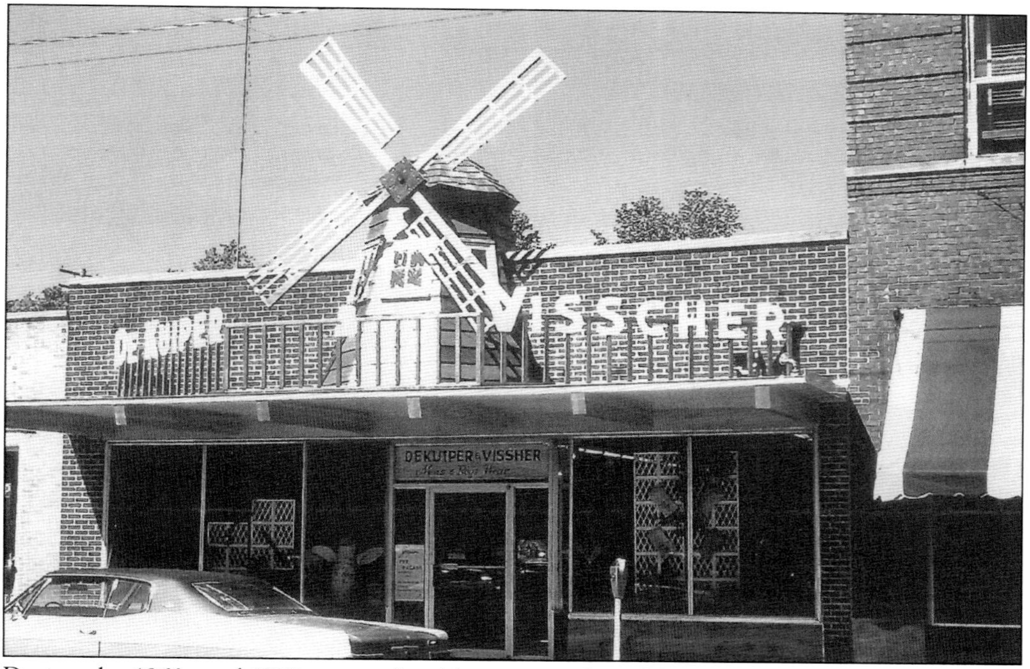

During the 1960s and 1970s, many local businesses along Main Street updated their facades. DeKuiper & Vissher, a men's clothing store at the time, was one such business. The company's updated look played on the Dutch heritage of the Newaygo County area by incorporating this large windmill into its storefront. With the windmill firmly in place, the building later housed the Dutch Bakery.

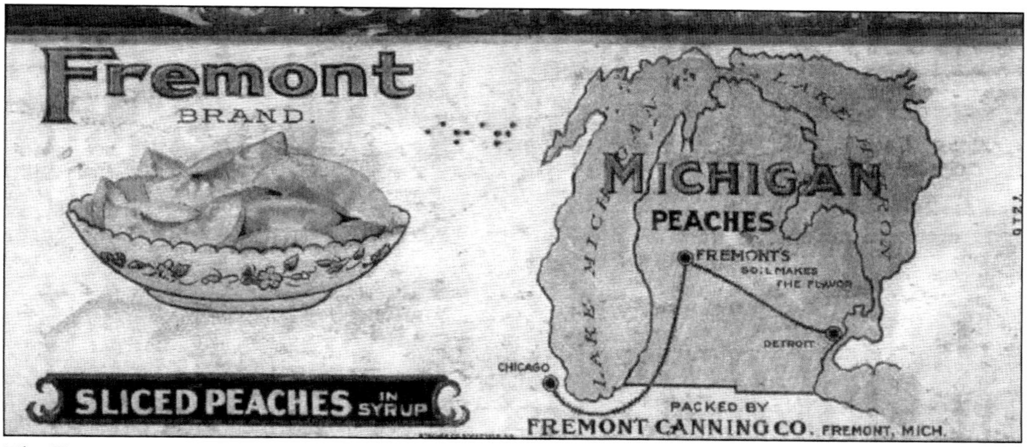

The Fremont Canning Company canned many items grown by local farmers, including vegetables, such as beans and peas, along with fruit, such as peaches and apples. This is a Fremont Canning Company label from a can of sliced peaches in syrup. The company was growing at the time and sending canned goods to Chicago and Detroit.

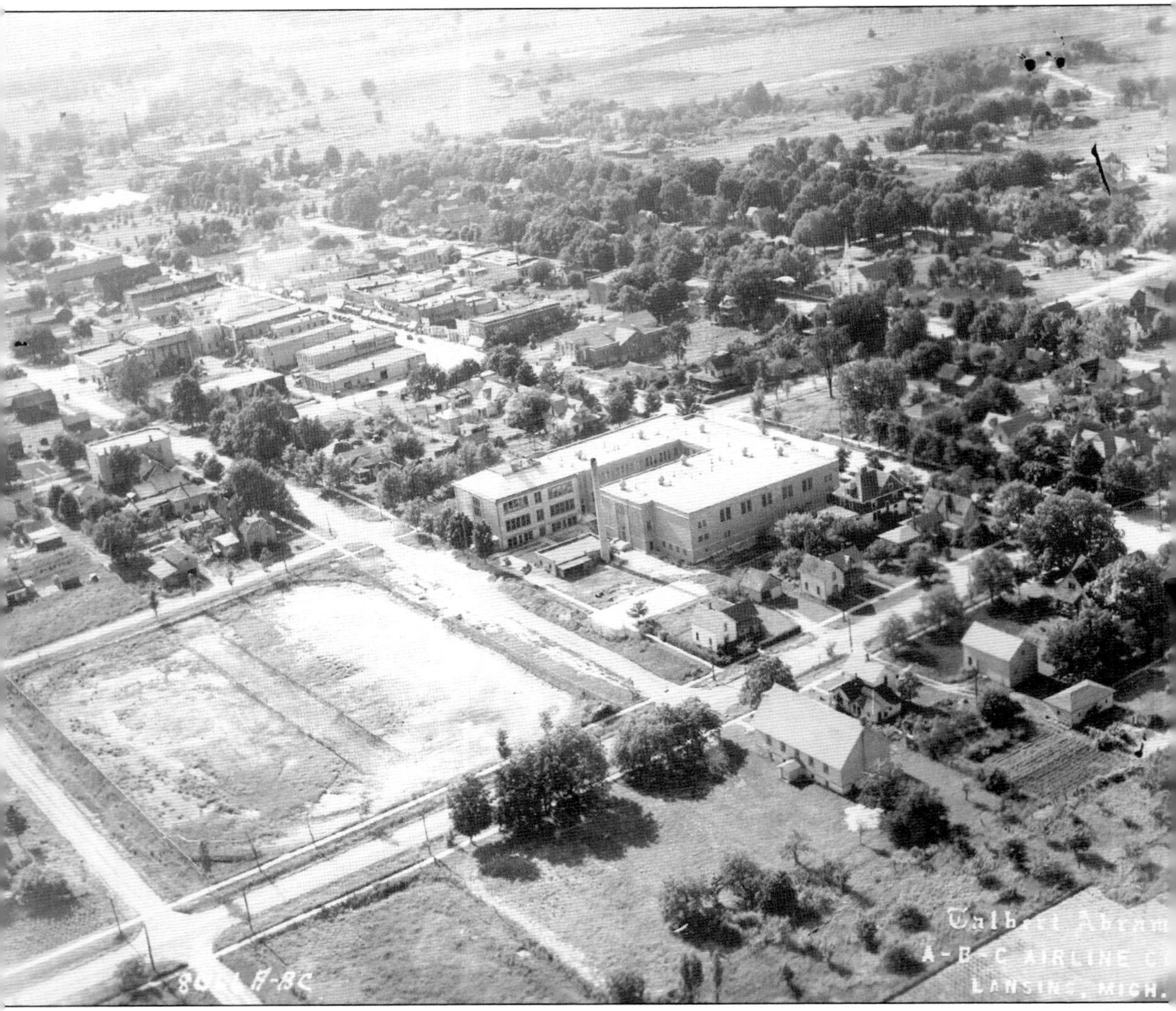

Here is an aerial photograph of Fremont looking west. Many companies offered cities and farmers the opportunity to get a photograph of their town or farm. Note the amount of open land surrounding Fremont, which is now developed. The bird's-eye shot also offers a great view of the school and football field at the time. The facilities have since expanded to keep up with the growing population.

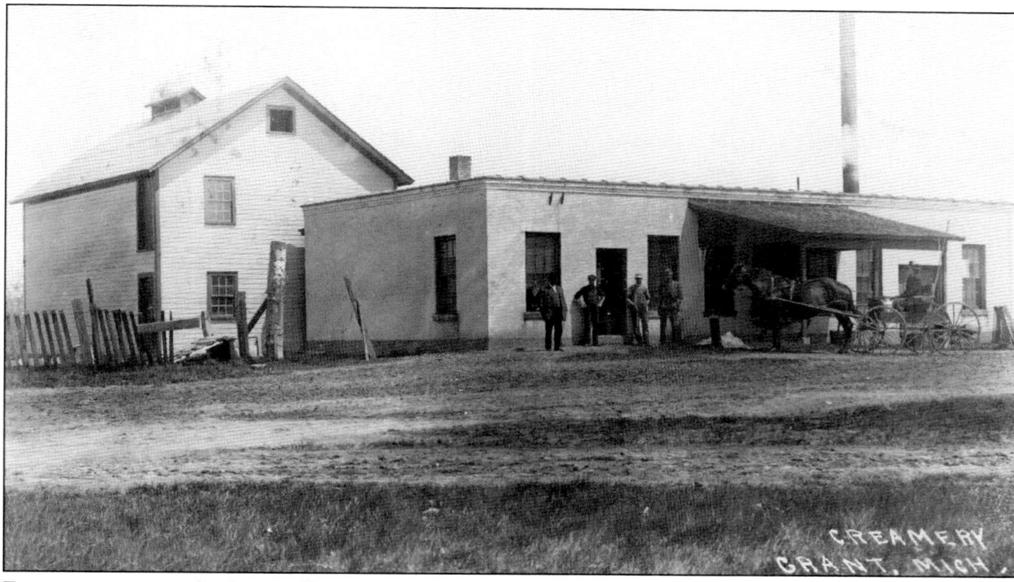

Every community had a small creamery, and many of these grew into much larger facilities as the population expanded. Newaygo County is in the middle of agricultural country and livestock farms. The creameries would process the milk, making cheese, cream, and dairy products, which were then delivered to the customer's door. The milk box, an item of the past, was a useful tool in the day of creameries. This one was located in Grant.

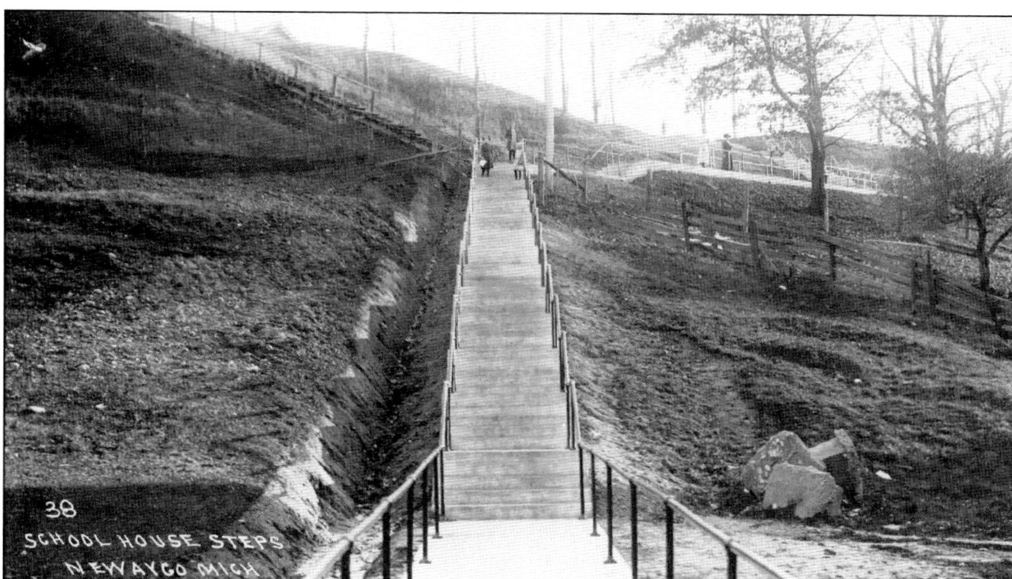

Many Newaygo students remember the steep stairs going up to the high school, which became a junior high school (eighth and ninth grades), then a middle school (fourth through seventh grades). The steps were originally built of wood, but as the years went by they were rebuilt with steel. Just when a person reached the top, they would find two terraces that also had steps to climb. It was always great thrill to race others up or down the stairs, a fond memory for many Newaygo students. The hill was fun to slide down in the winter, but care had to be taken, as there were many trees and a parking lot at the bottom.

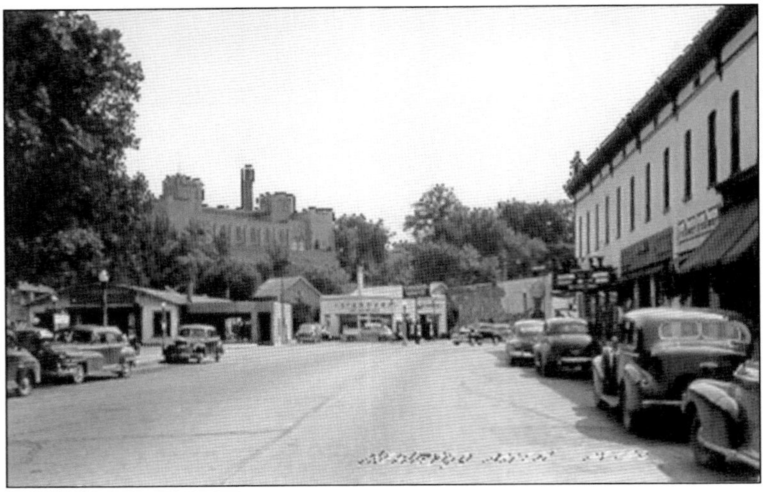

Downtown Newaygo has gone through many changes throughout the years. This photograph appears to show a busy day. The Newaygo School, on the hill in the back left, has become a landmark for people traveling through town. It has served as several types of schools, growing with the needs of the city.

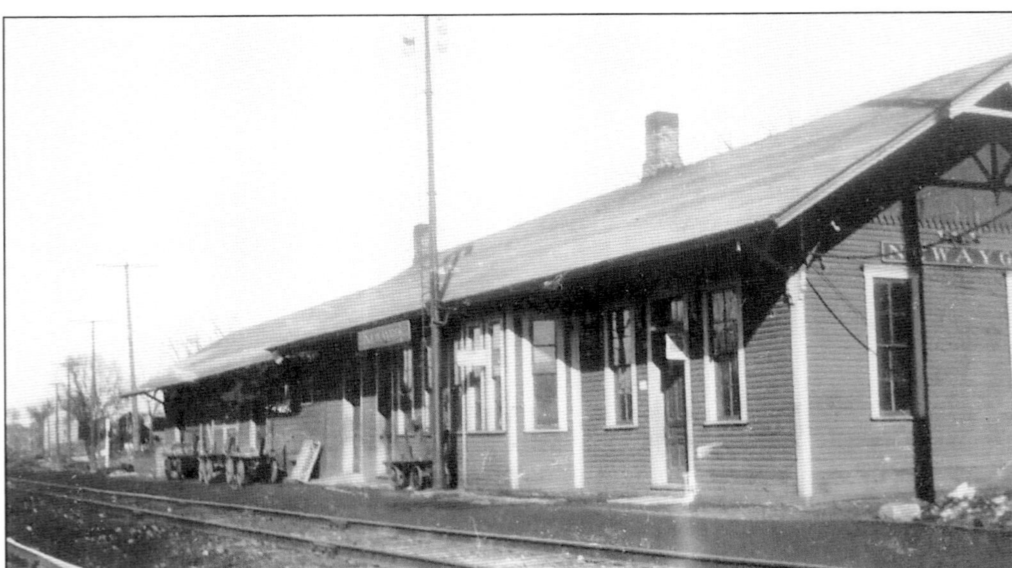

The Pere Marquette depot in Newaygo welcomed passengers for several years. The first railroad reached Newaygo on September 11, 1872, to great fanfare and celebration. Soon after, the village started to grow. In May 1992, the 120-year-old depot burned down in an act of arson. It was a sad ending to a beloved landmark.

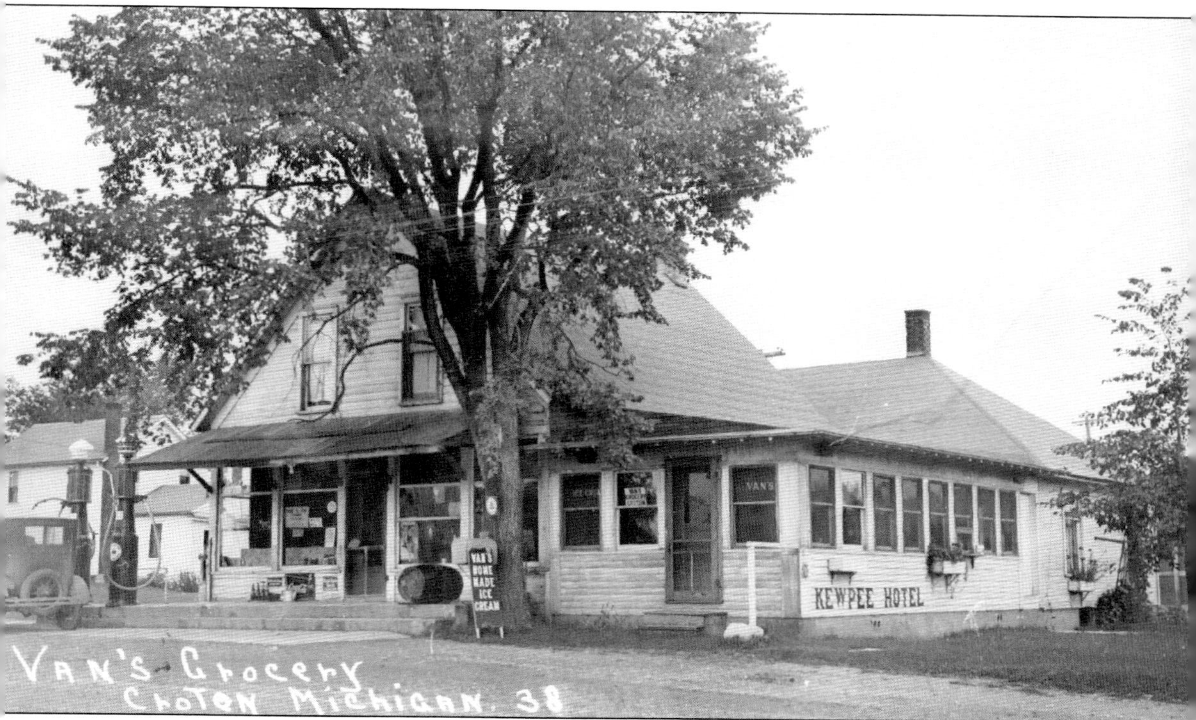

Croton is a beautiful spot. Formally known as the Forks, Croton became a destination of many vacationers. Van's Grocery was a long-standing convenience store that also offered sporting supplies, ice cream, and fuel for cars. The attached Kewpee Hotel, overlooking the beautiful Muskegon River, offered rooms for those needing a place to stay.

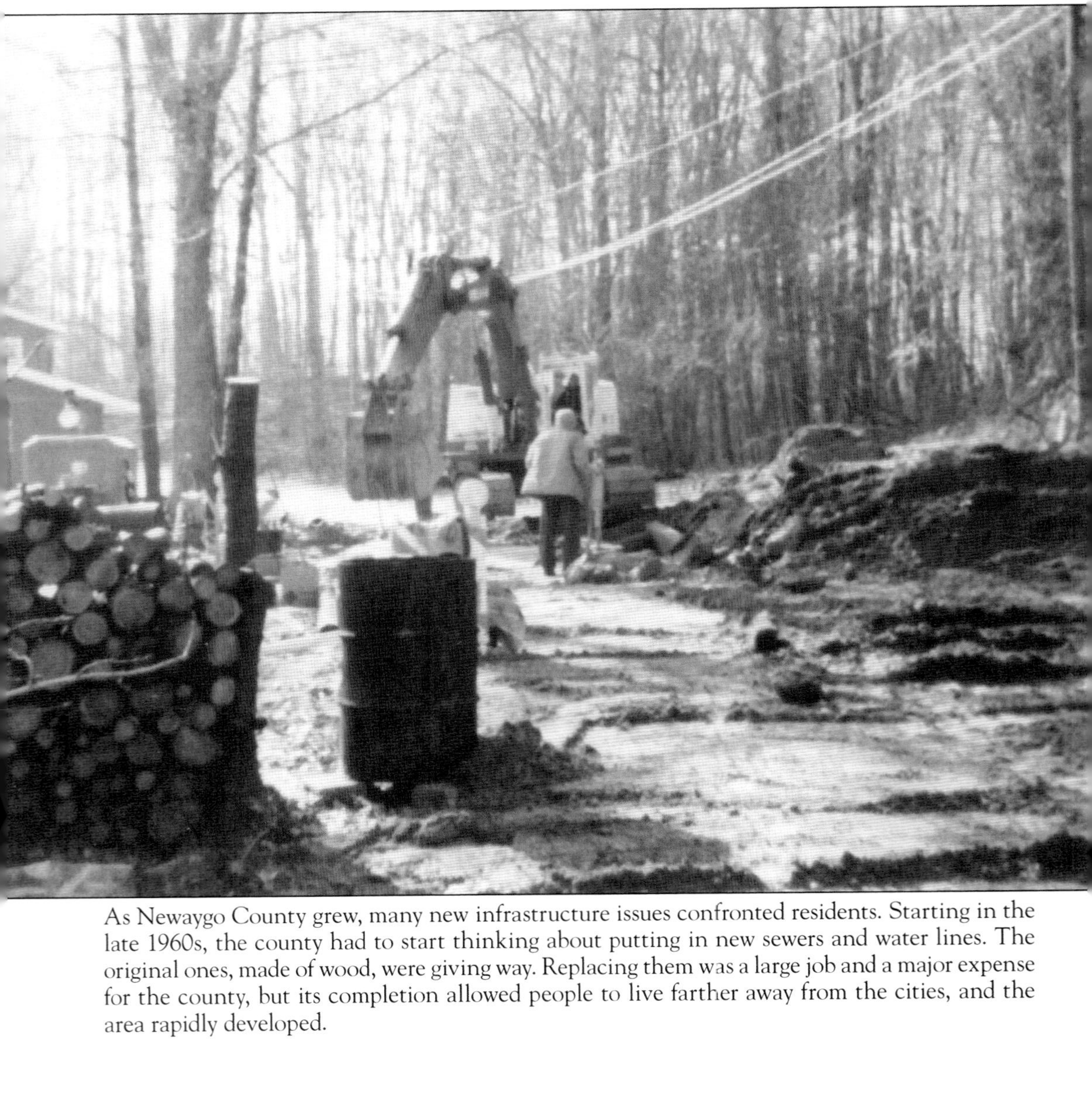

As Newaygo County grew, many new infrastructure issues confronted residents. Starting in the late 1960s, the county had to start thinking about putting in new sewers and water lines. The original ones, made of wood, were giving way. Replacing them was a large job and a major expense for the county, but its completion allowed people to live farther away from the cities, and the area rapidly developed.

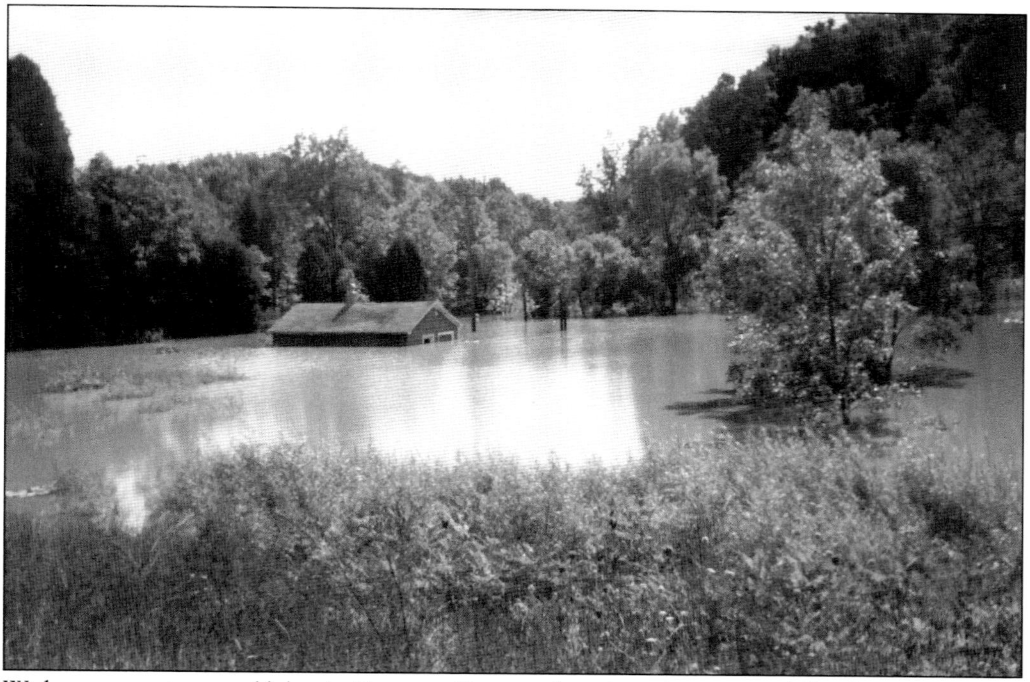

With so many rivers and lakes in Newaygo County, there have been several floods over the years. Many of them have caused the county to declare a state of emergency. For many residents, the beauty of the rivers and lakes override the risk. Unfortunately, the floods cause much property damage. Living on the lakes and rivers has given residents a great respect for Mother Nature.

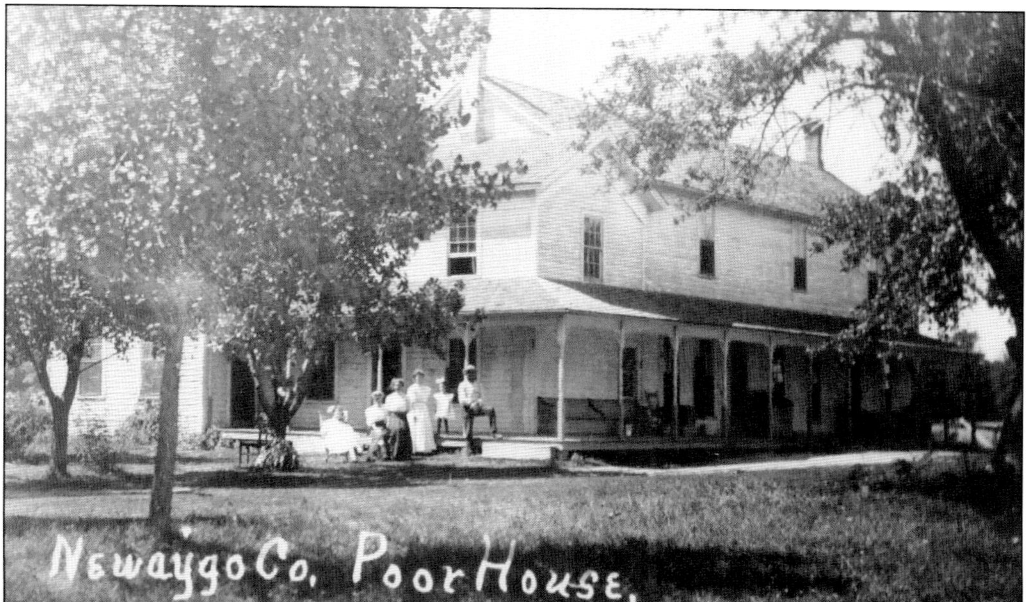

Newaygo County had two poor farms: one on the south side (pictured) and one on the north. The south-side poor farm was a little older and started to have maintenance issues, so residents and staff were moved to the north-side poor farm, which was a new brick building.

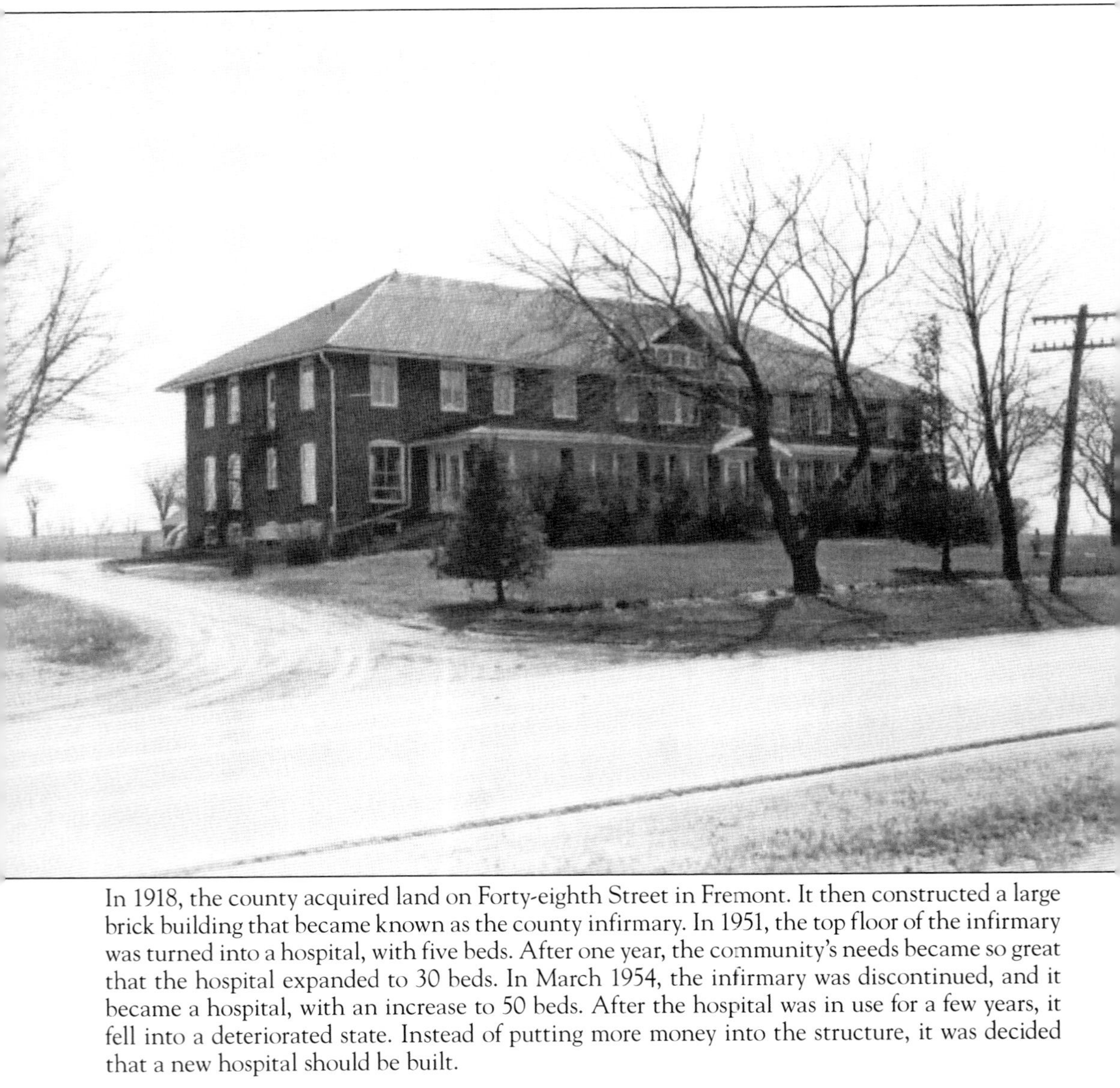

In 1918, the county acquired land on Forty-eighth Street in Fremont. It then constructed a large brick building that became known as the county infirmary. In 1951, the top floor of the infirmary was turned into a hospital, with five beds. After one year, the community's needs became so great that the hospital expanded to 30 beds. In March 1954, the infirmary was discontinued, and it became a hospital, with an increase to 50 beds. After the hospital was in use for a few years, it fell into a deteriorated state. Instead of putting more money into the structure, it was decided that a new hospital should be built.

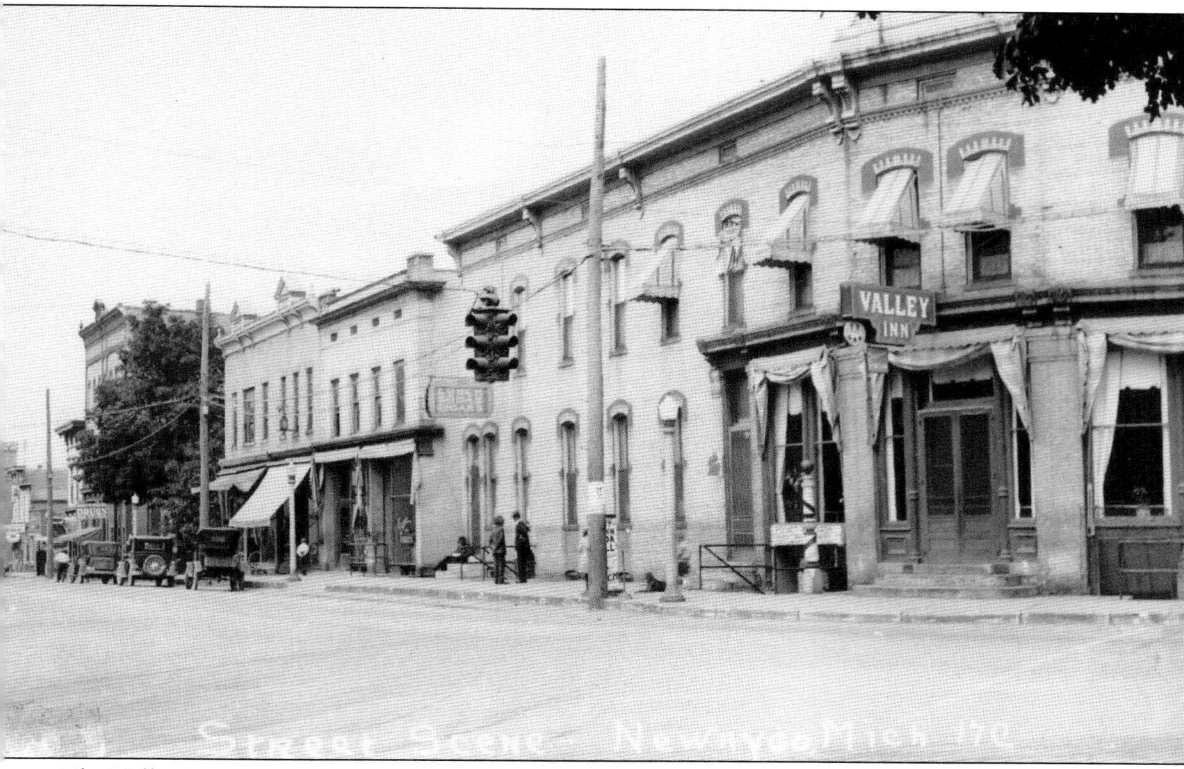

The Valley Inn was a part of the Courtright Hotel. It was a favorite spot for many people passing through town or spending a few days in Newaygo. In 1920, the town took down the stop-and-go light seen here after it had been in use for only a few months. It was replaced with a new flashing light.

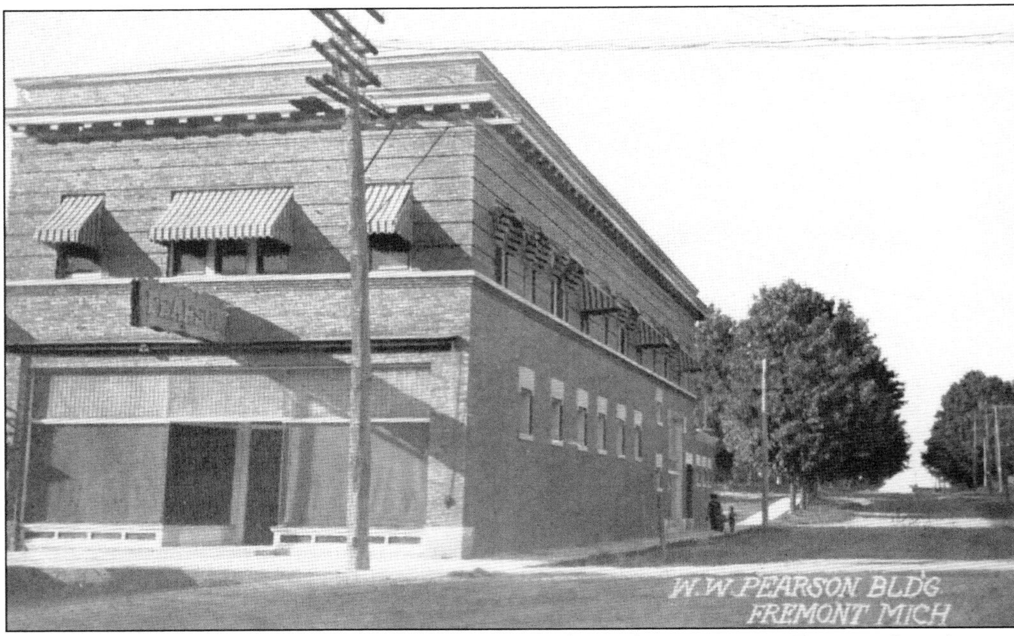

The W.W. Pearson Building, located on East Main and Merchant Streets in Fremont, has changed very little over the years. The lower level has been mostly used for commercial purposes, while the upper level is divided into several residential apartments. Note the old telephone pole that stands along the street in the days before the lines were buried.

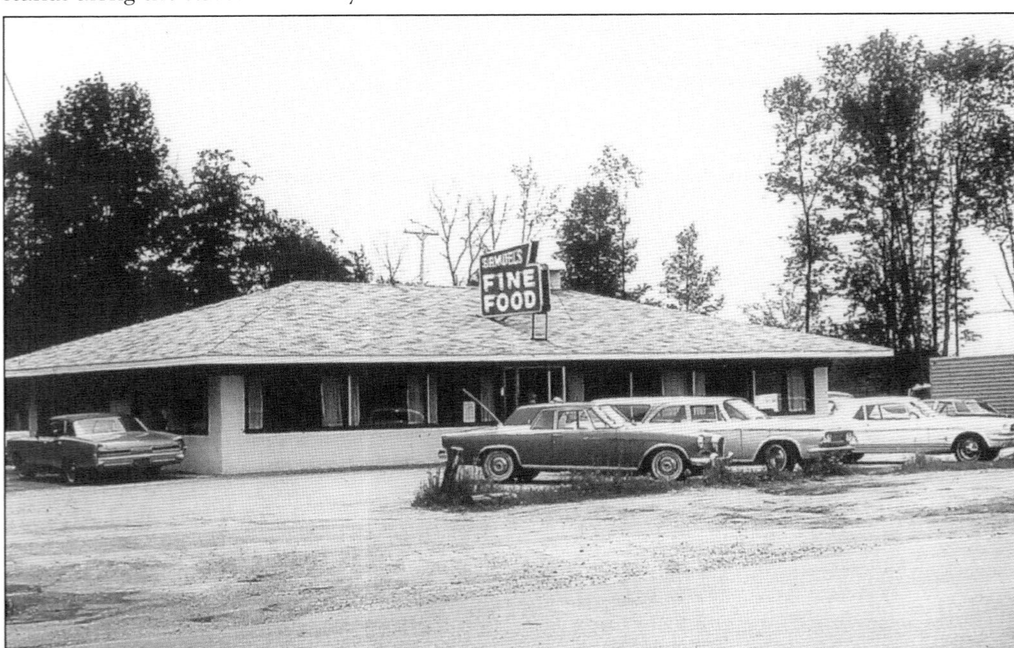

For many years, Samuel's Fine Food was a Fremont institution. It was at one time just a small diner in the downtown area. In the 1960s, it moved to the corner of Main Street and Connie Avenue. It expanded several times, including the addition of a banquet room. It remained a popular spot for family meals until it burned down in the 21st century.

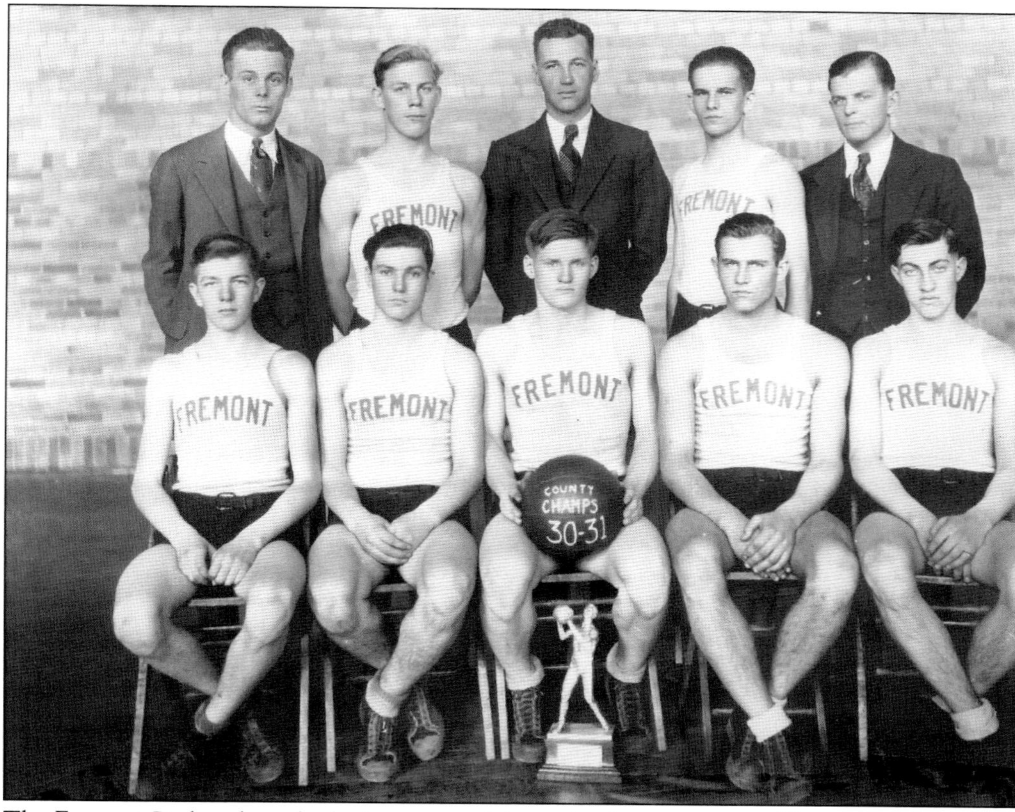

The Fremont Packers have had a long sports history in the community. The photograph above shows the 1930–1931 basketball team. Below, the 1931–1932 squad poses for a photograph. Among the players were Robert Geeting, Alvin Vredeveld, Clyde Dawes, and Cedric Sweet. Coach Lee led the guys into a 17-win season. The coach was quoted as saying, "The team showed plenty of spirit and fight."

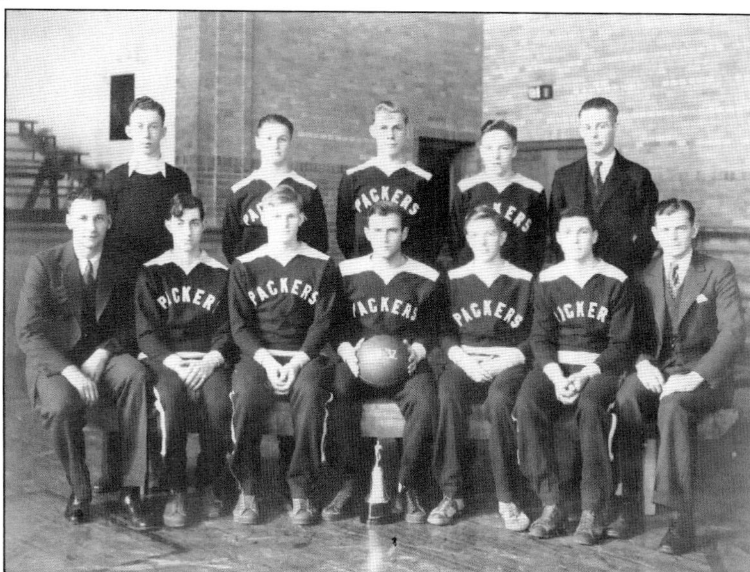

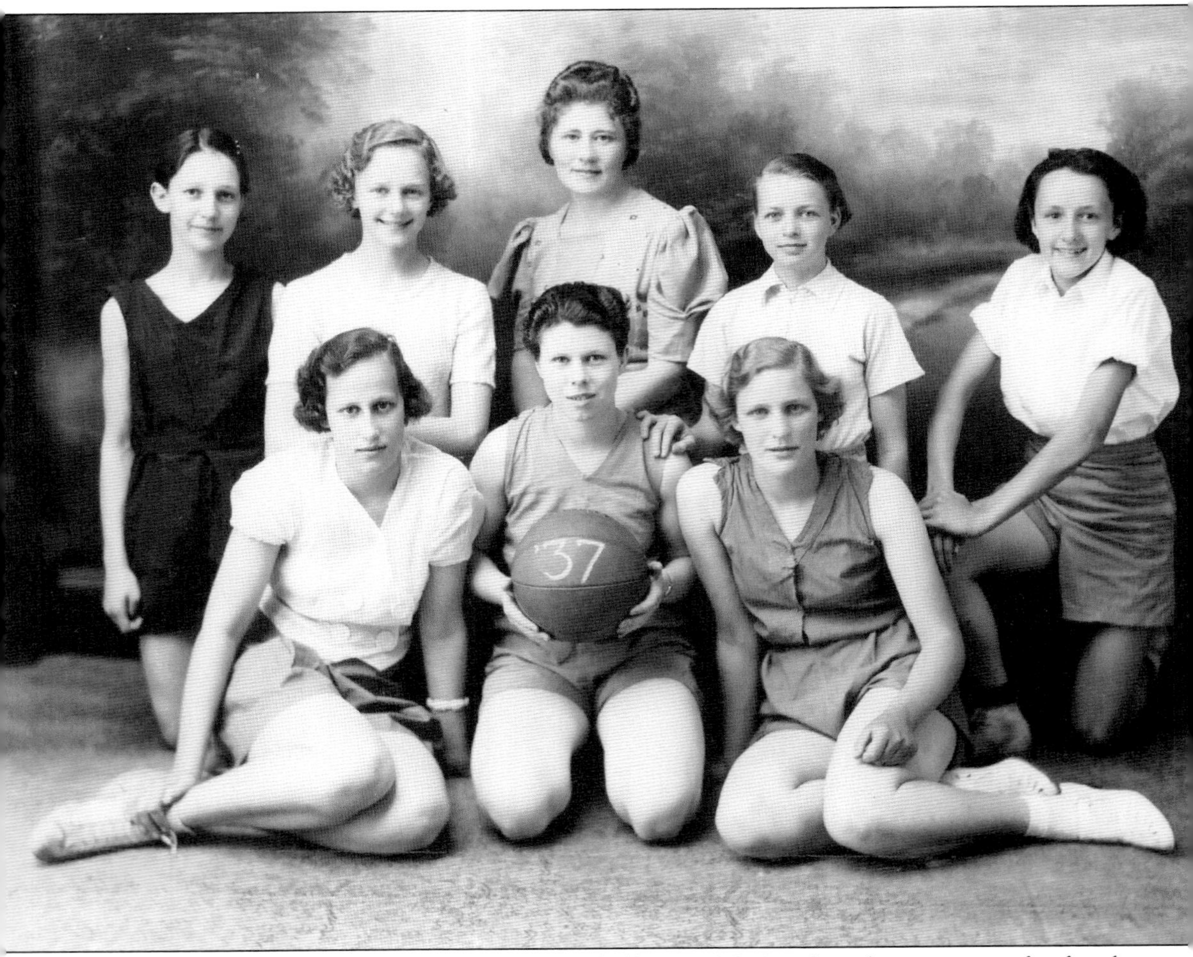

The Fremont Packerettes started playing basketball in 1945. Before that, there were very few female teams. This is a photograph of a 1937 girls' basketball team from Fremont. Many communities had their own teams, which played each other much as school teams do today.

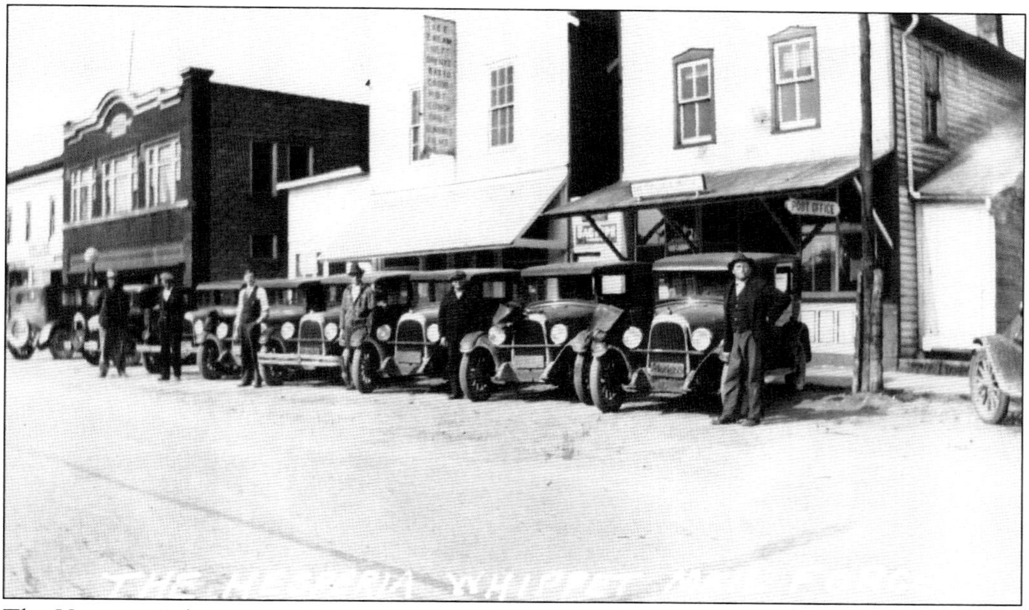

The Hesperia Whippet Mail Force poses in downtown Hesperia. Shown here are, from left to right, Harry Campbell, Frank Smith, Ben Somers, Sid Robertson, George Williamson, and Sam Klophenstein. These men delivered mail to people in the Hesperia area. With the majority of residents living outside of town, these mail carriers helped open up communication in the area.

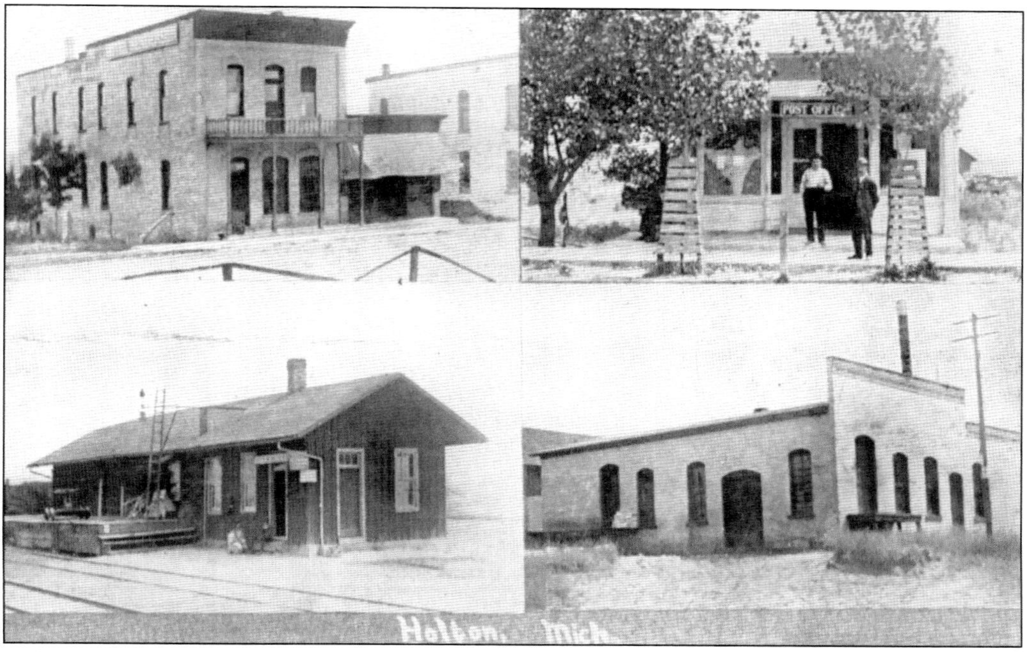

Holton is actually in Muskegon County, but since it is located so far from Muskegon, it has been adopted by Newaygo County. Holton has long been known as a town that sits peacefully between Fremont and Muskegon. Rich in history, it has always been an area thriving in agriculture.

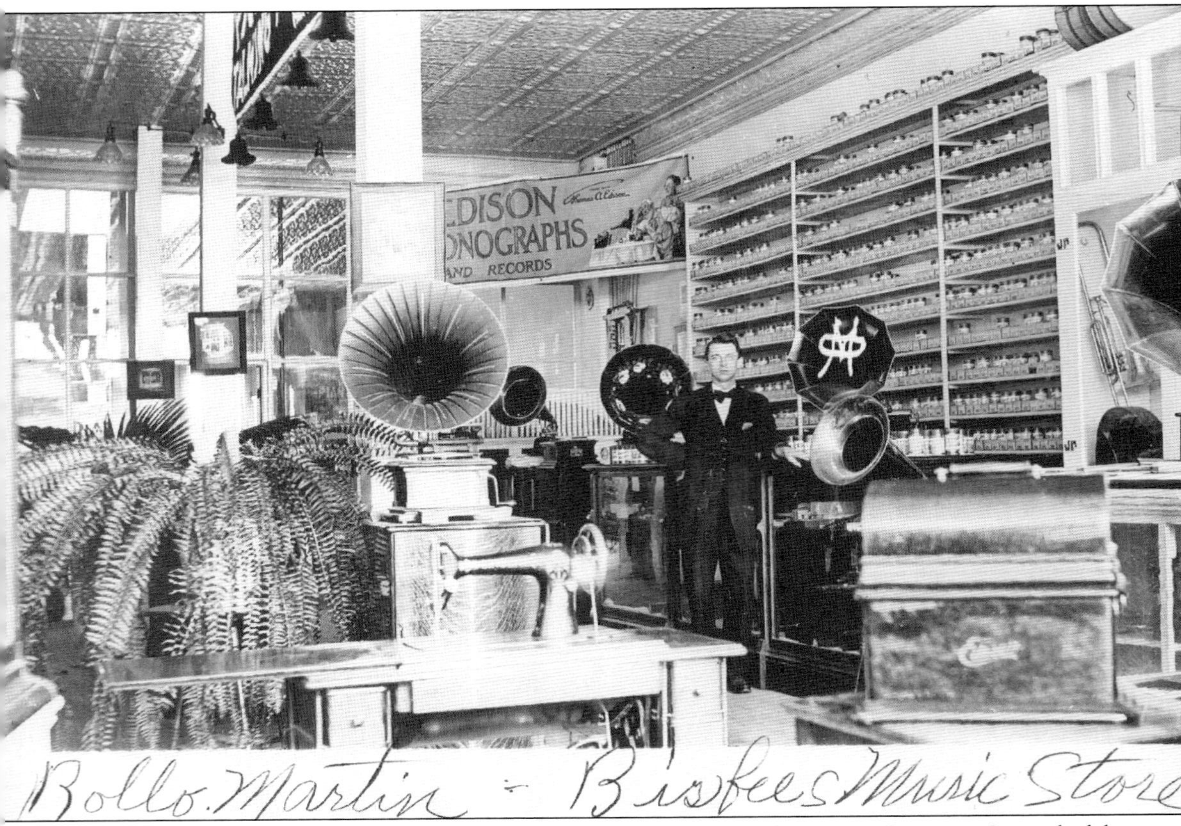

Bisbee's Music Store was one of the many businesses located in downtown Fremont. Several of the old buildings in Fremont still retain distinctive tin ceilings. Rollo Martin, one of the employees at Bisbees's, is almost lost amid all of the phonographs. Note also the several different styles of horns on the phonographs.

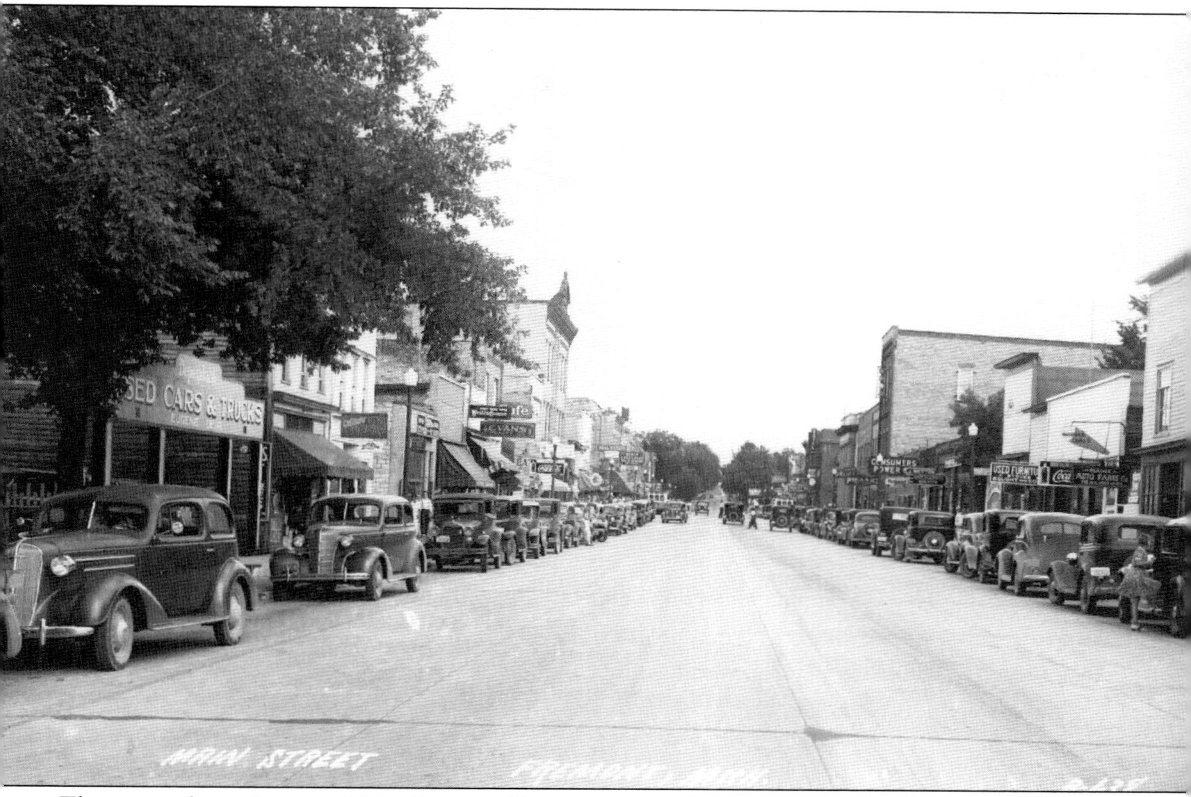

There were busy times on Main Street in Fremont, as can be seen here with all the cars at the west end. Many of these building still stand, although in many cases the facades have been altered. Among the businesses shown here are the used car and truck dealership (left foreground), Consumers Power (right), a used furniture store, and a drugstore.

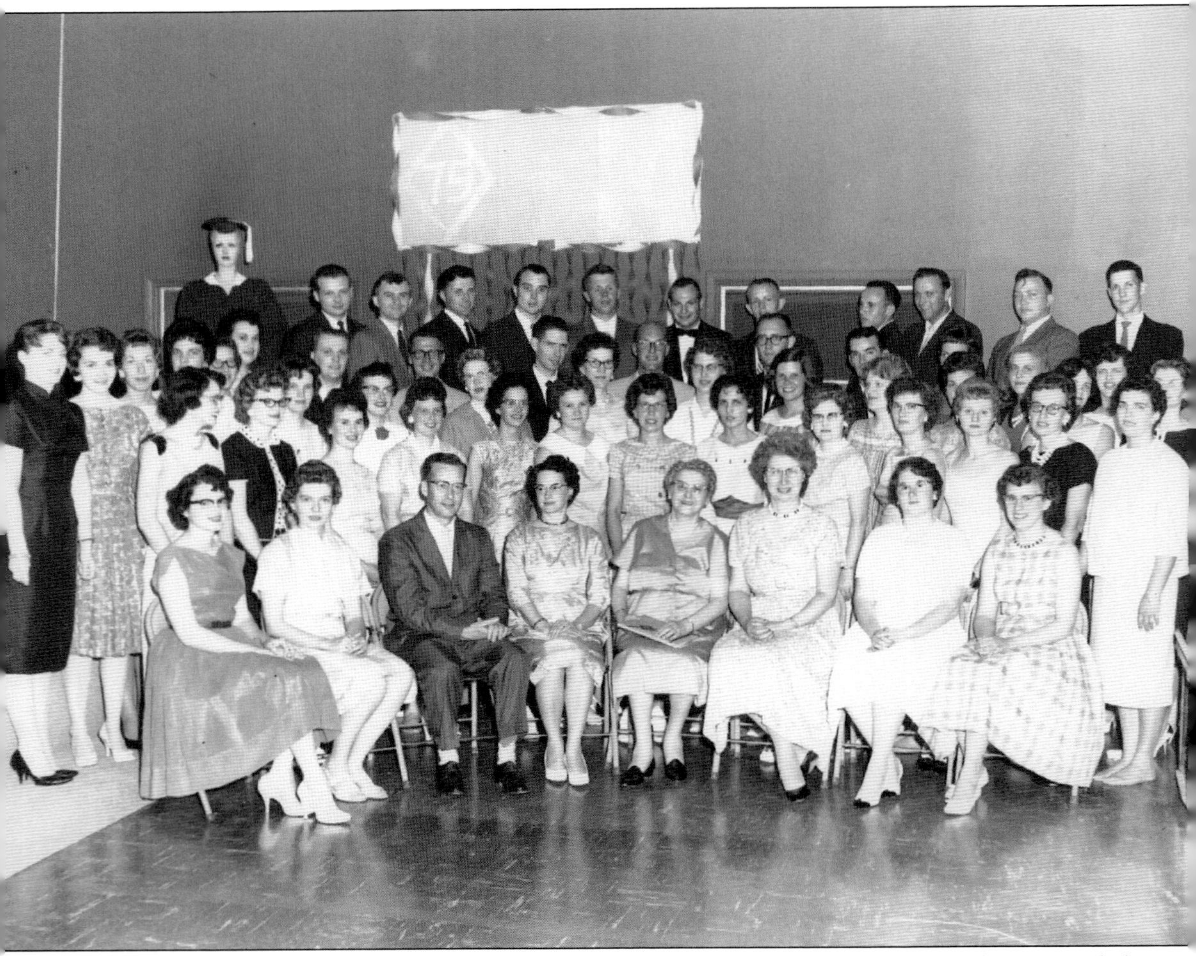

Even before the consolidation of the county schools was complete, many rural students attended high school in Fremont. The Fremont High School class of 1954 is seen here at its 1961 reunion. Some of the classes continue to meet, year after year, to reminisce and share news.

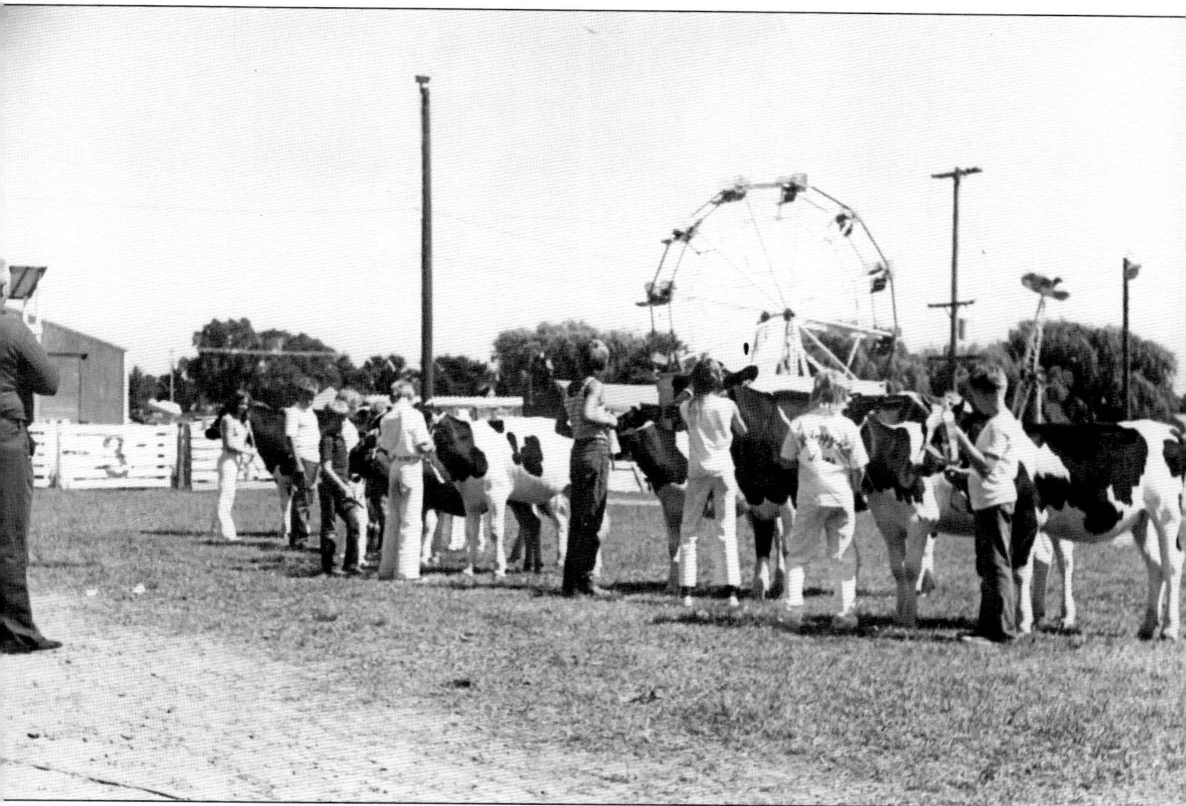

The Newaygo County 4H fair has been going strong for over 50 years. County youth participate in many categories, including baking, sewing, garden produce, and farm animals. There is always a lot to take in at the fair. This 1970 photograph shows fair participants beginning their dairy showmanship.

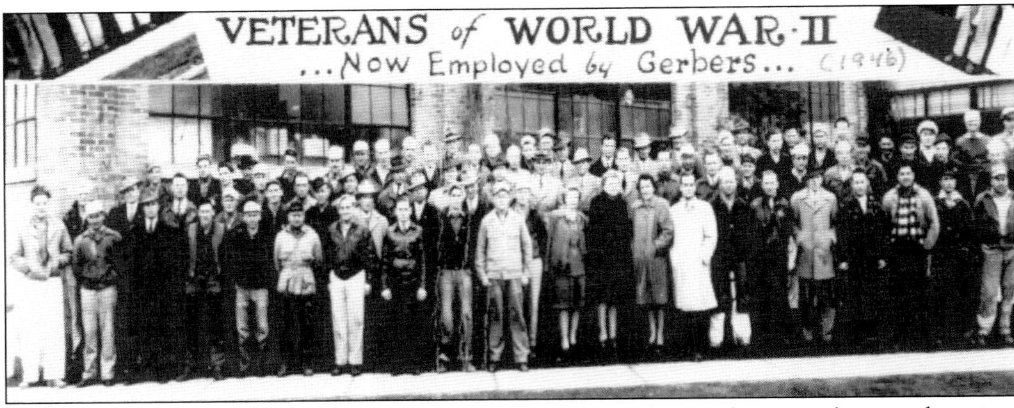

During World War II, Gerber Products Company lost many of its employees to the armed services. The company continued to support them by sending out its monthly newsletter to soldiers away from Newaygo County. After the war, the company welcomed them back with open arms. This 1946 photograph shows World War II veterans employed by Gerber's.

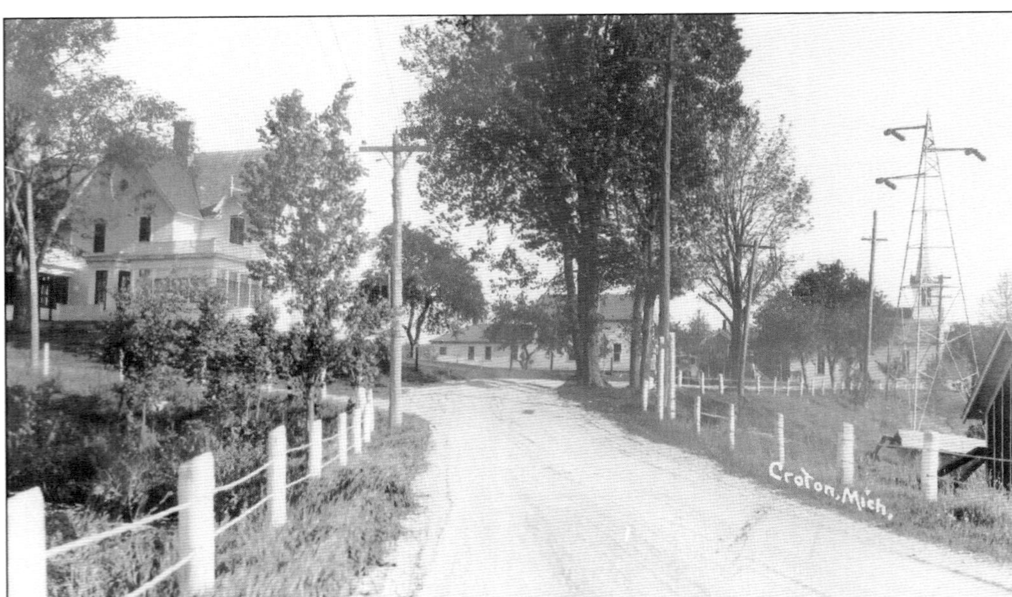

Croton, located along the Muskegon River, is home to the Croton Dam. On the right in this photograph is the power pole for the high-power lines that ran straight from the power plant. Visible along the road are old-time barricades of short wooden posts with metal cables running through them. This simple style of barricade has been upgraded many times over the years, from wood posts to metal and back again.

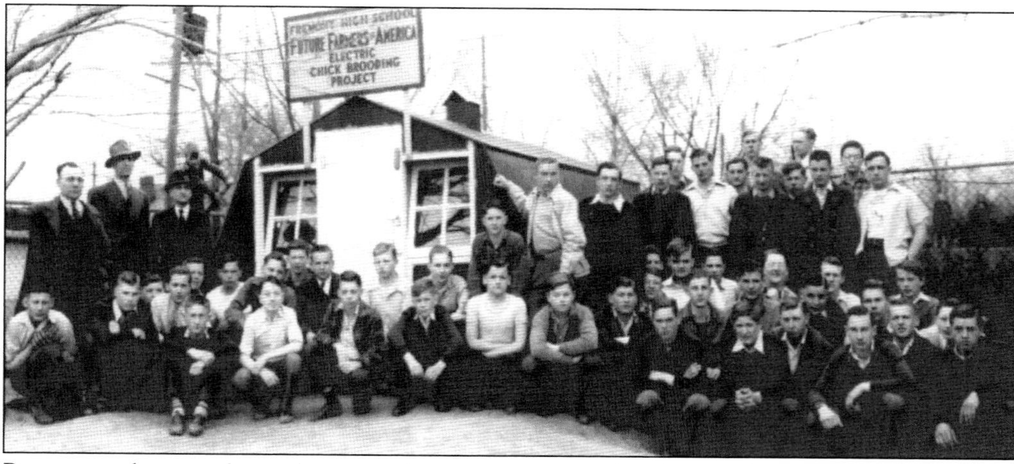

Being a predominately rural county, Fremont's chapter of the Future Farmers of America (FFA) has been a very active participant in the learning process for boys and girls. Here, students and advisors pose in front of the building housing an electric chick-brooding project. FFA provides opportunities for young farmers to learn leadership skills that carry them through whatever they do in life.

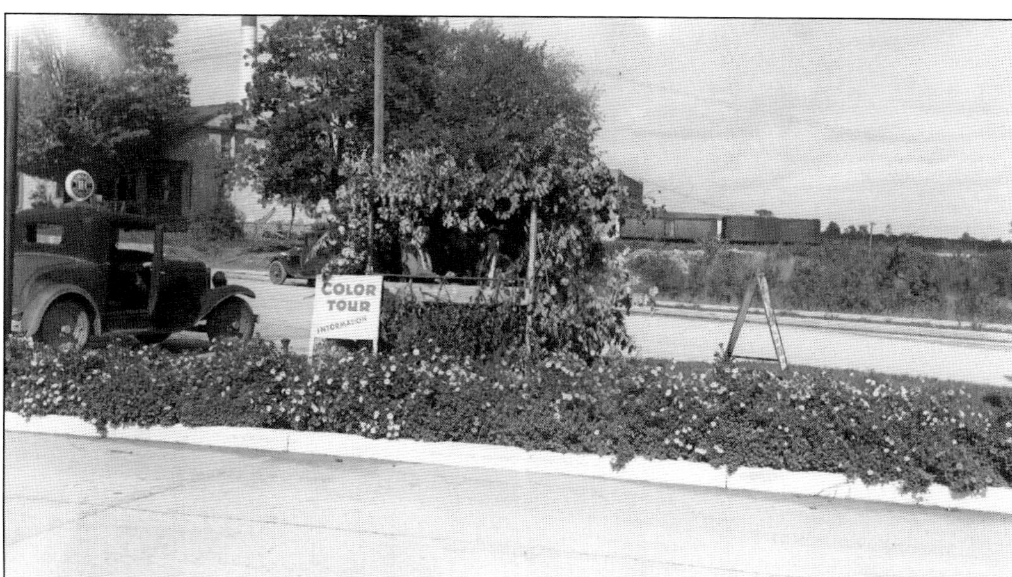

One advantage of being a mostly rural county is the glorious colors of the trees in the fall. With maple, beech, oak, dogwood, sassafras, and many other trees growing in forests and wood lots alongside of the pines, color tours were a popular way to spend a spare afternoon in the family automobile each autumn.

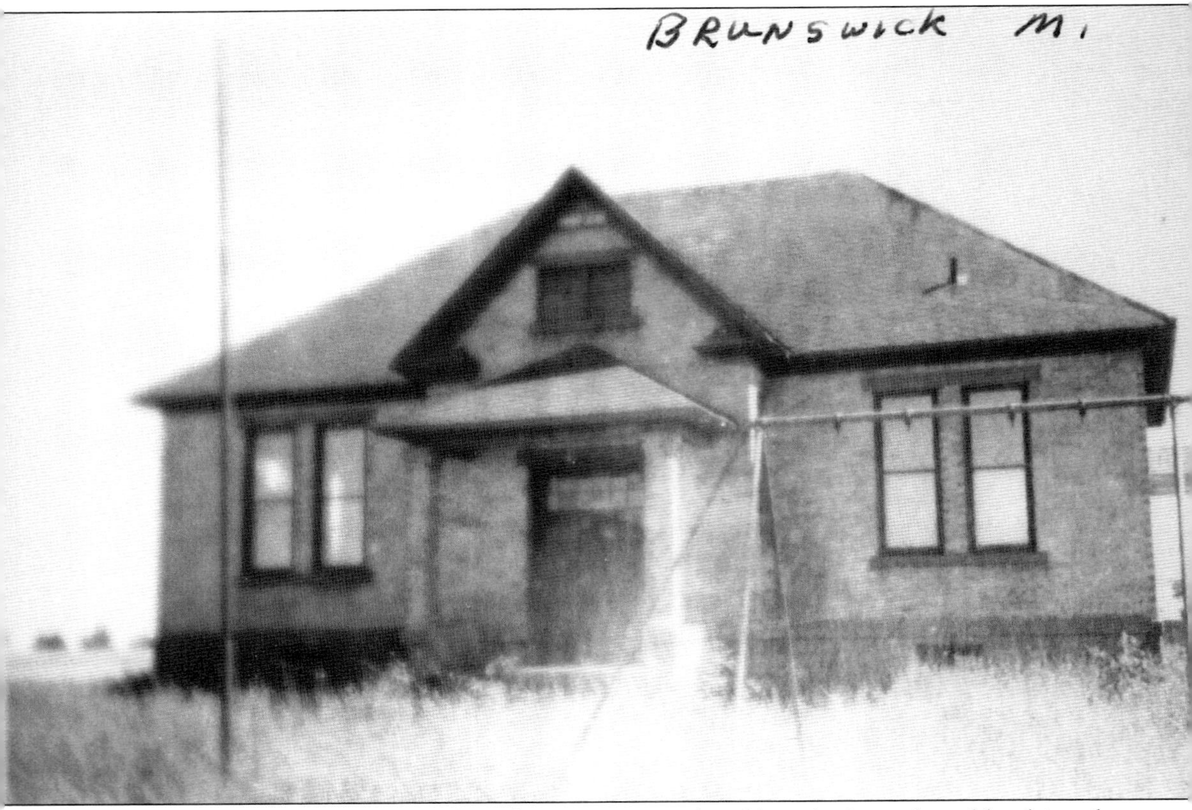

Brunswick, on the Newaygo and Muskegon county railroad line, looks nothing like this today. When the photograph was taken, it was bringing to market 10 carloads of peaches a day. The area remains an active agricultural region. Brunswick may have become smaller over the years, but it is still a vital part of the county.

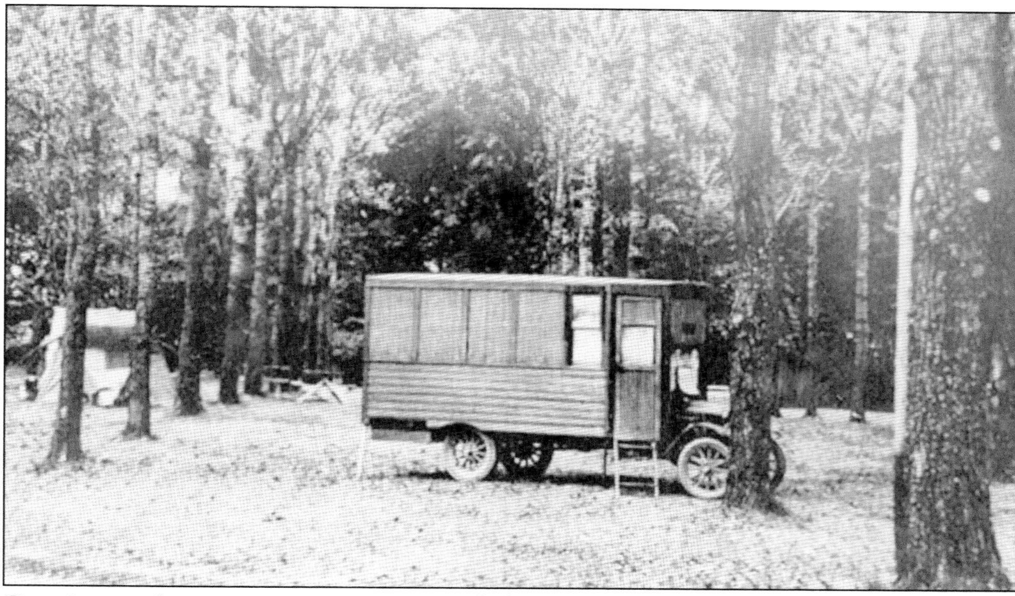

Camping is a favorite summer activity. People became very creative in developing new ways to enjoy it and make life more comfortable. This early motor home is parked by Fremont Lake for a summer getaway. Many people started building their own motor homes in the 1940s, and they were also made available for purchase.

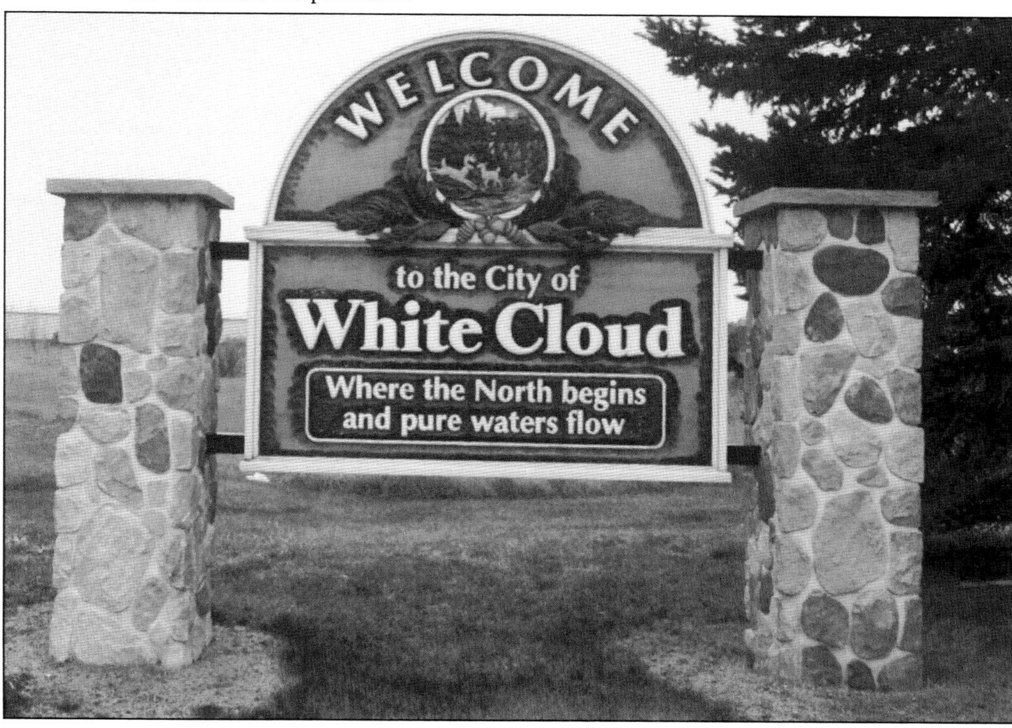

This sign declares White Cloud to be "where the North begins and pure waters flow." The sign has been updated in the last few years. The old wooden sign that greeted visitors as they entered White Cloud was a landmark and will always remind residents and travelers that they truly are in the land of the North Country and pure water.

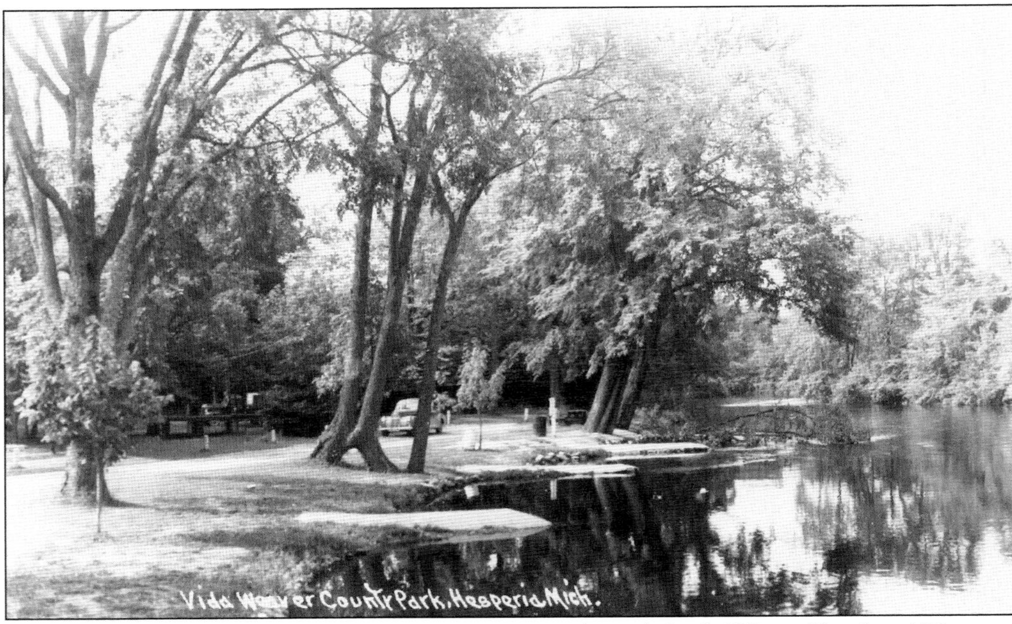

The White River flows through the county, passing through both White Cloud and Hesperia. There are several parks along the river, including Vida Weaver Park on the east bank of the White River in Hesperia. Vida Weaver was a doctor and a relative of Daniel Weaver, the founder of both Fremont and Hesperia.

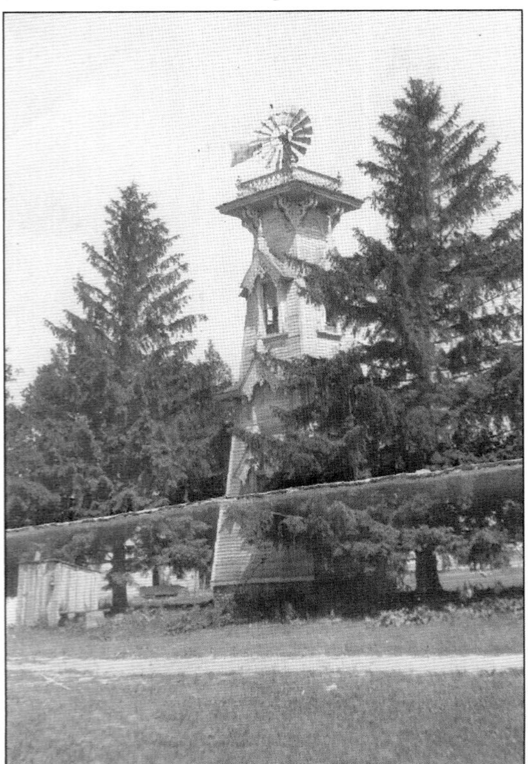

The Ensley Windmill Tower was built by Benjamin Ensley, one of the most prominent early citizens of Newaygo County. Ensley came to the area in 1857, having purchased land in southern Newaygo and northern Montcalm Counties. His farming operations proved extremely prosperous, and Ensley soon erected several imposing farm structures, including the renowned windmill tower. After his death, the farm was subdivided among several heirs, and most of the original buildings were demolished; however, the tower was still standing when, in 1966, it was moved to the Windmill Gardens Museum Village in Fremont. Its ornate brackets and scrollwork were subsequently restored.

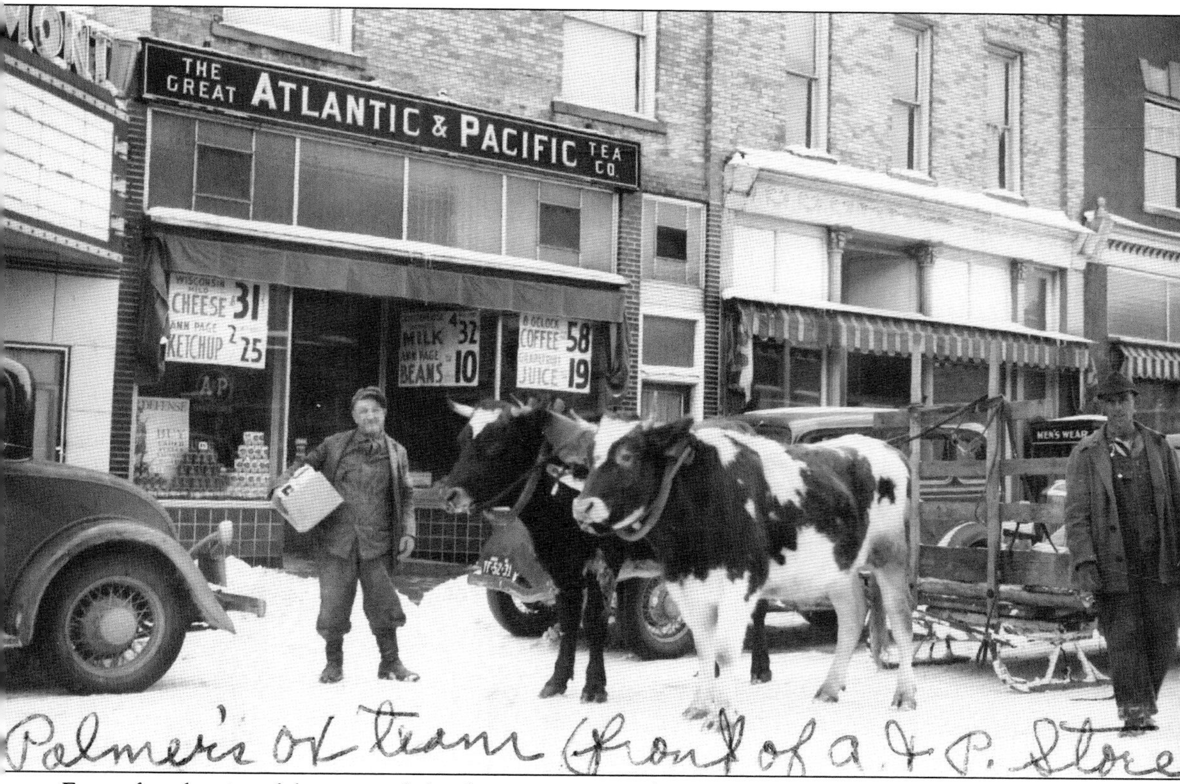

Even after the rise of the automobile, there were times when cars just could not compete with the older modes of travel. Pictured here in front of the Atlantic & Pacific Tea Company (A&P) store is Mr. Palmer with his oxen team. The runners on the sleigh on the right indicate that Palmer had a snowy way into town.

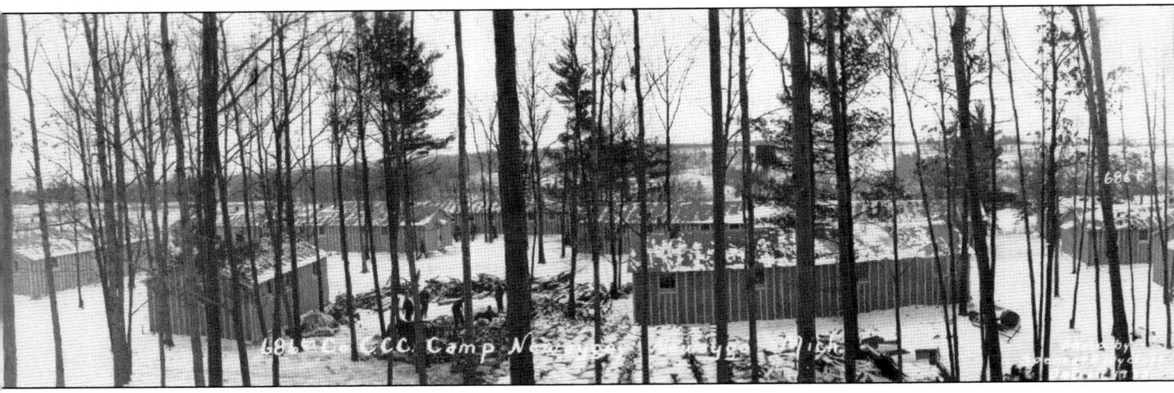

During the Depression, the Civilian Conservation Corps (CCC) provided work for unemployed boys and men when the country was having economic struggles. Here are photographs of CCC Camp Newaygo. There were numerous camps in the Newaygo County area. The results of CCC laborers' hard work are still visible in the trees they planted and the many state parks on which they worked.

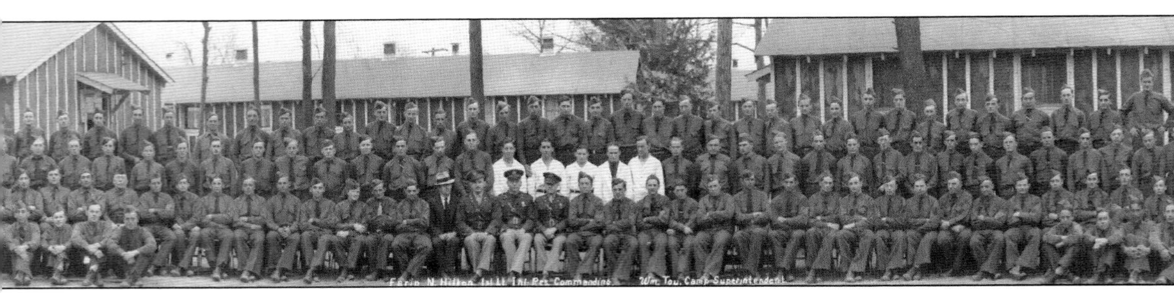

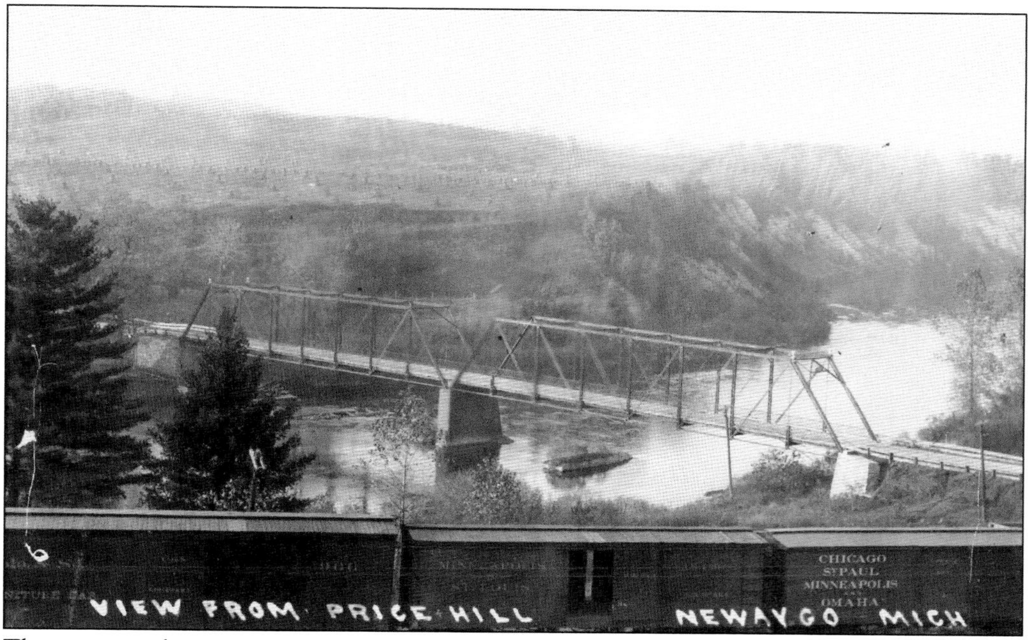

This is a view from Price Hill, high above the old bridge over the Muskegon River in Newaygo. The bridge served Newaygo for many years and was a major span across the river. It was replaced in 1953 with the present structure. The new bridge sits peacefully between Fremont and Muskegon. Holton is filled with history and has always been an area rich in agriculture.

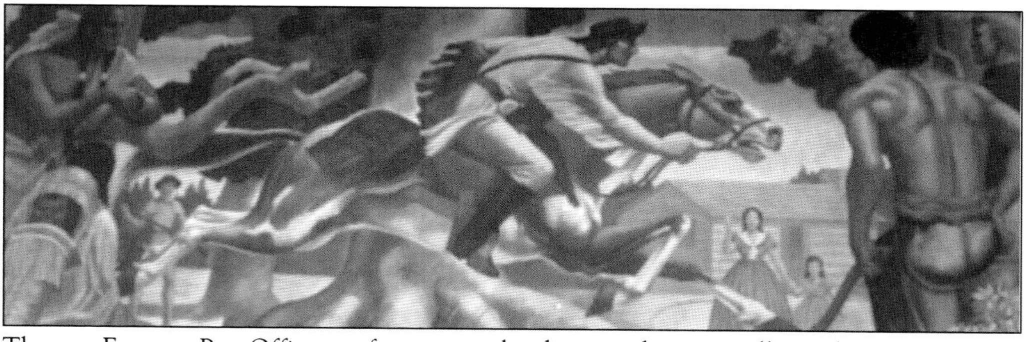
The new Fremont Post Office was fortunate to be chosen to house a wall mural. Often mistaken for Works Progress Administration art, post office murals were actually executed by artists working for the Section of Fine Arts. Commonly known as "the Section," it was established in 1934 and administered by the Procurement Division of the Treasury Department. Headed by Edward Bruce, a former lawyer, businessman, and artist, the Section's main function was to select art of high quality to decorate public buildings if funding was available. By being placed in public structures, the art was made accessible to all people. The artists were selected based not on need but rather judged by other artists. They were not told what to paint, just guidelines, with items of local interest preferred. Fremont's mural, painted by Lumen Martin Winter in 1938, is titled *The Pony Express.*

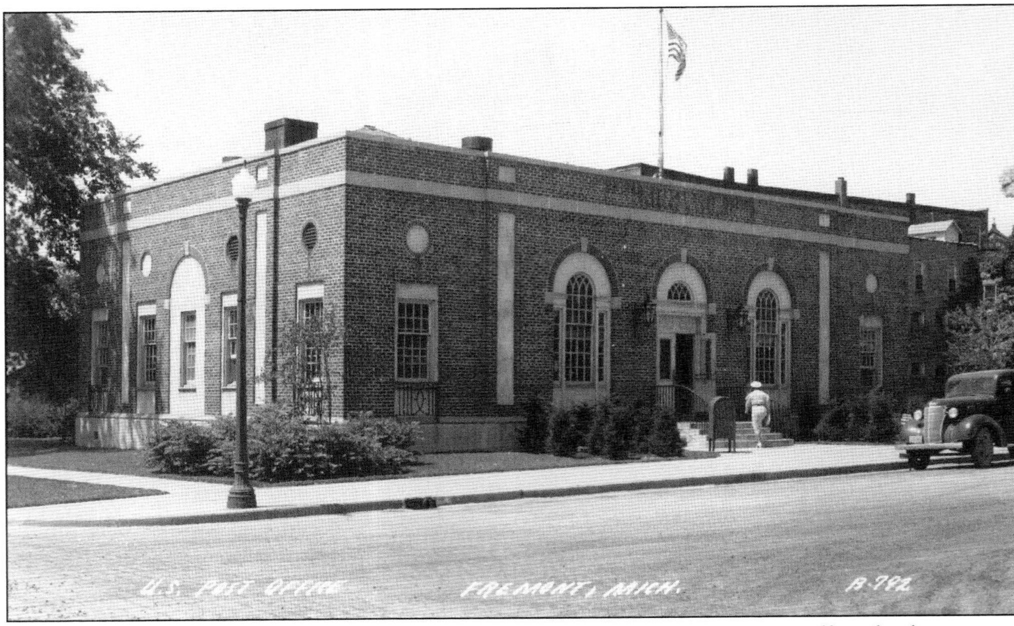

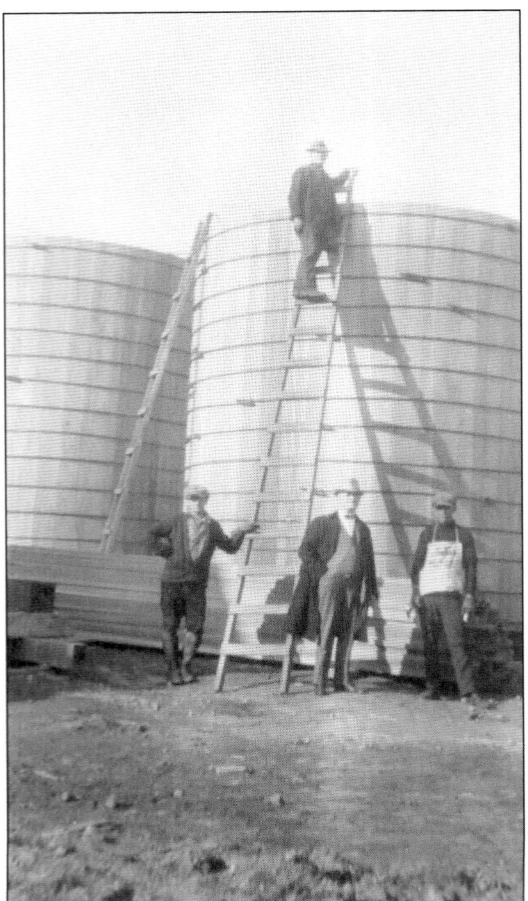

Fremont's current post office, built in 1938, was one of many post offices constructed during the New Deal. It is home to one of the Art Deco murals that were part of the Section of Fine Arts. Both the artwork and the building provided jobs during a time when many were finding employment hard to obtain.

Here are vinegar vats at the Grant Canning Company. With an abundance of apples, products like vinegar became an important part of the economy. The county is home to many orchards, and fruit became an important industry. Apples were used for many things, including vinegar, apple juice, applesauce, and baby food.

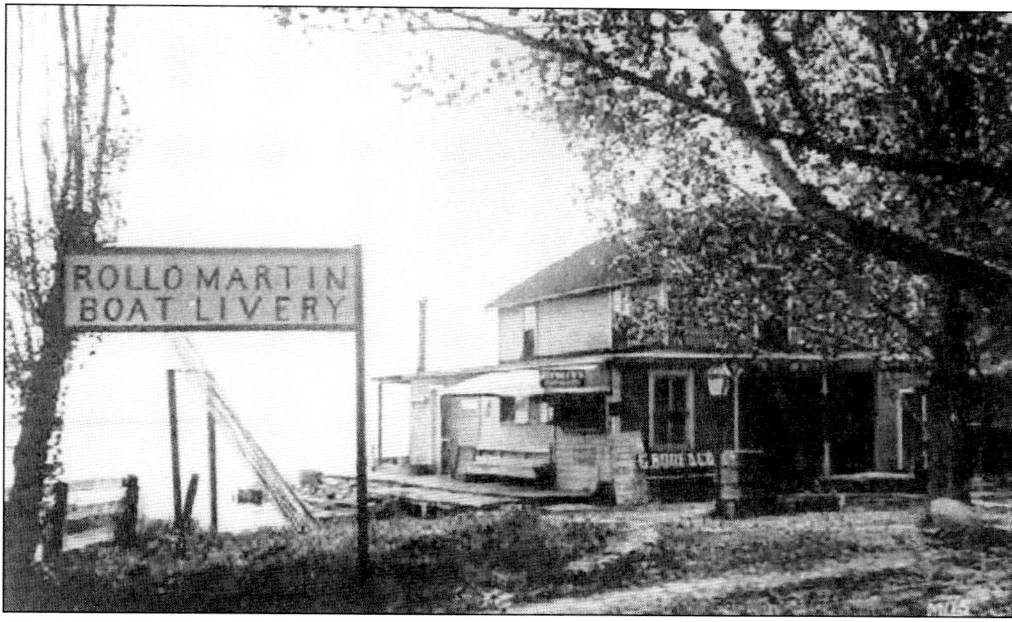

As people came to enjoy more and more leisure time, Fremont Lake became a popular destination. Rollo Martin Boat Livery, located on Fremont Lake, gave visitors the chance to enjoy the water without needing to maintain and transport their own boats. Martin's livery would rent out boats to the public for fishing or just a relaxing day on the water.

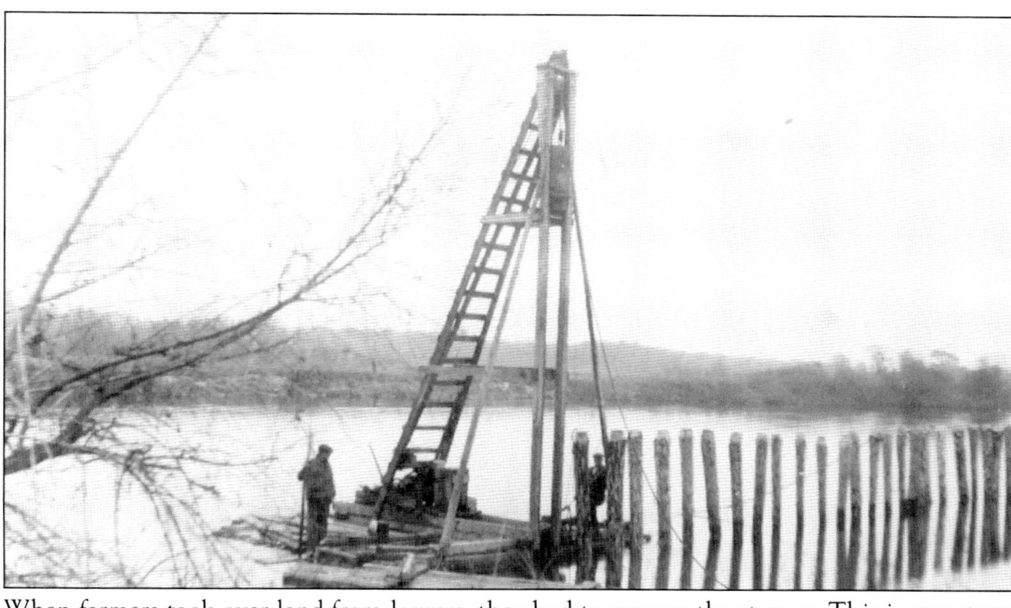

When farmers took over land from loggers, they had to remove the stumps. This is one stump puller, a lever-type device, near White Cloud, Michigan. Newaygo County was logged heavily, and many areas were clear-stripped, leaving land barren and susceptible to erosion, as all the topsoil blew away.

Consistent with our mission to preserve history on a local level, this book was printed in South Carolina on American-made paper and manufactured entirely in the United States. Products carrying the accredited Forest Stewardship Council (FSC) label are printed on 100 percent FSC-certified paper.